Being TEXAN

Celebrating a State of Mind

By Jeff Carroll

Lone Star Publishing
Bryan, Texas

This is a work of non-fiction. The people and places are real and the incidents reported are either a matter of widely accepted theory or found in public or private records. All history, however, is a matter of perspective. This is especially true of "folk" history, where there may be many different interpretations of the same material.

This is a revised, expanded version of a work originally published in a limited edition by Author House, Inc., 2006.

Cover & Book design by Jason Carranza
Index prepared by Jonelle Carson
Set in Sabon

Interior illustrations by Jason Carranza, Lillian Cowden, Suzy Keller, Gary Manthei, Nathan Smith, and Sam Woodfin

This book is printed on acid-free archival paper.

Published by Lone Star Publishing
2023 S. Texas Avenue
Bryan, Texas 77802
www.LoneStarPublishing.net

Library of Congress Cataloging-in-Publication Data

Carroll, Jeff.
    Being Texan : celebrating a state of mind / by Jeff Carroll.
        p. cm.
"Revised, expanded version of a work originally published in a limited,
private edition by Author House, Inc., 2006."
    Includes bibliographical references and index.
    ISBN 978-0-9794354-4-7
    1. Texas--Social life and customs--Anecdotes. 2. Texas--Biography--Anecdotes.
    3. Texas--History--Anecdotes. I. Title.
F386.6.C37 2009
976.4--dc22

                                    2009012314

                            CIP

10 9 8 7 6 5 4 3 2 1

Dedication:

With thanks to
Paula and Deborah
Who, with great patience and not a little constructive criticism,
read these stories first ...

and to
My Students,
who listened to them for so many years

Acknowledgments:

These stories would not exist were it not for the thousands of people who lived them, recorded them in pen, pencil, or memory, and then passed them on to future generations to be preserved by others. Although they did not think about it at the time, they lived the true essence of *Being Texan*.

Being TEXAN

Foreword

Texas Before 1500

The Spanish Period: 1500 – 1821

Mexican Texas and the War for Texas Independence: 1821-1836

The Republic of Texas: 1836-1846

Early Statehood and the Civil War: 1846-1866

Advancing the Frontier: 1866-1900

A New Century, New Frontiers: 1900 – Present

Afterword

Bibliography

Resources

Index

"The legends of our people rise like smoke.
Sit beside me and learn,
For I am Keeper of the Flame."

"Walks Alone"
Tickanwatic shaman

Foreword to This Revised Edition

Being Texan has almost nothing to do with where one was born or lives today. Being Texan is, as many authors have written, "a state of mind." It has something to do with an outlook on life that suggests that, no matter what the hardship, there was, is, or will be a way to work it out. It has something to do with accepting responsibility. It has something to do with recognizing flaws and failures and rising above them. It is simply the process of living well, despite what the world throws at us.

Is this uniquely Texan? Of course, it is not. Many scholars argue that Texans are no different from other people and the "Texas Mystique" is no mystery at all, simply a matter of egocentrism. So be it. They are entitled to their opinions just as I am to mine. Although I think a book like this could be written about any other state, I also think the flavor would be somewhat different. Try inserting any other state name in the title—it just would not have the same ring to it.

Being Texan is a collection of stories about people. Some of them are people that you already know, and some are not. Whoever they were, wherever they came from, and whenever they arrived make little difference. They all contributed something toward making Texas what it is today— good, bad, or indifferent. They all became a part of the much larger story of Texas, just as you who read this today are living your part of the story.

All of these stories have appeared before in some form. Some come from my newspaper column "Legendary Texas," some from the scripts of my radio program by the same name, some from my first five volumes of the *Legendary Texas* series of books, and some from the published notes for my Texas History classes at Texas A&M University and at Blinn College.

Some stories may not appear to be politically correct by modern standards, but we do the past a great disservice if we judge them in that light. This is "Folk History," a history of the people. The people and the stories should be judged, if at all, in light of what was common and acceptable in their time. Good anthropologists realize that when dealing with different cultures, one should never judge things as "good" or "bad," but simply recognize them as being different.

Readers frequently ask if the stories are true. Ultimate truth is a concept argued by theologians, philosophers, and historians. This is not a scholarly work with footnotes to justify everything I say. I have edited all of these to make them as factual as I can, but I will not claim an absence of errors. After all, these are stories of people reacting to changing situations; no one will ever know exactly what they were thinking about at the time, unless they tell us in some way. If someone believes something to be *true*, acts upon it in that belief, and then writes about it in a letter or journal so that others' lives are influenced by it, it then becomes its own version of "truth" for those people.

History is a matter of perspectives, not an exact science.

I arranged these stories in chronological order so that they flow in a single line, like chapters in a continuing story. In this revised edition, I have added a few more stories to fill some of the gaps in the time sequence. Those who read them for pleasure may find the sequence easier to follow than it was in the five *Legendary Texas* volumes. Those who use these stories to illustrate and supplement material in accredited textbooks will find it easier to correlate the material. For these students and teachers there are appendices dealing with the Texas Essential Knowledge & Skills (TEKS) required in Texas schools, as well as suggested strategies, activities, and references to aid the learning process. This revised edition also contains an Index to help folks find particular people, topics, etc., and a rather limited Bibliography of sources for further reading.

History does not happen in a vacuum. No matter what is happening in Texas, there are other things going on in the world. I preface each story with a few comments to try to put things in context. Who knew, for instance, that while Texans and Tejanos fought for Texas independence, other wars in Europe would send thousands of newcomers to the Texas frontier? Who knew that what we call the "French and Indian War," that took place mostly in upper New York State and the Ohio River Valley, would ultimately lead to the abandonment of Franciscan missions throughout Mexico and the American Southwest? The more we know about history, the more we are able to put the pieces of the puzzle together, until a much larger picture begins to appear.

Look around you. All of the folks you see going about their everyday affairs are, in their own way, contributing to the story. I urge each one of you to keep some kind of record of your life. That way, your part of the story will not be lost. Think about it for a minute. What are some things that you remember from when you were younger that you just don't see or hear about today? What new things are taking place in your life? How do you react to the change?

You are a part of the story. By living your life, you, too are *Being Texan.*

Jeff Carroll
Bryan, Texas
April 2009

Texas Before 1500

A Beginning

There remains a great deal of argument between Bible scholars and science over the age of the Earth and those who inhabit it. Whether the Earth has been around a few billion years and its human inhabitants a few hundred thousand, or they both came into being about 6,400 years ago, is a matter of perspective. I don't see either side yielding any ground to the opposition. In this case it makes little difference. Both sides of the argument will, I think, agree that Texas was fairly well populated a long time ago. During the closing days of a period in which they hunted the mega fauna of the time with spears, these first Texans left their marks on the land. Perhaps that is also open to argument. I don't know. But, I do not think one can argue about the presence of our first manufacturing industry.

Paleo Indian flint crafter
by Lillian Cowden

1

We don't know who he was. Or, *"he"* may have been *"she,"* or it may have been a case of *"they."* But, whoever, he, she, or they were, they built our first industry—one that lasted a long time. We need to give these people names, but the names generally available today are not very satisfactory. They lump too many different people into one category and call all of them "Paleo Indians," which simply means "old Indians." These people brought the first manufacturing industry to Texas before the invention of the wheel and long before the Christian era. It was here, it flourished, and you can see evidence of it today on the slopes above where the Canadian River was dammed to form Lake Meredith.

In a way, we owe our first introduction to this ancient industry to a wandering cowboy named Allen (or "Allie") Bates. Sometime between 1877 and 1880, Allie moved a few head of his cattle up on the Canadian, where grazing was good, and built a dugout cabin in one of the dry washes that fed into the river. Soon that dry wash became known as Allie Bates Creek, and that was how it appeared on maps furnished to Dr. Charles Newton Gould, a geologist from Oklahoma, who surveyed the area between 1903 and 1907. What Dr. Gould found changed not only the map of the Panhandle, but it also changed the way we think about those humans who occupied the state a long time ago. They were not as primitive as we once supposed.

What he found was a ridge of very special dolomite, a kind of limestone, stretching for about 125 miles from the Texas Panhandle into Oklahoma. This ridge was especially visible in the walls above Allie Bates Creek, and so, since he had to call it something on his map, Dr. Gould named it "Alibates dolomite."

Obvious even then, but not understood, was the fact that other people had been there long before Dr. Gould, or even Allie Bates. Above Allie Bates Creek, in an area where geologic pressure and chemicals in the rock

Flint points
by Lillian Cowden

2

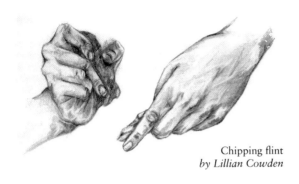

Chipping flint
by Lillian Cowden

had turned the white dolomite into crystal-hard and beautifully striped and mottled pink chert, was the remains of a quarry—not a small one, but a big one that required the work of many people for a very long time.

Now, Alibates Chert is unique. Geologists have never found anything quite like it anywhere else on earth. This is where the industry part comes in. According to the dictionary, industry means "any branch of trade, business, production, or manufacture." That certainly fits the situation. That chert was quarried in Texas, manufactured into a valuable product, and then traded throughout the South and Southwest. Lithic artifacts made from Alibates Chert are found from Savannah, Georgia, to San Diego, California. Weapon points, knives, scrapers, hammers, and other tools made from Alibates Chert found their way into the Clovis, Folsom, Agate Basin, Plainview, Angostura, Eden, Scotts Bluff, and Harrell cultures at the dawn of our prehistory and were still manufactured and used when the Spaniards introduced more efficient killing implements of iron in the 1500s.

How far back does this go? Well, people of the Clovis Culture, first identified about 150 miles west of Allie Bates Creek near Clovis, New Mexico, used Alibates Chert tools to kill and butcher the woolly mammoth and giant bison at the receding edge of the last ice sheet.

Every year archaeologists learn more about these people who created the first Texas industry. In many ways, they were just like we are. They were *homo sapiens*—that means "reasoning, thinking humans." They appear to have lived in family-based clans, which may have moved seasonally to take advantage of changing food supplies. Their primary source of food seems to have been the *mega fauna*, the really big game of the time, including mammoths and giant bison. Killing such big animals required "reasoning and thinking" abilities to make-up for lack of size and strength. Herds or individual animals were, if possible, attracted or frightened into boggy areas where their very size became a disadvantage, or they were stampeded over cliffs or into ravines. The actual killing was performed with relatively short spears tipped with stone points crafted for the purpose. The manufacture of these projectile points required a high degree of skill and great patience. They were not the products of accident.

3

As I said in the beginning, someone first found that one source of Alibates Chert. Someone learned to quarry it and turn it into items of great value, and someone carried those items perhaps a thousand miles or more to use and to trade. If that isn't industry, then the dictionary and every chamber of commerce in the world is wrong.

Don't just take my word for it. Alibates National Monument is located right up there on Lake Meredith, where Potter and Carson Counties come together northeast of Amarillo, Texas. The National Park Service has tours that will take you to the site, but you should check ahead on the dates and times. Down at the Panhandle Plains Museum at Canyon they've got a good display on the topic. Check it out—it kind of takes you back!

Texas Clovis point
by Jason Carranza

Something Happened

A long time ago something happened. We don't know exactly what it was, but we know it happened rather quickly and changed the earth. Of course, a lot of people have theories and the cultural folklore of people all over the globe often allude to it, but the fact remains—we just don't know. What we can see are the results. It brought a quick end to the Pleistocene time period and an end to the last (so far) ice age. It brought global warming on a scale unimaginable by politicians today. Sea levels around the world rose at least 300 feet as the glaciers melted. Vast moraines, or mountains of gravel, remained to mark the extent of earlier glaciers. Cool, wet, and lush forests and prairies turned to deserts. The mega fauna, the really BIG GAME of the Pleistocene, became extinct throughout the earth and some were quick-frozen in new ice caps with food still in their mouths. Here in North America and Texas it brought an end to the culture of our first human inhabitants, the ones we call Paleo-Indians.

The people who replaced the Paleo-Indians were of the same genetic stock, but their culture was quite different. Before "something happened," Texas was a veritable paradise of flowing streams, mild climate, and abundant food. The Paleo-Indians, who hunted the giant bison, the woolly mammoth, and other big game, and those who cooperated in creating our first industry up at the Alibates Chert quarries, suddenly faced an environ-

4

Paleo Indian family
by Suzy Keller

ment similar to what we find today in the Trans-Pecos Sonoran Desert. It was an environment with few of the resources necessary for survival. Water was a primary limiting factor.

Limiting factors fall into two categories—resources and conditions. Any resource necessary for survival is a limiting factor, especially if it is in limited supply. Water, food, and shelter are prime examples of such resources. Conditions such as climate and other environmental hazards are also limiting factors.

When the climate changed, the lush vegetation disappeared, and the big game died out or moved on. In the absence of the mega fauna, food became a limiting factor of importance only slightly less than water. The Paleo-Indians simply could not easily adapt, and they left few survivors. For lack of a better name, we call them Early Archaic Indians.

Early Archaic Indians lived in small, family–sized groups and enjoyed little or no cooperation with their scattered neighbors. In fact, almost every neighboring family was in daily, mortal competition for the resources necessary for survival. If a family controlled a source of water it would, naturally, fight to keep that control. They ate anything to maintain life, including insects, mice, grubs and worms, seeds, fruits (when available), and any other small game. Rabbits, when they could be found, were about the largest game, along with the occasional deer. The people moved as necessary to find water, food, and shelter, in that order. Since the most obvious sources of water were the scattered small streams, most folks lived along their banks in shallow wind-and/or water-carved caves or under rock overhangs. They wore twisted and braided grass aprons and sandals and little or nothing more, because even the skins of the rabbits were used as food. Life was short and precarious. This very primitive lifestyle existed throughout Texas, and, in some parts of the state, until long after the arrival of the Spanish. In other words, the Early Archaic Indian lifestyle lasted a very long time for some people.

Then the climate began to change again, slowly this time, moving from east to west. In far East Texas more rainfall meant more plants and animals and more people. We call this stage of development the Middle Archaic. People could again live together in larger groups and cooperate on hunting expeditions and in the harvesting of prickly-pear cactus and pecans. They were still migratory, but they didn't need to travel as far to meet their needs, so they often returned to old campsites. They had a bit more in the way of clothing and shelter. Pottery made its appearance, as did the ritualistic burials of the dead, suggesting the beginning of a belief in an afterlife. It took about another 2,000 years for this climate and social change to reach as far west and south as a line roughly drawn from Dallas to Austin, to San Antonio and on to Victoria. On that line the change seems to have stopped.

By that time, the moderating climate in East Texas was such that the people there entered what we call the Late Archaic period. Resources supported a large enough population to stimulate the beginnings of tribal development and a level of social stratification, where some made the decisions for the group and others carried the burden of the work. Trade routes opened between groups, which began to lay claim to certain geographic regions. Agriculture began as an accident when people returned to old campsites and found food growing from abandoned garbage piles.

Annual rainfall in East Texas continued to increase, and, about 2,000 years ago, people living north and east of the Trinity River entered the Neo-Archaic stage of development. They lived in highly stratified social systems with organized government, religion, and agriculture, in permanent villages made up of permanent homes. These people represented the southwestern-most expansion of the Mississippian Culture that had permanent cities of thousands of people as far north as the Ohio River Valley and in Illinois. Then, about 700 years before the arrival of the Spanish, something again happened in West Texas.

This time it had very little to do with a change in climate. A new kind of people migrated into Texas from the North. We call their arrival the "Athapascan Intrusion." The genetic origins of the Athapascan peoples are found in Asian Mongolia. Apparently, they migrated into Northern Alaska and the Northwest provinces of Canada. Many of their descendants and traces of this migration are still there—there is even a Lake Athabasca in Canada. Then, about 1,400 years ago, the group split and about half of them began migrating south down the eastern slope of the Rocky Mountains. When they reached the point where Denver, Colorado, is today, they split again. Those who went to the Southwest—Utah, Arizona and western

New Mexico—we today call the Navajo. Those who came south into Texas and eastern New Mexico we call the Apache. By 1500 they had killed, absorbed, or run out most of the earlier peoples with whom they came into contact. Being a people accustomed to the mountains and plains, they rarely ventured east of the Edwards Plateau area of Central Texas.

Available resources were the key to population growth then, just as they still are today. Loving County in far West Texas has an annual rainfall of between three and four inches and a total population of about 70 people. Cass County in East Texas has an average rainfall of about 49 inches and a population of about 40,000 people. They are both basically rural areas, unlike Bexar, Harris, or Tarrant counties. Of course, there are other factors involved—but you get the picture.

The land and its resources are like the settings on a stage before a play begins. They determine where the people can go and what they can do when they get there. It has always been that way.

American bison
by Nathan Smith

The Spanish Period: 1500-1821

1500—Homefolks

The year of 1500 was not especially important in world history. Pope Alexander VI sold new indulgences to support a crusade against the Turks, and the first black-lead pencils were used in England. The first Caesarean childbirth operation on a living woman was performed in Switzerland by a pig gelder, and a lot of other folks were born, and a lot of others died. Some were important, and some were not. There were the usual wars and revolts, regicides, patricides, fratricides, and suicides. Explorers began to realize that there was a lot more to the "New World" than they supposed. However, it wasn't until September of 1519 that Magellan set sail on the

Indians of Texas circa 1500
by Suzy Keller

9

voyage that would prove to most folks that the Earth was round. It was a pretty ordinary year. Perhaps because nothing happened of monumental importance to confuse us, the year 1500 makes a good dividing line between pre-history and history in our part of the world.

For something to be "Historic" there must be people who leave a written record. "Prehistoric" refers to any time when people do not leave written records. Thus, for something to be prehistoric does not necessarily mean that it is very old. It simply means that the people involved left no written records to explain their activities. Here in Texas that dividing line came about 1500. There were many people here at that time, and they had been around for thousands of years; but except for pictographs on rocks, they left no written records. Those written records, the accounts of the first European explorers, began about 1519.

Who were those Texans who greeted the first explorers? How many of them were there? What were their lives like? Well, in some cases, we will never know, because they passed from the scene before anyone wrote about them. At best, we have a list of about 900 different tribal names gathered by early explorers, and many of these are no doubt just different names used for the same people. So, unless you are an archaeologist dealing with a particular site for which you have a name, we must lump many groups of people together based on similar lifestyles and give those large groupings names that we can handle. Although there may be many sub-tle differences between the components of these groups, they had more in common with each other than with their neighbors.

Coahuiltecans
by Suzy Keller

Most of the South Texas brush country (the *brasada*) below the Nueces River and the desert land of West Texas was occupied by scattered bands of people we will call *Coahuiltecans*. They existed at a very primitive level, most of them trapped in the Early or Middle Archaic stage of development. Just as it is today, water was the primary limiting factor then, followed by a shortage of food for much of the year. They lived in small family groupings that rarely exceeded a dozen or so. Each family unit was the mortal enemy of every other family, because they were in daily competition for the limited resources necessary for survival. They wore little in the way of clothing, because they had little from which clothing could be made. Woven grass or yucca fibers made aprons that, along with braided grass sandals, completed the wardrobes of adult males and females. The children wore nothing. For food they ate anything they could find. Ants, insects of all kinds, birds, mice and rats, lizards and snakes, occasional rabbits, and the roots of some plants made up much of their diet. About the only time of the year when there was plenty of food was in the summer, when pods of mesquite beans and the fruit of the cactus were ripe. Unfortunately, this coincided with the driest time of the year. The Coahuiltecans could not take advantage of this abundance because they had to stay close to their dwindling water supply.

Like many of the small animals they hunted, they lived under rock overhangs or in brush piles. They had little in the way of personal property and little time to enjoy what they had. Some of them apparently killed female children at birth simply because they represented an extra mouth to feed. Some apparently ate their neighbors on occasion. Life was short and probably generally unpleasant, but because they had nothing with which to compare, it was what they were used to.

Karankawa
by Suzy Keller

The *Karankawa* lived in a relatively narrow band along the Gulf Coast, south of Galveston. There are several different spellings of that name, but don't worry about it—all of them are correct. The Karankawa were the most outstanding physical specimens in Texas in 1500. Men and women alike averaged well over six feet in height, and their bodies were well formed. While some lived in wandering bands, many lived together in larger tribal groupings of 100 or more, controlled by a shaman, or religious leader. Like the Coahuiltecans, they wore little in the way of clothing. Males remained nude for most of their lives; before the age of puberty, girls wore deerskin smocks, but adult women wore only braided moss aprons below their waists. Both men and women covered their bodies with tattoos made by piercing the skin with cactus thorns and rubbing rancid alligator grease mixed with soot from the fire into the wound. These wounds festered, of course, and, when healed, left three-dimensional geometric outlines of scar tissue.

Life was much better for the Karankawa than it was for their neighbors to the west. There was abundant water and food. They hunted all manner of game with long bows and arrows that were often four feet or more in length. They were excellent fishers and left islands of oyster shells to attest to their harvests of shellfish. Alligators were such an important part of their diet that they assumed mythical status in Karankawa society. Rancid alligator grease, liberally applied to their skins, protected the folks from mosquitoes and sunburn.

Their living shelters were brush arbors (*ramadas*) made of poles with brush, grass, or anything else on top to provide shade. They made small boats by hollowing logs with fire and used oyster shells to scrape away the burned wood. In these they poled their way from island to island and to the mainland.

Children were the wealth of the family and the tribe. If a child died for any reason, the whole tribe mourned for a year and parents cut fingers from their hands.

Early in their contact with Europeans, the Karankawa got a bad reputation as man-eaters. Lurid accounts of Karankawa cannibalism appeared in books throughout Europe. Most Europeans were so afraid of this, that the Karankawa were hunted and killed to the point of extinction. Europeans just didn't understand that there are basically two kinds of cannibalism. The first kind is for food value, and is rather rare. The other kind is performed as a part of semi-religious ritual. This ritualistic cannibalism is quite common throughout history, in many societies and in many parts of the world. Look at it this way: if you consider that there is something special about *you*—something that sets you apart from all other people— and that this special something is responsible for your intelligence, bravery, honor, etc., then you're on the right track. Now consider that when you die, all of that is lost to your family, your friends, and your community. You may not realize it, but you now have the answer. Within the Karankawa culture they believed that when you died everything that was special about you was lost *unless* everyone else in your group ate a small portion of your flesh. When they did that, you did not really die; that special something that was *you* lived on in others. It worked for your enemies, too—

12

Tonkawa
by Suzy Keller

if you killed an enemy and ate a bite, you got some of his energy and bravery.

Central Texas, an area roughly bounded by the Nueces River on the south, the Trinity River on the North, today's I-35 on the west, and the coastal lands of the Karankawa on the east, was the home of people we call the *Tonkawa*. Actually, they called themselves *Tickanwatic*, which means *"the most human of people."* The Tonkawa lived in a land of plenty, with an abundance of water in many streams, springs, and rivers. They had an almost constant food supply in the form of fruits and nuts and the wild game that fed and drank in the same land.

As a rule, the Tonkawa lived in family-based clans and moved about through the course of the year within a relatively small area. Summer took them to the drier ridges, where the prickly-pear cactus, grapes and berries, and other fruits, such as wild plums, were abundant. In winter they sheltered in the valleys to escape the weather and to gather pecans and acorns. They usually returned to the same camping spots every year. Their standard shelter was the tipi covered with skins. They cooked their food, wore more complex clothing than their neighbors, and acquired more private property.

Apache
by Suzy Keller

Regardless of the relative levels of the two civilizations, the Tonkawa were actually far more cannibalistic than the Karankawa. They often held a true cannibalistic feast after a battle in which they killed or captured enemies. Despite this habit, they adapted well to European culture; many served later as military scouts for the army and the Texas Rangers.

In 1500 most of Texas to the west of a line drawn from today's Fort Worth to San Antonio, to Eagle Pass and on to El Paso, was claimed and sparsely occupied by the eastern branches of the *Apache*, who were the eastern-most extension of the Athapascan Intrusion. We are not sure of the date, but they apparently came from the far north into the area around 700 AD. Their warriors, among whom there were many women, were fierce fighters. They tended to kill, run out of the country, or absorb their neighbors. They were primarily nomadic, following the buffalo herds on their winter migrations into the area. They planted small gardens in the spring and summer. They brought with them the laminated re-curve bow and the domestic dog, which was at that time the only satisfactory beast of burden in North America. They wore minimal clothing, but that included knee-high moccasins similar to the "mukluks" of the Far North.

Jumano
by Suzy Keller

Two small and very different groups of people that we know by the same name existed like islands in the sea of the Apache. The Spanish called them both *Jumano*, and that didn't help much because, as I said, they were quite different. One small group lived in the vicinity of present-day San Angelo, near where the Concho joins the Colorado River. They remain something of a puzzle because, at that time, they appeared to be a culture in decline, one that had lost its will to live. The Apache tended to leave them alone, because they just didn't act like normal people. They hunted only enough to keep from starving and rarely practiced any form of agriculture. There is really not much to say about them, except that they existed.

The other group we know as Jumano lived along the Rio Grande below today's El Paso. They were the most southeastern extension of the Puebloan Culture of New Mexico. They lived in permanent adobe *pueblos* (towns) ruled by a tribal council and shaman. They practiced an advanced form of agriculture based on complex irrigation systems and had a social system that divided the labor among all of the people who shared in the harvest. The Apache also left them alone most of the time, but I suspect for a different reason. Cyclic weather patterns in the Southwest dictate that there will be a drought about every 7-10 years. During these times the buffalo herds, on which the Apache depended for food, did not migrate to the South, which meant that the Apache went hungry. In drought times they raided the pueblos for stored food but didn't kill the people, because they knew that, when the next drought came around in another 7-10 years, they could come back and do it again. For the Apache, the Jumano of the pueblos were rather like a savings account in the bank.

In a strange twist of fate, these two groups we call Jumano joined together about 100 years later to become the *Tigua*. Their descendants still live in the El Paso area today.

If you look at a botanical map of Texas, you will notice a long tongue of heavy vegetation entering Texas from Oklahoma above Fort Worth and generally following the west side of I-35 south until it runs out on the Edwards Plateau. We call this the "Cross Timbers" region, and it was the

Wichita
by Suzy Keller

15

Caddo
by Suzy Keller

home to a very large, but loosely organized group we call the *Wichita*. This isn't an accurate term, because it really applies to only one of a collection of several hundred remnant and refugee populations.

Texas was not much like their ancestral home, and being woodland Indians, they didn't do well on the prairies. They fled the upper Midwest around the Great Lakes, forced from their homelands by expanding pressure from other tribes in eastern North America. Pushed steadily south, they were trapped by a combination of geography and hostile inhabitants.

There were a lot of them, but they represented such a wide variety of languages, cultures, religions, and organizational patterns that they were unable to capitalize on their numbers, and so remained a rather weak people, harassed by enemies and competitors on all sides.

North and east of the Trinity River the land belonged to the *Caddo*, part of that great *Caddo-Hasinai* Confederation that occupied much of Louisiana, Arkansas, and Missouri. These, in turn, were a part of the even greater Mississippian or Mound-Building Culture of the Mississippi, Tennessee, and Ohio River valleys.

The Caddo were the most culturally advanced residents of Texas in 1500. Each local community was part of a true political confederation made up of semi-autonomous towns, with a highly stratified social order based on agriculture and bound together by agreements of mutual aid. The mounds they built for ceremony, living

Attakapans
by Suzy Keller

and burial, were replicas of those found throughout the central part of the United States and served the same purposes. Towns were permanent, as were the tall, cone-shaped houses thatched with river cane. It was a matriarchal society in which one's social position was dependent on the mother, not the father, and where women could and did rise to positions of tribal control.

Of all of the counties in Texas, only one is named for a woman—Angelina. She was Caddo and governed her people well. The Spanish called her a "sagacious" woman.

Occupying a small coastal corner of Southeast Texas and slopping over into southern Louisiana to the Mississippi, were the *Attakapans*. They were a curious, war-like people who kept to themselves, hunted and fished in the swamps where they also practiced some agriculture on the dry islands. They spoke a language unassociated with any other in North America. Some cultural geographers contend that their language stems from ancient Phoenician, and that they may well have been descendents of shipwrecked Phoenician sailors from the eastern Mediterranean Sea. Certainly, such could be the case, because Phoenicians were the greatest world navigators of their day.

That brings us full circle. Remember that in any of these groups there was a great deal of variation and that they were lumped together because they had more in common with each other than with their neighbors.

The question remains: "So, OK, we've got a lot of different groups of people. Just how many people are we talking about?"

Of course, we will never know. From almost the beginning of this time period in 1500, the church was interested in how many souls there were to save; and the government was interested in how many there were, who, as slaves, represented a possible profit. Historians and anthropologists, and all manner of agencies and disciplines, have worked on the problem ever since. Although there is a lot of argument and the total is revised almost every year, a partial consensus estimates a total population of today's Mexico and the American Southwest circa 1500 of about 50 million people. About 30 million of these were in today's Mexico, where the Central Valley was the most densely populated spot on earth. That leaves about 20 million to divide between Texas, New Mexico, Arizona, a little tip of Nevada, and the southern half of California.

Certainly, there were places where no one lived. There are places like that today. Likewise, there were places where the available resources allowed abundant populations. You can make up your own mind about how to divide those folks between Texas, California, and the desert areas; but if we give Texas only one fourth of the total, which equals 5 million people, that was equal to the population of Texas according to the modern census of 1930. Any way you look at it, there were a lot of people of different cultures here in 1500. This was their home, just as it is yours today.

1544—Martyr

In November of 1528, Alvar Núñez, Cabeza de Vaca, and a handful of other survivors from the ill-fated expedition of Pánfilo de Narváez to Florida, were washed ashore near today's Galveston. For several years local groups of Karankawa Indians of the area kept them as sort of a combination of captives and honored guests until Alvar Núñez and three companions escaped to the interior. They wandered westward and south. Finally, in May of 1536, they encountered other Spaniards on the west coast of Mexico. These were the first Europeans to walk across Texas. Alvar Núñez was the first to leave a written account. Actually, he left several written accounts of that trip. They don't agree with each other.

You see, the Narváez expedition expected to find the same riches that Hernán Cortéz found in Mexico. When the only survivors of the Narváez expedition reported that there was no gold in Florida and no great riches in the brush and desert of South and West Texas, they were thrown into prison in Mexico City. Obviously they were keeping the news to themselves until they could go back and become as rich as the king himself. In order to get out of prison, Alvar Núñez hinted that, while they had found no riches, they had heard about them—seven cities of gold.

The Spanish Church wanted a piece of the action and sent Father Marcos de Niza with Estevanico (the Moorish slave who had been with Alvar Núñez) as a guide to check it out and locate the golden cities. Historians can only guess where they went. Indians somewhere killed Estevanico (maybe) and Frey Marcos didn't leave much of an account other than to state that he had actually seen the golden cities. The golden cities were there, somewhere in the American Southwest. The Church said so. All that was left was for an expedition to find and conquer them in the name of Spain. Thus, in 1540 Francisco Vásquez de Coronado set out from Central Mexico with 300 horsemen, 70 foot soldiers, a handful of priests and lay brothers, three secretaries, and about 1,000 Indians.

"November 30, 1544: After four-year's travel on foot away from civilization, a lifetime of service of one kind or another to Church and king, far from the green

Cabeza de Vaca and his three companions, *by José Cisneros*
courtesy UTSA's Institute of Texan Cultures at San Antonio (Calleros Estate)

19

*hills and groves of Andalusia in the Spanish homeland—
so much time and preparation to end so suddenly. Not
everyone can be a martyr. First you have to believe in
something—anything—strongly enough to fight to defend
it. Then you must die in the process."*

Juan de Padilla was a soldier back there in Spanish Andalusia. That
is, he was a soldier until God tapped him on the shoulder and said, *"Follow me."* He became a priest and a member of the Franciscan Order. But
he knew a soldier's life, and he felt the call of adventure in the New World.
Down in Mexico he put his two lives together and served as a guardian in
the monasteries of Tulancingo and Zapotlan.

Then came January 6, 1540, when Alvar Núñez reported tales of sev-
en golden cities in the unknown country to the north. Frey Marcos de
Niza corroborated the story, and Governor Mendoza appointed Francisco Vásquez de Coronado to lead an expedition of conquest. Such an expedition needed God's guidance. It needed men strong in body, as well as
in faith.

Father Juan de Padilla was one such man.

Near the end of April of 1540, the expedition set out into the deserts
and mountains of Sinaloa, Sonora, and the American Southwest. Through
the lands of the Yaqui, Zuni, and Hopi they wound their way. Some saw
the Grand Canyon. Some saw the fortress rock of Acoma. Others followed
the Rio Grande northward through the pueblos of New Mexico. Frey Juan
walked all the way, carrying his burdens, a soldier of the Church. They
spent the winter of 1540-41 at the Tiguex Pueblo in northern New Mexico, and in the spring, moved eastward. They crossed the Sangre de Cristo
Mountains and the broad valley of the Pecos River. Then they climbed the
escarpment onto the *Llaño Estacado*, the "staked plains" or "Caprock" of
the Texas Panhandle. They found no golden cities, only endless grass and
sky, and the buffalo that they called *cíbolo*.

In Palo Duro Canyon, Coronado held council. The men and horses
were worn out and food was scarce. The summer was half gone, winter
was coming, and they were far from home. There were no cities of gold,
only the buffalo wallows that the men derisively called the *Cities of Cíbolo*.
Much of the expedition was ordered to start back toward Mexico, while
Coronado and a chosen few, including Frey Juan, went *más allá*, further
on. In July they found Quivira, a few brush and mud huts of those we call
the Wichita, in a bend of the Arkansas River in what would one day become Kansas.

Then came the retreat. They hadn't made many friends among the Indians they encountered along the way, and that turned their struggle to re-

turn to Mexico into a brutal slog. Back on the Rio Grande in northern New Mexico, Coronado's expedition disbanded. Most of the men made it back to Mexico, but Father Juan de Padilla decided to stay. For two years he, with a few companions and converts, remained. There was God's work to do and there were souls to save.

He did his best. Cut off from the questionable civilization in Central Mexico by over 1,000 miles of desert, he decided to go even farther into the interior. He retraced the expedition's route into the Texas Panhandle, into that endless sea of grass, where scattered Indians were finding their first horses—those lost by the expedition.

Even today Lipscomb County up on the Oklahoma border is a harsh, semi-arid, and lonesome country. They have an average annual rainfall there of about 23 inches, but sometimes the rains don't come.

On November 30, 1544, near the site of today's town of Higgins, hostile Indians killed Father Juan de Padilla. His companions buried him under a pile of stones. Almost a hundred years before the first successful Anglo colony was founded on the Atlantic Coast, Texas had its first Christian martyr—a former soldier of Andalusia.

1598–Rio Grande Thanksgiving

During the 1500s Spain was the richest nation in Europe. Despite a variety of wars, the riches that flowed into Spain from the New World were beyond the wildest dreams of anyone. Even Columbus, who died penniless and in disrepute, had not dreamed of what the conquest of the Americas would mean. The New World was, indeed, "The Promised Land," as far as Spain was concerned.

Since Francisco Pizarro had found great wealth in South America and Hernán Cortez had done the same in Mexico,

Don Juan de Oñate
by Suzy Keller

21

no one doubted that more golden opportunities awaited those who dared to enter what we now call the United States. Although the expeditions of Alvar Núñez, Cabeza de Vaca, Francisco de Coronado and Luis de Moscoso Alvarado found little reason to return, there were still others who dreamed of riches and empire.

Roasted duck, goose, and turkey, corn pudding, squash and pumpkins, venison and buffalo, and prayers of thanks—is this our first Thanksgiving with the Pilgrims in the Plymouth colony? Not exactly, but it was Thanksgiving. It was a first, and it beat the Pilgrim Fathers by over 20 years.

On an early morning in April of the year 1598, a ragged and thirsty party of eight armed scouts approached the cottonwoods that fringed the Rio Grande just below where the city of El Paso stands today. Their task of trail-marking completed, they rolled in the water with their horses, two of which were carried away by the current, and two of which drank too much water and died. With or without horses, their job was to wait for those who followed the trail they had made across the Chihuahuan Desert from the interior of Mexico to *El Paso del Norte*, the Pass of the North, which led to the open lands of the newly appointed governor of Spanish New Mexico, Don Juan de Oñate.

This was no small undertaking. When the governor's expedition arrived at the river on April 26, it was not designed to explore but to occupy and colonize. There were soldiers and servants, women and children, the clergy, and many high-wheeled ox carts filled with belongings. There were herds of cattle, horses, sheep, goats, and pigs. Four years in planning, the expedition had toiled across the barren Chihuahuan Desert, and its members had suffered great hardship. Now it was at the gate, the pass to the promised land of New Mexico.

These hardy *pobladores*, or pioneers, would form the first non-Indian settlements in the American Southwest. It was a time for celebration and thanksgiving.

The colonial Spanish were a legalistic people. Laws of the Church and the Crown required ceremony. So be it. When Don Juan de Oñate came before his people on the 30th day of April, 1598, he wore one of his six complete suits of armor and was welcomed with a fanfare of trumpets. A representative of the Church on one side, and of the Crown on the other, led him by the hand across the river. He stooped to pluck some herbs from the soil, signifying that he would make the land produce. The royal decree was read aloud to grant him authority. He then called upon, *"the one and only true God,"* the *"Holy Mother of God,"* the *"Divine Trinity,"* and St. Francis to bear witness as he proclaimed his legal authority to govern the land. He stooped, picked up, and threw stones to signify that he would protect his claim. He enumerated the purposes of the colony and encouraged all to serve him as worthy subjects.

Then, in the name of God and the King, he declared, *"I take possession once, twice, and thrice of the lands of the said Rio del Norte, without exception whatsoever, with all its meadows and pasture lands and passes—and all other lands, pueblos, cities, villas, of whatsoever nature now founded in the kingdom or province of New Mexico and of all its native Indians—all jurisdiction, civil as well as criminal, high and low, from the*

Arrival of priest, soldiers, and Indians at El Paso del Norte, *by José Cisneros courtesy UTSA's Institute of Texan Cultures at San Antonio (Calleros Estate)*

23

edge of the mountains to the stones and sand in the rivers and the leaves of the trees." He knelt and prayed for blessing and strength. The soldiers fired a volley with their weapons, and a cross was planted by the river. The ceremony of *La Toma*, "the taking," was complete. Only then could the people of his colony cross the river.

Thus began our first Thanksgiving.

Father Alonso Martínez sang a mass and followed it with a sermon. Then there was a play, hastily written and rehearsed by Captain Don Marcos Farfan de los Godos, and a parade of all members of the colony, dressed in their finest. Don Juan de Oñate led the group as governor, followed by a crucifer, a royal standard bearer, the trumpeters, and the royal secretary, whose job it was to ensure that all appropriate taxes were paid to Church and State.

Polished armor and horse trappings glittered in the sun. Ribbons adorned the polished horns of oxen, whose bellowing added a bass note to the descant soprano screech of ungreased wooden cart axels and the bleatings and squeals of sheep, goats, and pigs. They all marched in review before the cross.

Then came the feast of thanksgiving with the finest that they had brought and the best a bountiful land could provide. Local Pueblo Indians contributed corn, melons, squash, and turkeys. The festivities and feasting lasted almost a week.

Ahead lay more deserts, difficulties, and an unseen future. But, for a time, there was rejoicing and the opportunity for rest.

If you have the opportunity, visit El Paso during the last week of every April and participate in their annual reenactment of our oldest Thanksgiving.

1632–The Blue Visitor

Back in 1927, J.B.S. Haldane, who spent a lifetime trying to explain science to unscientific minds, expanded on Shakespeare when he wrote, "I suspect that there are more things in heaven and earth than are dreamed of, in any philosophy." Certainly, there are things that happen for which there is no logical explanation. In a way, they are provable only by their result. This is that kind of story. In a way, it makes no difference whether you believe it or not. The situations leading up to it appear to be true and the result is a matter of historic fact. How you get from "Point A" to "Point B" is your problem.

In 1598, Don Juan de Oñate established the first Spanish settlement in the American Southwest a few miles north of where Santa Fe, New Mexico, is today. Despite assorted wanderings by explorers, this was the only real Spanish toehold. With Oñate were several Franciscan priests, who found the job of Christianizing the Indians an uphill drag because of the tendency of other colonists, and Oñate's government officials alike, to rape, pillage, and plunder, to say nothing of the attempts of the Church to destroy all semblances of native religion. For twenty years their efforts went unrewarded. The religious fields of the Southwest were simply not ready for the harvest.

Then came the strangers.

There were about 50 of them, and no local Indians knew who they were. They simply appeared one day from over the *Sangre de Cristo* Mountains in the East and, through a use of universal sign language, requested instruction in "The Faith," baptism, and a mission among their people. Surprisingly, they already showed a rudimentary knowledge of the Gospels and the Sacraments of the Roman Catholic Church. For the priests, this was the best news in years. They went into high gear and, for a few days, gave as much instruction as they could. Then, after a short time, the Indians disappeared into the night and the desert. No one knew who they were or where they came from. It was as if they had never existed.

The next year it happened again, and then again, and then again, on an irregular basis.

Meanwhile, in 1602, near the tiny Spanish town of Agreda, a girl was born into a family of minor nobility. She was the first-born daughter of Francisco Coronel and Catalana de Arana. She was baptized as María Coronel and, early in life, showed a high degree of

Maria de Jesus de Agreda, the Blue Visitor
by Suzy Keller

25

piety and a thirst for knowledge. At 16, María convinced her parents that they should convert the small family castle into a convent for Franciscan nuns. She must have been very persuasive because her father became a friar and her mother a nun in the process. At age eighteen, the persuasive young lady took her religious vows and the name María de Jesús de Agreda. She donned the rough brown habit of the Franciscan order and the outer cloak of coarse blue cloth of her own order.

At that time, the New World was much in the news in Spain. It was a world of riches to conquer, filled with souls to save. One hundred years before, the Roman Church promoted the belief that all Native Americans were *"savage beasts in the shapes of men"* and no more human than the *"birds of the air or the beasts of the fields."* By 1600, however, European church officials recognized in the natives a "Divine Spark" that could be fanned into the flame of true humanity, *if* an individual were to receive instruction in The Faith, to be baptized, and become a communing member of the Roman Catholic Church. María wanted to be a part of this new crusade. She wanted to go to the New World as a missionary, but it was impossible. Her simple order was poor, and, in any case, women were not allowed to go as missionaries.

According to Carlos E. Castañeda, whose *Our Catholic Heritage* is a "must read" for Texas historians, María dedicated herself so completely to religious contemplation that, as early as age 18, she began to drift into a series of catatonic comas that lasted from a few hours to more than a week. The first time it happened, folks thought she had died and were preparing her body for burial when she woke up and scared everyone there beyond belief. On awakening, she was as puzzled as anyone else, but after it happened a few more times, she explained. She said that, in dreams, she was transported to the New World where she taught the gospel to several groups of native people. Afraid that something might be wrong with something that seemed so right, María told of her dreams to her confessor, Fray Sebastian Marcilla of Agreda. He, in turn, forsaking the sanctity of the confessional, told his superiors.

Miracles are not unknown to readers of the Christian Bible, and many religions accept the concept of miracles and an "out of body" experience. The word spread. King Philip IV of Spain himself visited María on several occasions, and, with the encouragement and blessing of the Roman Catholic Church, sent investigators to the New World to search for evidence.

Meanwhile, back in New Mexico, Fray Alonso de Benavides and his assistant Fray Juan de Salas contemplated the mystery of the occasional visits of Indians from the East who, by then, were called Jumanos. At the same time, Fray Alonso contemplated with even more enthusiasm his imminent replacement in this spiritual wasteland and a return to Spain and home. During the 1600s, the colony in New Mexico was about as far from Spain as you could get. News and supplies reached the New Mexico missions only once every three or four years. So it was that in July of 1629, Fray Alonso received Fray Diego León, who came as his replacement, but also brought a question about any miraculous appearances. Even the visiting Jumanos were questioned about it.

"*Of course,*" they said. No one had ever asked that before. They said that was why they came on a regular basis. They'd been sent by a beautiful woman, dressed in a robe, "*the color of the sky,*" who appeared often among their people, taught them, and sent them in search of salvation.

Now, whether you believe in miracles or not, you must accept the bottom line. Fray Juan de Salas and Fray Diego León, acting on what the Jumanos said, returned with them to their country, about 300 miles southeast of Santa Fe. There they were welcomed by a large congregation of Indians near the junction of today's Coleman, Concho, and Runnels counties, where the Concho flows into the Colorado. There the priests stayed for several months, preaching and teaching, and, ultimately, baptizing about 2,000 Indians. When they received emissaries from other tribes of the area who told the same story of a "lady in blue" and made the same request for a mission, they left for New Mexico and promised to return. In 1632, they were back, in company with a few soldiers, and, near today's San Angelo they established the first Roman Catholic mission in Texas. Although the mission lasted less than a year, it created a foundation of faith, and when new missions were established on the Rio Grande in 1680, there were Jumanos there to participate in the work of building.

However, back in Spain, there were problems. When the reports of the investigation returned, things had changed. María de Agreda was no longer a teen-aged neophyte. She had become the Mother Superior of her order, and, more importantly, she had become the most outspoken European advocate of women's rights, both in the Church and in secular walks of life. Her writings offended both Church and Crown, and she had become what we would call today "politically incorrect." Although she was able to describe, to the satisfaction of the priests who had been there, certain localities and people in the New World, the church officials were not about to give special recognition to someone who questioned Roman Catholic policies regarding the role of women in society.

María de Jesús de Agreda died on May 24th, 1665, and was buried in her cloak of blue, "*the color of the sky,*" but that isn't the end of the story.

In the 1680s, word came to the Viceroy of New Spain that the French, under the leadership of René Robert Cavalier, Sieur de La Salle, had established a colony on the coast of the Gulf of Mexico. Alonso De León ultimately made five expeditions to find and destroy the French colony of Ft. St.

Louis down on Garcitas Creek near Port Lavaca. He was too late. A combination of disease, lack of food, and Indian attack had already destroyed the colony. After destroying what remained of the French fort and finding a few French refugees living among the Indians, De León and the priest of the expedition, Father Damián Massanet, led the Spanish into East Texas in search of other possible French incursions.

On the banks of the Neches River they met a large congregation of Indians of the *Nabadache* tribe, a Caddoan group, who indicated that their fathers had told them that one day the Spanish would come bearing the Word of God. In questioning, they indicated that "the lady in blue" told their fathers. As an immediate result, the mission of *San Francisco de Los Tejas* was consecrated in May of 1690 near the present sites of Augusta and Weches in Houston County. Later reports from Indians along the Sabine River indicated that a mysterious "lady in blue" had brought comfort to their villages during an epidemic of smallpox.

Indeed, a ghostly "blue visitor" is said to have appeared to people in need throughout Texas as recently as 1944. Truly, as Haldane implied, strange things do happen.

1675–The Mass of Father Larios

By 1670, both France and England had established claims to the northern Atlantic coastline and Canada and were expanding to the West and South. The Hudson's Bay Company was chartered in England in attempt to wrest the Canadian Indian trade from the French. Meanwhile France had its hands full in a war with the Dutch. While the English and French fought an undeclared war against each other in North America, they became allies in the war against the Dutch in Europe. Sweden and Denmark were at war in Europe, and, while everyone was busy elsewhere, England annexed both New Holland (changing its name to New York) and New Sweden (which became New England).

Meanwhile, for all practical purposes, Spanish interest in the American Southwest during the sixteenth century was confined to a few explorations in search of gold and silver and the establishment of their settlements along the Rio Grande near today's Santa Fe. Most Spanish officials, if they thought at all of the area we call Texas, decided that there was nothing here worth the trouble of finding and keeping it. "Not so," thought wealthy humanitarian Don Antonio Balcárcel Rivadeneyra y So-

tomayor. While the rest of the world fought wars over gold and trade, he wanted to save souls.

Don Antonio Balcárcel Rivadeneyra y Sotomayor was more than just well-to-do. As a loyal supporter of Spain, he was an *encomiendado*, one of those specially designated to have kingly powers over a large area, and *alcalde mayor* (governor) of Coahuila. With these powers came responsibilities. One of these was to care for and Christianize the Indians. Don Antonio took his responsibilities seriously. While other representatives of the Crown did their best to rape, pillage, plunder, and rip the tags off of the mattresses of the Native Americans, Don Antonio tried to see what he could do to bring them the Word of God and make them productive members of society.

So, in the spring of 1675, he sent out a combination exploration and Christianizing party to penetrate what we now call Texas. The military leader of the expedition was Fernando del Bosque. With him went only ten Spanish soldiers. In addition, however, other members of the expedition included Lazano Agustin, who was the governor of the Indian pueblo of *San Miguel de Luna*, twenty lay brothers from the mission of *Nuestra Señora de Guadalupe* at Monclova, Fathers Juan De Larios and Dionisio de San Buenaventura, and over one hundred Christianized Guyquechele Indians.

On May 11, they reached the Rio Grande at a spot a few miles below today's Eagle Pass. They did not, and could not, know that within fifty years, there would be a major mission and presidio complex on the site called *San Juan Bautista* that would anchor the southern end of a royal road connecting many missions in Texas. In 1675, there was nothing but the dust, the

Father Juan de Larios
by Suzy Keller

29

river, and a few scattered bands of Coahuiltecan Indians who had not progressed beyond the nomadic stage of hunting and gathering.

Bosque took formal possession of the river in the name of the king, named it the *Buenaventura Del Norte*, and planted a large wooden cross. Then came representative Indians from farther into the interior. They requested instruction in The Faith and baptism for their people. Perhaps, like the Jumanos before them and the Caddos afterward, the mystical "blue lady" sent them, but no one asked. Instead, the party crossed the river and entered what we now call Texas.

Three days later, Bosque ordered a camp established on the Nueces River near today's Uvalde. There, they unpacked a portable altar, complete with altar cloths and silver furnishings, and prepared for a Mass. On May 16, 1675, Father Juan De Larios sang what the Roman Catholic Church recognizes as the first high mass celebrated in today's Texas.

In all, the mass attracted over 1,000 adult Indians, and 55 infants were baptized. Throughout the next month, the expedition made six stops in Texas and sang masses at each, returning to Mexico through today's Edwards County. By the middle of June they were back in Mexico making their reports. When Alonso DeLeón made his journey into Texas twenty years later in search of René Robert Cavalier, Sieur de LaSalle, and his French colony, he followed much the same path as that of Father Larios when the Cross led the way.

1700–Angelina

The last time anyone bothered to count them, there were 254 counties in Texas. That's a whole bunch. The U.S. Bureau of the Census also estimates that those 254 counties contain almost 20 million people and that women outnumber men by a rather wide margin. Now, the point of this is that, with all of these counties and the majority population of women, only one county is named for a woman. She was a Native American and her name was Angelina.

Angelina was, in all probability, a member of the *Assinais* or *Téjas* tribe, which was, in turn, a part of the Caddo/Hasinai Confederation. We know more about the Caddo groups than any other Indians in Texas during the early days of European settlement because they were, by far, the most culturally advanced. They had a highly stratified society, an advanced political system and religion, and practiced what can only be called "scientific farming," in which there was crop rotation and irrigation. In addition, women played a very important role in the society, often rising to the status of chief or high priest.

At a time when most other Native Americans in Texas lived a nomadic lifestyle, these folks lived in permanent villages with long-lasting, two- and three-storied domed homes, and raised mounds for temples, burials, and other important functions. In fact, the member groups of the Caddo/Hasinai Confederation were an extension of the advanced cultures of the Mississippi and Ohio River basins, which seemed to have cultural, if not genetic, ties to the mighty civilizations of Central America.

But, back to Angelina.

Our first written record of Angelina comes from the indomitable Father Damián Massanet, who, in 1690, established the first Spanish mission, *San Francisco de las Téjas*, in East Texas up in Hamilton County. In 1691 he described her as an *"Indian maiden with a bright intellect and possessing a striking personal appearance,"* who *"expressed a desire to learn the Father's language."* So it was that, in 1693, when Don Domingo Terán de los Rios ordered the abandonment of the mission, Angelina returned to Mexico and was baptized and schooled at the mission of *San Juan Bautista*, a few miles below today's Eagle Pass.

By 1713, Angelina was back among her people, not only able to speak Spanish, but also French. There, she became the pivotal focus around which both France and Spain revolved in their attempts to control trade in the area. She was an interpreter for and a confidant of Louis Juchereau de St. Denis', the intrepid French explorer, and she was probably the one who directed him to *San Juan Bautista*. His dealings there make another story, but he returned to East Texas with a new bride and leading the Spanish expedition that created six new missions. Among those who came with him, Father Isídro Felix de Espinosa spoke of Angelina's help as coming from *"a learned Indian woman—reared in Coahu-*

Angelina
by Nathan Smith

31

ila." Fray Francisco Celiz described her as a *"sagacious Indian woman interpreter,"* and Fray Juan Morfi recorded that *"one Angelina who has been raised on the Rio Grande and spoke both Spanish and the Texas languages"* served as his interpreter.

When Francois Simars De Bellisle sailed from France in 1719 and was shipwrecked in Galveston Bay and captured by Attakapan Indians, it was Angelina who ransomed him and claimed him as a husband. Francois, being fresh from France, didn't understand the situation and didn't really appreciate his salvation. You see, many of the important women who led the Hasinai tribes had six or more "husbands," or male consorts, who did menial work around the house, provided food and companionship, and stayed out of the way when they weren't needed.

Ultimately, he was "rescued" by Angelina's old friend St. Denis, who probably explained that in France it was usually the other way around.

Within a short time, Angelina led the official party to welcome the new Spanish governor, the Marqués de Aguayo, and took up permanent residence at the mission of *Nuestra Señora de la Purisíma Concepcíon de los Hasinai.* Some of the records of the missions were destroyed, and we don't know for sure what happened to Angelina. We do know that European diseases swept through the Native American population of East Texas like wildfire, killing thousands. By 1750, the Caddo/Hasinai were only shadows drifting like smoke through the pines of memory. Angelina, however, was not forgotten. The Angelina River was named for her, and, later, Angelina County took its name from the river, as did the Angelina National Forest.

1716–The First Trail North

There is probably no period in our history as a state or a nation that made a greater impact on our culture than that era of the cowboy and the trail drives. This is remarkable because that period lasted only about 20 years, from 1866 to 1886. During this time, over ten million cattle made their way from Texas to the railroad loading pens of Kansas, or to stock the northern ranges, or to feed those Native Americans confined to desolate reservations. This was the high tide of the cowboy myth.

But there were other cattlemen who came before the cowboys of the classic American myth, just there are still those who make their livings with horses, cattle, and personal independence.

Suggest a cattle drive and our minds reflect pictures of John Wayne types in big hats moving steers from the Texas Brush Country, or *brasada*, to the Kansas railheads. These drives made an indelible imprint on our society, our culture, and our imaginations—but they weren't the first. Take away the railhead. Replace the big hat and six-shooter with the sword, lance, and armor of the Spanish conquistador, and you come closer to the real "firsts" of the cattle drives.

illustration by Nathan Smith

Remember that the Spanish Empire was old in the New World before George Washington and Thomas Jefferson were born. The sands of time had covered many Spanish trails before Stephen F. Austin came to Texas. During the late 1600s and early 1700s, Spain established, maintained for a while, abandoned, and re-established a series of missions and presidios in North East Texas and Western Louisiana in response to French influence in the same area. Among these outposts were *Nuestro Padre San Francisco de los Téjas* near the Neches River, *Nuestra Señora de la Purisíma Concepcíon* on the Angelina River, *Nuestra Señora de Guadalupe de los Nacogdoches* at Nacogdoches, *San José de los Nazonis* near Cushing, and *San Miguel de Linares de los Adaes* near the site of present-day Robeline in Louisiana.

Los Adaes was the end-of-the-line, only 18 miles from the French post at Natchitoches on the Red River. Within a few years it became the first official seat of Spanish government in Texas, our first capital, and it boasted a mission, a presidio manned by Spanish troops, and a village of women, children, tradesmen, and farmers brought all of the way from Central Mexico—more than a thousand miles over *El Camino Real*, the Royal Road.

East Texas was full of game and the small farms produced corn, beans, and melons in abundance, but it wasn't quite the same as it had been in Mexico. The colonists needed more of the food that they had been accustomed to back home. In the summer of 1721, 145 years before Charles Goodnight turned his steers toward the North Star, five herds gathered at the *San Juan Bautista* Presidio below the Rio Grande and slightly downstream from where Eagle Pass is today. In the first herd were 300 cattle. They were followed closely by herds of horses, pigs, goats, and sheep. The helmeted cavalry of Spain rode flank and drag. On October 20, 1721, they arrived at *Los Adaes*.

During the years before its abandonment in a gesture toward economy, *Los Adaes* was trail's end for many herds, including one of 4,000 horses, which re-supplied the Spanish cavalry posts all the way from the Rio Grande. By order, in a sort of Noah's Ark in reverse, a pair of each of the animals driven along the trail—cattle, horses, sheep, goats, and pigs—was turned loose at each major stream crossing and told to go forth and multiply. The objective was to provide a future population of animals that would not have to be driven all the way from Mexico. The wild horses and cattle of South Texas came from this stock, as did the "Piney Woods Rooter" pigs of East Texas. The sheep and goats didn't seem to make it.

State and federal highways cover most of that first trail today, and, although the land remembers, S. Omar Barker, the poet, said, "... *few there be, with eyes to see, those tall men riding still.*"

34

1719—The Great Chicken War

Once upon a time, the capitol of Spanish Texas was a presidio in northern Louisiana near today's town of Robeline. It stayed there, on paper, for a very long time, but in practice it rarely functioned in that capacity. In fact, despite the attempts by Spain to establish missions and colonies in Texas, few met with much success. Texas was just too far away from the centers of Spanish culture and government. The Native Americans resented the Spanish insistence that they become Roman Catholic and productive members of Spanish society, and Texas was just too close to the French in Louisiana.

You see, back in 1685, when René Robert Cavalier, Sieur de La Salle, established the ill-fated French colony of St. Louis down just north of today's Port Lavaca, the Spanish thought their colonial world was coming to an end. They sent out expeditions to find and scratch the French itch. One thing led to another, and on June 3, 1690, Spanish priests sang their first *Te Deum Laudamus* at the first Spanish mission in East Texas, *San Francisco de Las Téjas*, near today's Weches. Although they also established a second mission a few miles away, the entire operation was not a rousing success.

illustration by Nathan Smith

Since there was, at that time, no sign of French activity, the Spanish moved back to the *Rio Bravo del Norte*, today's Rio Grande, in 1693.

Then came Luis Juchereau de St. Deniś. He was a French trader and an explorer in the mold of La Salle himself, and the governor of French Louisiana down in Mobile sent him up the Red River to check out trade possibilities with the Indians and to find out where the Spanish had gone. In that capacity he established a fort and trading post in a village of the *Natchitoches* Indians on the Red River in 1713 and went looking for business.

You've got to understand that the French and the Spanish wanted entirely different things from the New World. The Spanish wanted to occupy and control the land and its resources and turn the Indians into God-fearing, tax-paying subjects of the king. The French, on the other hand, wanted trade, with anyone, anywhere, and at any time. Imbued with a belief in the "noble savagery" of the Indians, the French wanted them to remain wild and free as trading partners. So, in his quest for trade and the location of the Spanish, it is not too surprising that the wanderings of St. Denis led him to the gates of the mission/presidio complex of *San Juan Bautista*, just downstream from today's Eagle Pass on the Rio Grande. As a Frenchman trespassing on Spanish territory, he was subject to arrest, torture, and execution for trespassing.

Things did not look bright for St. Denis. After many trials and tribulations, more than a little swashbuckling romance, and the application of a strange Spanish legal loophole called *Obedezco, Pero No Cumplo*, "I obey, but do not comply," the viceroy in Mexico City hired St. Denis to lead the Spanish back into East Texas and into northern Louisiana itself. There later, in 1716, Diego Ramón, the new grandfather-in-law of St. Denis and the second appointed governor of anything called Texas (Don Domingo Terán de los Rios was first), established the mission/presidio of *San Miguel de Linares de los Adaes* just a few miles from the French trading post at Natchitoches.

All went rather well at the mission for a while with the somewhat illegal—but cozy—arrangement of the French trading post supplying the Spanish capital. It was a long way to Mexico City, however, and both the Spanish Church and government decided that there should be a way station and rest stop along that long road. On May 1, 1718, Martín de Alarcón, who had replaced Ramón as the governor, established the mission of *San Antonio de Valero* on the banks of the San Antonio River. Nearby were the presidio of *San Antonio de Béxar* and the *Villa San Fernando de Béxar*.

I don't know if Alarcón ever visited his official capital at *Los Adaes*. I rather doubt it. There was no good reason for him to have done so. By 1719 there was almost no one there, and the population dwindled to a priest, a lay brother, and one ragged soldier who tended the mission's stock. The Indians of the area much preferred the jolly French over at Natchitoches, because they didn't insist on changing them. They stayed away from the mission in droves.

Then war broke out (again) between France and Spain in Europe. On a frontier where no one cares about such things, war is boring. While pondering their fate over a few drinks at Natchitoches, Captain Blondel of the French army and a squad of his soldiers decided one night to raid the chicken house at the Spanish capital. In the end, it didn't do much to boost Blondel's reputation, but it changed history. When they arrived at *Los Adaes*, only the lay brother and the ragged Spanish soldier were at home. Seizing the opportunity, the French soldiers raided the mission's hen house and in the excitement of flying feathers, drunken fumbling, and *fowl* language, Blondel's horse threw him. The lay brother escaped.

You may remember the story of Henny Penny, who ran to tell the king that the sky was falling. Soon Goosey Lucy and Turkey Lurkey and the rest of the barnyard critters were in an uproar.

That's exactly what happened as a result of Blondel's chicken raid. The lay brother escaped to the next mission on the Spanish chain with the word that a French invasion force was right behind him. One by one, every Spanish mission in East Texas was abandoned and the refugees straggled down the long road to the San Antonio River, where they made applications to re-establish their missions in that safer location.

Today, there is a pleasant little park outside of Robeline, Louisiana, that occupies the site of the first capitol of Texas. But, as a result of what became known as "The Great Chicken War," new missions bloomed along the San Antonio River, and the Villa San Fernando de Béxar became the cultural center of northern New Spain.

1720—*La Pobladora*

When Father Antonio de San Buena Ventura Olivares received permission from the Spanish Crown and the Roman Catholic Church to establish a mission along the San Antonio River in 1718, it was supposed to serve not only the local Native Americans, but also become a resting point for caravans of supplies headed North along El Camino Real for the Spanish missions in East Texas and Northern Louisiana. When Martín de Alarcón, the governor, established the Presidio San Antonio de Béxar, one mile to the north of the mission during that same year, the ten families who accompanied the soldiers formed the Villa de Béxar that ultimately grew into today's city of San Antonio. The "Great Chicken War" brought more missions and presidios, but no civilian population. Soon, the Villa de Béxar became San Fernando de Béxar, the first legally recognized municipality in Texas.

The Spanish authorities had great hopes for the settlement, but to make it permanent, they needed more people. Sometimes we forget where they found them, and, not only who they were, but also how important they turned out to be.

Maria Betancour
by Nathan Smith

Imperial Spain had a major problem. The Spanish claimed lands as far north as Oregon, but they couldn't occupy them. After the first rush of conquistadors, who sought God, gold, and glory (not necessarily in that order), there were few people in Spain who wanted to help colonize the New World. In Mexico, fewer still wanted to leave their homes and travel to the North, where there were always threats of Indian attack, and where the living was hard. Without settlers, Spain could not hope to hold her empire against incursions from the English, the French, and even the Russians.

So, they tried a variety of things. The authorities offered prospective Mexican colonists incentives of land and stock. That didn't work. Then they sent convicts and their families. Most of these, however, didn't want to remain after the terms of their incarceration were over. They tried to settle peaceful Indians from the Central Valley of Mexico, but that didn't work either. The authorities demanded *"men with families,"* but few would take the risk of settling along the northern frontier.

Then came the "Great Chicken War" with the French in Louisiana. The few settlers and those who served and protected the missions in East Texas and northern Louisiana retreated, and there were more missions established along the San Antonio River, but with only a few more families.

Finally, in desperation, someone had an idea. Alone in the Atlantic Ocean, off of the West Coast of Africa, are the Canary Islands. The people of the Canary Islands were considered to be of Spanish descent, but their genetic heritage came from shipwrecked seamen, perhaps as far back as the Phoenicians or the Romans. The islands, claimed by Spain, were becoming crowded. After all, there wasn't much land there to farm, and supplying the growing population was becoming a problem. The answer seemed simple—stock the frontier settlement at San Antonio with Canary Islanders and solve two problems at one time. But who would lead the way?

Maria Betancour was born in 1703, in the same year that Archduke Charles became the king of Spain. As was the custom of the time, she married young. By 1731, she was a young widow with five children and no prospects of bettering her station in life. She had nothing to lose and all to gain by leaving the Canary Islands and establishing a new home. She was outspoken, and because she had to be to survive, a leader. When she first applied to go to the New World, her request was refused. The government wanted *men*, with families, to protect the frontier. But none stepped forward. Maria argued that she was as capable as any man, and, in addition, if they would let her go, she would round up additional families. Despite the official instructions to send men with families, it was Maria Betancour who led thirty-one Canary Islanders to San Antonio in 1731, where they formed the first truly civilian population. As a part of the bargain with the Crown, each family received grants to both farm and pasture land and town lots. Building started immediately.

Maria named the main square, around which all Spanish towns were built, *"Plaza de las Islas"* in honor of their homeland. Soon, the settlement bloomed with trees and flowers and gardens of fruit. The town along the San Antonio River prospered and became the leading outpost of Spanish culture in Texas.

Maria married Lorenzo de Armas and had five more children to add to the growing population. Before she died in 1779, Maria Betancour was recognized as *"La Patrona,"* the protector, and *"La Pobladora,"* the founderess or colonizer.

Today, all of San Antonio honors Maria Betancour during annual celebrations, and to be able to trace your heritage to her sons or daughters or to the people she led is quite a great honor.

1755— The De Miranda Report

Perhaps the oldest and most persistent lost treasure story in history tells of seven fabulously rich cities of gold where people lived in golden houses and ate off of golden plates. Incised clay tablets from the Sumerian Empire five thousand years ago suggest that these cities exist in the trackless reaches of the Mongolian desert. Persians thought they were in China. Alexander The Great thought they were in India. Crusaders were convinced they were in central Africa, ruled over by a Christian king, Prester John.

When the Spanish found more wealth in South and Central America than anyone could imagine, they looked for still more. The report of Alvar Nuñez (Cabeza de Vaca) suggested that the greatest wealth in the New World would be found in the central portion of today's United States. This, of course, led to the Coronado expedition, which found nothing but sky, grass, and buffalo. However, the search for wealth—and for legendary golden cities—continued.

Bernardo de Miranda y Flores arrived in San Antonio in 1755 as the vice governor of the Spanish province of Texas. The year of 1755 was the high point of Spanish missionary activities in Texas, but there were also troubles with hostile Tonkawa, Apache, and the new kids on the block, the Comanche. Somehow, the promise of converting Indians into productive members of Spanish society had never materialized, and the whole Spanish experience in Texas was costing the Spanish royal treasury a *lot* of money. So it was that, before he was fully settled, Bernardo de Miranda received orders from Governor Jacinto de Barrios y Jauregui to take a small expedition and explore the Llano and Colorado rivers in search of reported outcroppings of silver.

With 12 soldiers, an Indian guide and interpreter, and five "businessmen" from San Antonio, de Miranda set out on his quest. Apparently they traveled down Honey Creek to the Llano River and then on to the Colorado before returning to San Antonio in mid-March of 1756. There he filed his report on the expedition. It was the stuff of which dreams are made, and not only changed the immediate course of history, but has excited imaginations ever since.

According to the report, the expedition found a "mountain of silver" which de Miranda named *Cerro del Almegre*—a hill of red hematite, in which there was a cave. He entered the cave, which he named the Cave of St. Joseph of Alcazar, and found a vein of silver more than two yards wide and of immeasurable thickness. Nearby, he said, were additional outcroppings of silver so numerous that he promised every citizen of Texas a claim. Ore samples he brought back did, indeed, show high concentrations of silver. In addition, reported de Miranda, a trusted *Apache* told him that *más allá*, further on, west on the Colorado, there were two mountains, *Los Dos Almegres*, filled with silver so soft that it was easily cut with a knife.

The mines reported by de Miranda were, however, never opened or, indeed, officially visited again by the Spanish. Although the viceroy authorized de Miranda to do so in 1757, and although the silver ore samples looked promising, there were no more expeditions. Other events intervened, and de Miranda faded from the story. One might say that a variety of circumstances conspired against de Miranda and made it impossible for him to follow his dream. Some say he died while on another expedition into East Texas.

A few years earlier, Captain Felipe de Rabago y Terán, *commandante* of the presidio *San Francisco Xavier de Gigedo* on today's San Gabriel River near Rockdale and Cameron, had been implicated in the murder of the local priest and the ultimate abandonment of three missions in the area. But the commandante had friends and family in high places. Instead of being punished, he was chosen to lead the expedition to establish a new presidio and mission on the San Saba River, just below today's Menard. You see, down in Mexico, Pedro Romero de Terreros, a wealthy mine owner,

illustration by Nathan Smith

41

thought that Capt. Felipe was a heck of a nice guy and offered to pay for the whole enterprise as long as Capt. Felipe led the troops and his cousin, Fray Alonso Giraldo de Terreros, was in charge of the mission. Pedro Terreros had heard of the de Miranda report and decided that he would take a shot at the *two* reported mountains of silver rather than just one.

The mission on the San Saba and its companion presidio were established in 1757, but the Apache, for whom the mission was built, stayed away. The presidio was completed, and, somewhere in the vicinity, a mine produced some silver.

Today we know that the site is on the northwestern edge of a geological formation known as the Llano Uplift. It is the most highly mineralized part of Texas and has seen a variety of mines operated throughout our history. On March 16, 1758, over 2,000 combined Comanche, Wichita, Bedias, Tonkawa, and other Indians attacked both the mission and the presidio. There were few survivors, and the mission and presidio were abandoned, as well as, apparently, the silver mine.

In the fall of 1759, an attempt to punish those involved by attacking a large Indian encampment on the Red River was such a failure that Spain never again challenged the Indians of the southern plains tribes. The San Saba mine almost faded from memory, as did the de Miranda report, because more important things were happening on the world stage.

History never happens in a vacuum. In 1756, while de Miranda made his report, a French battle fleet attacked the British stronghold of Port Mahon on the little island of Minorca in the western Mediterranean Sea. For all practical purposes, this was the opening salvo in what is known in Europe as the Seven Years' War, and in North America as the French and Indian War. On one side were Austria, France (and her Indian allies in North America), Russia, Sweden, and Saxony; and on the other were England and the Prussia of Frederick The Great. For a change, Spain wasn't really involved. It had a few problems of its own.

In 1759 King Ferdinand VI of Spain died, and, because of intermarriage of royal families, a Frenchman named Charles, of the Bourbon Dynasty, became Carlos III, the new "Bourbon king" of Spain. Carlos III thought he had inherited a rich empire. He was wrong. For over 200 years Spain had squeezed its New World colonies dry. Certainly, some wealth was still coming in, but it was going out even faster.

About the time that Spanish forces were defeated by the Indians on the Red River, King Carlos III sent the Marqués de Rubí over to the New World colonies to find out what had happened to the money. His report to the king identified two parts of the Spanish venture in the American Southwest which were not only unproductive, but were costing Spain more money than it could afford. The Spanish crown accepted and acted upon his recommendations.

The first failure was the mission system—the Marqués noted that the missions were costing the crown over a million *reales* a year but were producing few converts among the Indians. He recommended that all the missions should be secularized. As a result, over 100 missions in Northern Mexico and the American Southwest closed their door, their lands were divided among the few Indian converts in the area, and their buildings were abandoned. In Texas only three missions survived to become parish churches—one in San Antonio, one in *La Bahía* (today's Goliad), and one near El Paso.

The second failure was the Spanish effort to colonize the plains and the wilderness. The Marqués reported that the high cost of providing protection against hostile Indians was not worth the very minimum result; he recommended that the colonies on the fringes of empire should be abandoned. Here in Texas, royal troops marched to northern Louisiana, did an about-face, and swept all Spanish citizens they could catch back below the San Antonio River.

Finally, to make matters more difficult, the Seven Years' War ended in 1763 with the signing of the Peace of Paris. France lost. England claimed all of Canada and all of French Louisiana east of the Mississippi River, except for New Orleans. Although France and Spain were normally enemies, they were both Roman Catholic nations. Since a Frenchman was on the throne of Spain—and to keep the rest of French North America out of the hands of the "heathen" English—France gave Spain its entire claim to Louisiana west of the Mississippi. Short on funds, and with a new boundary to defend against England, Spain rushed most of its resources to the Mississippi River. Texas was mostly forgotten for the next forty years.

Fast forward to the beginning of the Mexican War for Independence from Spain in 1810. Among the many attempts to free Texas from Spanish rule, the most successful, at least in the beginning, was the Gutiérrez-Magee Expedition from Louisiana, known as "The Republican Army of the North." Under "The Green Flag of Freedom," the army was made up of Anglo-American soldiers of fortune, Indians of the Five Civilized Tribes, disaffected Mexican nationals, and a few Spanish renegades.

The Republican Army captured Nacogdoches and La Bahía, but then, under somewhat suspicious circumstances, the army's commander Augustus Magee died. Leadership fell to Gutiérrez, a Spaniard named Toledo, and an Anglo-American named Kemper. Momentum was on their side, and they captured San Antonio and secured the surrender of Governor Salcedo.

Then Gutierrez made a mistake. He ordered that all Spanish officials and their families be executed. Their throats were cut, and their bodies were left in a ditch along the road from San Antonio to Floresville. This action really split the army. Many went back to the United States, and a few went further west to see the country. In doing so, those who left escaped the largest and bloodiest battle ever fought in Texas. Spanish forces met the adventurers along and near the banks of the Medina River, just south of San Antonio, and the Spanish annihilated the Republican Army. After the dust settled, Texas had less than one third of the population it had had a year before.

Among those who escaped the battle was a fellow named Harper "Harp" Perry from Mississippi. Don't confuse him with Col. Henry Perry, also from Mississippi, who was one of the leaders of the army. Harp, along with another Anglo-American and a few Mexican nationals, wandered into the Llano Uplift area and either stumbled on de Miranda's "mine" or the one operated by the folks along the San Saba. No one lived in the area. The Comanche war trail into Northern Mexico was much further west. The Apache were gone, and remnant bands of Wichita and Tawakoni rarely went into the country that had for so long been a stronghold of their enemies.

In relative peace, Harp's little group mined silver ore, melted it down, and poured it into hollow river cane to make ingots that resembled today's structural steel re-bar. From time to time over the next few years one of the group would travel to San Antonio with a few of these odd-shaped silver ingots and trade for necessary supplies. In this way folks in San Antonio were reminded of the de Miranda report—but no one, not even the famed James Bowie, was able to follow the trail to the mine.

Then what they had feared from the beginning came in the night. In 1834, an Indian attack on the mine killed everyone except Harp, his partner, and a Mexican girl. Supposedly, these survivors took what they could carry and buried nearly a ton of the oddly shaped ingots on top of a nearby hill, then *"lit a shuck"* for St. Louis, where the partner married the girl and opened a saloon. Harp went on to New Orleans and missed the Texas War for Independence, living well on his share of what they had salvaged from the mine.

We don't know what happened to Harp over the next 30 years. He returned, a much older man, to the Llano Uplift country in 1866, after the Civil War. A lot of things had changed. Not only could he not locate the site where the buried silver was stashed, but he also could not find the ruins of the old smelter. On his way north with a herd of cattle, in an attempt to locate his old partner in St. Louis, he died following an accident in camp.

Harp told his story around the campfire, and since then many have searched for both the mine and the buried bars, which would, today, look like tarnished lead. So far as is publicly known, no one has found either, but the search goes on as new generations are lured by the promise of the de Miranda report.

1800—*Los Mesteñeros*

You read a lot about the Anglo-American cowboy of the late 19th century. He's a very colorful part of the heritage of the Southwest. Less often do you read about the Mexican vaqueros, *those centaur-like people who taught the entire world how to handle large herds of wild cattle from horseback. Almost never mentioned are* los mesteñeros, *those rugged men who caught and trained the wild mustangs that made the whole operation possible. You just can't do them justice in a short article. There should be a shelf full of books on the subject. The least I can do is introduce you to an almost forgotten people.*

Remember that when Cortez defeated the Aztecs and married Montezuma's daughter, beginning in 1519, he established *La Raza,* the new race formed of mixed Indian and Spanish bloods. He also introduced the horse to the New World and, with it, the North African Moorish tradition of fine horsemanship. Men who depended on horses for their lives developed an affinity for them and a comradeship that we see only rarely today.

Spanish mustanger
by Nathan Smith

Through loss, theft, and design, the horses of the Spanish *conquistadors* spread throughout Mexico and the plains of the American West. Wild horse herds, while less numerous than the buffalo, excited wide attention. The Plains Indians, who measured their wealth in horses, became some of the world's best light cavalry. As time passed and the flood of wagons brought Americans to settle the West, the horse became even more important. The availability of those horses depended on the Mexican mustangers, *los mesteñeros*, who adapted the North African traditions to North America.

Many old maps labeled the area between the Nueces and the Rio Grande as the *Llaños Mesteños* or Wild Horse Prairie. Deep in the thorny thickets of the South Texas brasada, los mesteñeros built the *corral de aventura* (or pen of chance) about half the size of a football field, to catch mustangs. Long mesquite posts were set deep into the ground with the tops leaning inward. These were laced together with rawhide to provide a flexible but sturdy enclosure. V-shaped wings of similar construction led out for as much as half a mile from a narrow gate. In practice, a *recibidor* (or receiver) stationed himself at the outer end of each wing and an *encerrador* (or closer) waited, hidden near the gate. *Aventadores* (or starters) slowly encircled a *caballada* (herd of horses) and moved them within the wings. Once inside the wings, they stampeded the herd toward the trap so that the momentum of the stampede would carry them in even if some sensed danger and wanted to turn back. Once the horses were inside the trap, the encerrador closed the gate of poles and covered it with a blanket to discourage escape. In dry weather *corrales de espiar* (watch pens) were built at watering places and the horses trapped when they came to drink. On some occasions, a single, well-provisioned rider might follow a herd for weeks until accepted as part of the scenery. He would then either lead or drive the herd into an enclosure. Sometimes individual mustangs were roped from larger herds, and there were even times when snares were used to trap horses in the brush where they hid from the mustangers.

Many men had their own secret methods of training the mustangs once they were trapped. In practice, the method of throwing a saddle on a wild horse, climbing aboard, and letting it buck was hard on both horses and men. Things like that give action to movies and rodeos, and *jinetes* (broncobusters) did it occasionally for show, but when a herd numbered in the hundreds, or even thousands, simpler, less damaging measures prevailed.

Whatever their methods, los mesteñeros were acclaimed throughout the New World as the best providers of both working horses and those ridden for pleasure. Even General Zachary Taylor, on his way from Corpus Christi to the Rio Grande to start the Mexican War in 1846, made it a point to purchase mounts for his dragoons from los mesteñeros, the Mexican-American lords of the horse herds of Texas.

After the Civil War, the focus in South Texas shifted from horses to cattle, and many of the same tactics for capturing wild horses were used to capture the mossy-horned old cattle that were even wilder. Even so, folks needed a steady supply of horses for the men who drove the cattle herds up the trail. Each trail drive also involved a *remuda* (herd of remounts) of from three to five horses per man. These horses, sold at the end of the drive, were worth more than the individual cattle and made an extra profit, so los mesteñeros never really went out of business until barbed wire closed the open range.

1811—An Experiment In Learning

We frequently speak of Mirabeau B. Lamar as being "The Father of Education" in Texas. Certainly, he proposed what later became our current educational system (even though nothing was really done about it until long after his death), but the credit for recognizing the importance of free education and doing something about it should go to an important individual that we tend to forget. Another thing we seem to forget is the fact that, once upon a time, schools and the opportunity for education were things that people were willing to sacrifice for and were held in high regard.

Juan José María Erasmo de Jesús Seguín was born in San Fernando de Béxar back in 1782 and became an important man in Old San Antonio. He was a big landowner and, perhaps, the first to experiment with the growing of cotton in what is, today, Texas. In addition, he was a prosperous merchant and a member of the government, in which he served as one of the Royal Land Commissioners. It was Seguín who, later, after the death of Moses Austin, recognized Stephen F. Austin as the legitimate heir to the Austin Royal Commission and made possible the settlement of Austin's "Old 300" colonists. That was in 1821. Seguín pushed for free education before that.

In 1811 the citizens of San Fernando de Béxar chose Juan Manuel Zambrano to reestablish Spanish royal authority in the area after the failure of a local revolution led by Juan Bau-

Spanish colonial-period school
by Nathan Smith

47

tista de las Casas. To assist him, he convened a council of eleven men, including Seguín, on whose shoulders fell the responsibility for all local government. The Archives of Béxar report that one of their first moves was to authorize the construction of a schoolhouse costing 855 pesos and the development of a public school system. Seguín and José Antonio Saucedo drew the plan and made the rules. Today we squabble over what schools must provide and what is expected of the students. There was little room for argument in 1811.

Not every child could attend. Seguín's plan called for places for seventy students. Some of these would be selected for their ability and would attend free, the beginnings of a scholarship program based on scholastic merit and not on how well one performed in sports. Those students who could afford to pay one peso per month and those who could pay only four reales, or about fifty cents in today's money, occupied the rest of the seats evenly. The teacher received thirty pesos per month. The *Alcalde* (sort of a cross between a mayor and a city judge) and four *Comisarios de Barrio* (ward commissioners) were responsible for collecting the funds. The students furnished books, paper, seats, and other paraphernalia. The *regidores* (city precinct police) visited the school each day to take roll and note any infringement of the rules.

Classes met seven days a week, from six to eleven in the morning and from two to six in the evening. On Sundays and holidays the students arrived an hour earlier so that they could all attend church in a group. Punishment was handed out for breaking rules of conduct, for failure to study, and for not advancing in class. If a student did not show up for class, the regidores paid a visit to his or her home. If the student was not sick, then they arrested the parents for failure to control their child. Such violators of the rules swept the streets that night.

Nowhere in the plan was there a provision for "extracurricular" activities. School was considered a place to learn, not a social or athletic club. There were, however, "homecoming" days when past students judged the competency of the new crop. A census of the period listed 285 boys and 268 girls resident in San Fernando. With only seventy openings for each year it was an honor to have the opportunity to attend. A student who received that honor but who failed to advance in his or her class was publicly flogged and then arrested for theft, for stealing the opportunity from another student who could not attend.

This experiment in learning was successful. They went to learn, and learn they did.

1818—Old Brit

There is a popular misconception among Anglo-Americans that the first of their kind came to Texas under the protection of Stephen F. Austin after 1821. Those families that filled his commitment to the Mexican government were called the "Old 300," and there is much social acclaim attached to a familial connection with them. Actually, Austin never really filled that contract. There were only 297 "families," but that was close enough for the government work of the period. And, in truth, he did arrange for most of those to come to Texas. Long before that, however, there were many Anglo-Americans living within the boundaries of Texas along the Red River and in such centers of commerce as Nacogdoches and San Antonio. There were also those who came earlier and were living independent lives on land that became a part of Austin's first empresarial grant. At least two of these families convinced Austin that both he and his colony would benefit from their continued presence.

A lot of folks said he was a little bit strange, but that could be applied to many, if not all, of the early settlers in Texas—and, perhaps, to many of us today.

James Briton "Old Brit" Bailey was born in North Carolina in 1779, and he came by his fighting spirit naturally. He was a direct descendant of that barelegged warrior of the Scottish Highlands, Robert the Bruce. Brit found the North Carolina highlands too tame and, at an early age, followed Daniel Boone through the Cumberland Gap into Kentucky's "dark and bloody ground," eventually moving on to the Mississippi. The War of 1812 made him a ship's captain in the U.S. Navy, and after that excitement was over, he grabbed his wife Edith and their six children and went to Texas, where he'd established himself on the lower Brazos River by 1821.

James Briton "Old Brit" Bailey
by Nathan Smith

Texas was in turmoil. After the Battle of the Medina River in 1813 and the revenge of Col. Joaquín de Arredondo, the population of the Mexican state of Texas was cut by two thirds. Texas ceased being a separate state in the Spanish system and became a province attached to the state of Coahuila. Mexico still wanted independence from Spain, so there were enough plots and counter-plots to keep officials so busy that no one paid much attention to Old Brit when he set up housekeeping on the Brazos, a few miles west of where Angleton is today.

As the first white settlers in the Brazos bottoms, Old Brit and his family fought Indians, drought, and Brazos River floods, and managed to carve out a good-sized plantation. Brit liked red, so all of the buildings—the house, the barn, the sheds, the crib, and even the "necessary"—were painted a dark, brooding red—like "Hell with the fires banked."

Now, Old Brit was a man of action and, once he got his plantation in order, life became boring. So, one fine day, he moved his long-suffering wife and her brood into a tent and burned down all of his red buildings—just so he could have the fun of building them again.

The Bailey plantation was located astride the old Spanish road that ran along the coast from the mission and presidio at La Bahía, now Goliad, to Louisiana. There it became a stopping place for travelers, noted for its great hospitality. That hospitality, however, had a price. Before being admitted to the ranks of honored guests, the visitor, be he priest or potentate or traveling peddler, had to engage Old Brit in a knockdown, drag-out, ear-chewing and eye-gouging fight in the front yard. This little ceremony completed, the reward was the best food and lodging within a week's travel.

About this time Stephen F. Austin came to Texas to claim the land that the Spanish government told his father he could use for settlement. It just so happened that Old Brit's plantation sat right in the middle of the grant. Stephen F. Austin was a picky man who took things very seriously. His contract said that he could only admit people of good repute. Somehow, Old Brit didn't seem to fit the bill. On October 3, 1823, Austin wrote to the Bailey family:

> *"You are hereby notified that you cannot be received as a settler in this colony and that you will not be permitted to live nearer the Brazos River than the San Jacinto nor nearer the Colorado than the Guadalupe. Sixty days are you allowed to remove your family and property."*

Later in the month, after receiving no response, Austin reported that he was compelled to remove Bailey because he was of poor character and had exhibited *"bad conduct."* He then had the poor judgment to go alone to evict the family.

"Isn't it true," asked Austin as he faced the muzzle of Brit's squirrel rifle, "that you once served a term in the Kentucky penitentiary?"

"Yup," Brit retorted, "but I'm not ashamed of that. It's the time I spent in the Kentucky Legislature that sets heavy on my conscience."

He said he'd come to Texas to lead an honest and solitary life and wished to be left alone. We don't know whether or not there was a fight in the front yard. No doubt, however, there were a few other comments exchanged and, perhaps, suggestions about the future, because Old Brit received legal title to his land a few months later. His family was duly enrolled as one of Austin's Old 300.

When he got bored and couldn't find anyone to fight, Old Brit drank. When he drank, he looked for new things to do. As the 1820s moved into the 1830s, he was excited because it looked like there'd be a new war with Mexico to provide entertainment.

Unfortunately, Brit didn't live to see Texas Independence. He lost his big fight to cholera in December of 1832.

Before he died, he told his wife, "I have never stooped to any man and when I am in my grave I don't want it said, 'There lies Old Brit Bailey.' Bury me so that the world must say, 'There stands Bailey,' and bury me with my face to the setting sun. I have been all my life traveling westward, and I want to face that way when I die."

According to local legend, he was buried in an eight-foot hole, standing up, wearing his buckskins and two pistols, and with his rifle in his hand, ready for the next fight. But he was not, as he requested, buried with his favorite drinking jug filled and ready for his trip. Some folks say that his long-suffering wife denied him that final wish. Others say that the slave who did the burying appropriated the jug in payment for digging the hole.

Here in Texas we have a variety of unexplainable natural, or perhaps supernatural, phenomena. The "Marfa Lights" are the best known, and there are similar manifestations in the Big Thicket area of East Texas. Down along the Brazos, the "Ghost of Bailey's Prairie" is fairly well known. It manifests itself as a wandering light at night, and those who claim to know say that it is Old Brit, still looking for his jug and a fight.

Jane Long, the "Mother of Texas"
courtesy UTSA's Institute of Texan Culture at
San Antonio (Winston Tarver)

1820—Mother Jane

Among the earliest religions are those based on the "Mother" figure. Whether she represented a fertility symbol or simply that from which all life springs, "She" has been the focal point of many cultures. Many nations claim to have sprung from "Mother Earth," so it is not surprising that certain ethnic and cultural groups choose to honor a particular "Mother" in their creation stories.

Before the battles at the Alamo and San Jacinto, there were many other attempts to tear Texas away from Spain or Mexico and open the way for annexation by the United States. Not the least of these was led by the handsome and dashing Dr. James Long in 1819, but this is only marginally his story. The real story here concerns his bride, Jane. Born the niece of powerful General James Wilkinson, the military governor of the Louisiana Territory, at sixteen she was society's darling, the beribboned belle, of many balls in Natchez and New Orleans. She was also deeply in love with Dr. Long.

General Wilkinson was one of those politicians who seems to have a finger in every questionable pot, but who always seems to receive advancement and riches anyway. It was he who, having negotiated the Neutral Ground Agreement with Spanish authorities—which promised that U.S. troops would stay east of a line running from the Arroyo Hondo to the Calcasieu River and on to the Gulf until a treaty could be signed between Spain and the United States regarding the western boundary of the Louisiana Purchase—sent a number of military expeditions into Spanish territory. The best known of these is the expedition of Lt. Zebulon Pike, which explored parts of Kansas, Oklahoma, Colorado, New Mexico, Mexico, and Texas, before returning to report. It was Wilkinson who instigated and supported the Gutiérrez-Magee "Republican Army of the North," which fought to separate Texas from Spain and was destroyed at the Battle of the Medina River, the bloodiest battle ever fought in Texas. He was the prime mover in the aborted Wilkinson-Burr Conspiracy to create a new nation between the Mississippi and the Pacific.

Officially, he was guardian of his niece, Jane. As a wedding gift, General Wilkinson promised to give Texas to the happy couple.

At her marriage to James, Jane promised to keep faith and to live by the promise of Ruth, *"whither thou goest, I will go."* Go she did, with Long, in a vain attempt to establish a free state at Spanish Nacogdoches. The attempt was a complete failure, and Long lost everything, even his horse. Jane, though, lost more—the life of their first child-to-be.

By 1821, they came back to try again, this time with a small band of followers, to a small mud-walled enclosure on that wind-swept bit of sand now known as Bolivar Point. (Take the free ferry there from Galveston, and today you will find a small marker near the old lighthouse.) There, living under canvas, they waited for reinforcements from New Orleans. This time, Long knew, was the right time. Mexico, fighting for its own freedom from Spain, was in turmoil. Many outposts were undermanned or abandoned. He must not wait! *La Bahía*, today's Goliad, was ripe for attack! With all of his men he sailed south toward Matagorda Bay. This time Jane could not go; he would only be gone for two weeks.

But the weeks grew into months. Others left, until there were only three in the mud-walled fort. Jane was there, with her second child, five-year-old Anne, and a young female slave named Kian, and the first stirrings of Jane's third child, yet to be born. Fall became winter and December's northers darkened the Gulf while, every day, Jane waited, always looking southward for a sail to appear.

Winter also brought a visit from the misunderstood, but dreaded, Karankawa, the occasional cannibals of the Gulf Coast. With a red petticoat flying from the flag pole, Jane drove them off with her only weapon, a small cannon—loading, firing, sponging, serving, and firing again, while she still watched southward, with hope, for the sail.

Sleet came, and, rare for the Texas coast, it was followed by snow. Always, there was the wind. The food was gone, but there were oysters, exposed when the north wind blew water from the bay. In the cold dark, Jane delivered her third child, a daughter, who would be claimed by some as Texas' first-born Anglo child. And the next morning, this "Mother of Texas" resumed her search for food and a sail.

A sail did appear, but not the one she wanted. Seeing the smoke from her fire, the crew of the schooner *Lively* came ashore and offered to take her with them. Where were they going? To Austin's colony. She had never heard of it. No, she would wait with faith. She had said that she would. He would return any day now.

Another schooner stopped with the same destination and the same offer. No, she would keep the faith. February brought sun, and April brought the spring. At last, July brought summer, and a new sail—but from the East, not the South as expected. It brought a friend from New Orleans, and he came with news that the wait was over. The sail from the South would never come. Dashing and dreaming young Dr. Long was dead in Mexico City's prison.

Jane had kept the faith, and, in a few years, she returned as a part of Stephen F. Austin's first colony. Although Jane's child was not the first Anglo child born in Texas, we still call her "the Mother of Texas," and the schools named in her honor are fitting monuments to her faith and dedication.

1821—The Case of the Cut-Rate Keelboat

The year was 1820. Under the terms of the "Missouri Compromise," Missouri could enter the United States as a slave state and Maine would enter as a free state, thus maintaining the balance of power in the United States Congress. This same Congress passed a new land law stating that public domain land belonging to the government in the new territories and elsewhere could not be sold to individuals for less than $1.25 per acre. Today, that seems a ridiculous price, but at that time, it placed the purchase of land beyond the abilities of all but large land speculators.

The United States was in the middle of its first major economic depression—the textbooks call it "The Panic of 1819." Without the protection of the courts, many people in the United States lost everything they had, even including their clothing. Few families had the opportunity to purchase land without going into debt to the speculators in the process. Then came 1821, and with it, a rumor that spread throughout the country. If you went to the Mexican province of Texas, you could get almost five thousand acres, Free!

Well, almost.

When most folks think of families going west to start a new life in a new land, they think of mile-long wagon trains with billowing canvas and lusty out-riders to warn of Indian attack. Certainly, these existed, but there were few wagon trains until the time of the California Gold Rush in the 1850s, and the big, organized immigrant trains didn't hit their peak of operation until after the Civil War. In the early days of Texas colonization, few came by wagon because there were few roads; some walked, and some came on horseback. Many came by boat.

The first seventeen men recruited by Stephen F. Austin for his colony came on the schooner *Lively*. They sailed in November of 1821 for the mouth of the Colorado River, but storms drove them off of their course. They finally managed to land at the mouth of the Brazos. When the *Lively* sailed away, it left them stranded. They tried to plant winter crops but those failed, and the men wandered off on Indian trails that they hoped would carry them back to the United States.

When Austin arrived in the spring, he hoped to find a settlement with crops in the ground. He found nothing. Then, Mexico won its independence from Spain, and Austin had to go back to Mexico City to renew his contract.

The *Lively*, meanwhile, went back to New Orleans for another load of passengers. This time it wrecked near San Louis Pass on Galveston Island. The passengers all survived, but the cargo of much-needed supplies sank with the ship. Friendly Indians helped them out and another schooner, the *John Motley*, which carried still more passengers, picked them up and landed them at the mouth of the Colorado. There they found no settlement and no one to meet them. The party split, some wandering up the river and some along the coast. According to one account, some starved to death and some managed to reach settlements inland. Meanwhile, Austin was still in Mexico trying to get official recognition for his colony. It was not an auspicious beginning.

During the spring and summer of 1822, several small ships tried to bring colonists to Texas. Some of them were never heard from again. Many of them, in the absence of good navigation charts, wrecked on the sand bars leading to entrances from the Gulf, stranding their crews and passengers on

illustration by Gary Manthei

55

the beach. Some, searching for the Brazos or the Colorado, found instead Galveston Bay and dumped their passengers there. They were the first to settle in the area that became the Galveston-Houston Metroplex.

Among those to arrive by accident in Galveston Bay were William "Uncle Buck" Pettus and his family. The Pettus family and a group of others arrived from Alabama on board the schooner *Revenge* in 1822. An elderly Frenchman, who lived alone and claimed to have been one of Lafitte's pirates, immediately accosted them and tried to collect taxes in the name of the Spanish government. They bought the old man off with food and supplies. Several more like him came out of the woods. Soon, more colonists arrived and, by the beginning of 1823, there were almost fifty families strung out along the edge of Galveston Bay and up and down both Buffalo Bayou and the San Jacinto River. In the autumn of 1822, another party arrived from Alabama.

These folks, about 34 in number, according to Pettus, who left an account of them, came from the vicinity of Florence, Alabama. They had heard of Austin's colony, and, rather than paying large sums and risking their lives with the captain of a schooner, decided to build a large keel-boat of the kind used along the Mississippi and Alabama rivers. The result was a square-ended, flat-bottomed scow, more like a large shoebox. It was 120 feet long and about 25 feet wide, with a single mast, oars, and long poles for pushing along when the wind failed. There was a tent-like canvas-covered shelter to protect them and their possessions from rain, and a large box filled with sand where they could build a fire for cooking without burning a hole in the bottom. They floated their way down the Alabama River to Mobile Bay, across Vermilion Bay, and then along the bayous and marshes of the Mississippi River and the coast. That they managed to get to Texas at all was a marvel.

Once they arrived, however, they were not happy. In fact, Pettus said they were *"greatly distressed."* Things were not quite as "settled" as they expected. Some folks wanted to stay, while others wanted to return to Alabama. Since each family group had chipped in time and money to build the boat, there was no easy compromise. Finally, they sawed the boat in half. Those who wanted to stay used the lumber from their half to help build shelter and, later, became recognized members of Texas society. The others, those who didn't like the hardship of building homes in the wilderness, patched their half of the boat, left, and headed back to Alabama the way that they had come.

They were never seen or heard from again.

Mexican Texas & the War for Texas Inpendence: 1821-1836

1823—An Adventure In Moving

James Fenimore Cooper considered himself to be a "modern" man. Certainly he was the first successful novelist to write in the United States, and his books still command a great deal of attention. Several of these formed what were called "The Leatherstocking Tales"—notably The Pioneers, *which was the first of the series printed in 1823;* The Deerslayer; *and* The Last of the Mohicans, *which followed soon after. The plots of these and others follow the central characters as they cope with the American frontier and move westward toward a horizon which ever moves before them. In the 1890s, Frederick Jackson Turner, who was among the most noted historians of his day, declared that the closing of the American frontier would, necessarily, bring about a change in the American character, as people found that they could no longer move to new land. Whether or not this prediction has come true is a matter of the perspective of the viewer, but no one can dispute the fact that "movers" built the United States.*

The Census Bureau tells us that we are a nation of movers—that the average family will move several times in search of many things, including different climate, different jobs, different schools, and different opportunities. So, what else is new? Our ancestors moved from the Old World to the New World, and we haven't stopped moving.

Today, moving is a big business—just pick up the phone, dial the number, and before you can hang up there's

Mary Rabb
by Lillian Cowden

57

a crew at the door. They pack everything (even your garbage), load, transport, unload, unpack it, and disappear. It wasn't always that way.

Mary Rabb came to Texas from Arkansas in 1823, the same year that Cooper published *The Pioneers*. She carried a baby, not her own, and rode on top of all her family's belongings that were, in turn, packed on a big, iron gray horse named Tormentor. She was a small part of a big migration to Texas in response to land made available by the new Imperial Colonization Law of the Empire of Mexico and the efforts of the land agent *empresario*, Stephen F. Austin. With her were her husband, John, his father, and several brothers and sisters with their families. One sister brought seven children. Having crossed the Red River in October, for over two months they worked their way south and west along the old "Trail of the Padres" and the *La Bahía* Trail until, in the middle of December, they reached the banks of the Colorado River at the bend that now circles La Grange. A few miles upstream they set up housekeeping at Indian Hill. But, the moving wasn't over.

Indian Hill was well named. The local indigenous population, a branch of those who called themselves Tickanwatic, "the Most Human of People," immediately appropriated almost everything that wasn't red hot. The immigrants lost their cattle, most of their horses, and most of their tools. They decided to move to an area closer to the "settlement," a spot below where Richmond now sits on the Brazos River.

On one old horse named Flucus, they packed their clothing and bedding, their only cooking pot, an iron skillet with a lid, and, on top, a spinning wheel made for Mary by John's brother, Andrew. Mary again rode Tormentor and others followed or rode depending on their ability. Along the way one pig was injured when Flucus stepped on its foot. A lame pig was of no use on the trail but would fatten up once they reached their new home. Since Flucus had done the dastardly deed, it seemed only fitting that he should carry the extra burden.

But, when they tried to tie the pig on top of the spinning wheel, both pig and horse objected. When they finally caught the old horse, the pig was dead, the cooking pot broken, and everything else was scattered for a distance of at least a mile.

Down on the lower Brazos, below today's Richmond, the mosquitoes and flies were so bad that, after a reasonable interval to give it a try, it was moving time again. This time everything was packed on a pony named Nickety Poly. Instead of a pig, two chickens rode on top of the spinning wheel. Behind the wheel, in the tied-up legs of an old pair of leather breeches, rode two hound dog pups. They traveled at night to miss most of the flies.

Sometime during the night the pups started to howl, and, since howling saddle bags were not within the cosmic view of Nickety Poly, he *"lit out"* for distant places. In the dark, no one could follow the trail. All appeared lost until, with the dawn, the bedraggled and rattled rooster tied to the spinning wheel still felt like crowing.

They built a new home about six miles below San Felipe, and Mary went back to spinning to make up for lost time.

Over the next ten years the Rabbs made at least five more moves—up the Brazos, over to the San Bernard, and again back to the Colorado. Several houses were washed away in floods, and several more children were born. Indians came and went, some with gifts and some for plunder. Crops flourished or were either washed away by floods or killed by drought. A loom was added to the spinning wheel. Whether in a log cabin or under a shady tree, Mary kept spinning and weaving, knowing that the next day, or the next week, or sometime, John would say that the time had come to move again. Following the Texas Revolution, they seemed to settle down on Rabb's Prairie in what is now Fayette County, not far from their first Texas home at Indian Hill. If you pass that way today, you'll cross Rabb's Creek and pass a sign for Rabb's Prairie.

The final move came after statehood, during the turmoil leading to secession and the Civil War. In 1860 they settled near Barton Springs at Austin, and it was there, in 1861, that John died. Mary could have moved back to more settled areas, but that would have been one move too many for her. There she stayed, and there she built a two-story limestone block home. At last, she had reached her horizon. Her adventure in moving was over.

1828—Three Legs and Courage

The semi-welfare state in which we live makes special allowances for many handicaps. This is a good thing because spirit and ability are not always dependent on one's physical aptitude for a job, and we would lose a lot if we relegated the handicapped to non-fulfilling roles.

Throughout history there have been those who, through determination, have overcome their problems for the betterment of all. Remember that the poet John Milton was blind, Thomas A. Edison was deaf, and General George S. Patton, Jr., was dyslexic. And then, of course, there was "Three Legged Willie."

Robert McAlpin Williamson rode into Stephen F. Austin's San Felipe colony in 1826. Like many another 22-year-old from the Deep South, he was looking for a growing land and the opportunity to grow with it. Under the terms of the Imperial Colonization Law of 1823 and the National Colonization Law of 1824, immigrants were invited to settle and were promised land grants in Texas if they were of good character and if they agreed to become Mexican citizens, to adopt the Roman Catholic faith, and to serve in the military if called upon to do so. Unlike most settlers who came to Texas under those conditions—strong, healthy, and whole—he was what we today would call "physically challenged." His right leg was withered, deformed, twisted at an angle to his body by polio, and only contributed to his balance with the aid of a third appendage, a strapped-on wooden peg. Today we would build for

Robert McApin Williamson
by Duncan Robinson, courtesy
UTSA's Institute of Texan
Cultures at San Antonio

him special doors, special ramps, and special facilities. Frontier Texas only offered him a special name—"Three-Legged-Willie."

In those days before independence, he practiced law and edited the first *Texas Gazette*. Its motto, "God and Liberty," worried many who sought conciliation with Mexico. But the people voted for him when he ran for office and elected him *Alcalde* (mayor and/or Justice of the Peace) of the San

Felipe community. With a fiery spirit people came to expect, he faced-down the Mexican government and released William B. Travis and Patrick Jack from prison at Anahuac. Closer to home, he designed, he surveyed, and established a new town at the muddy *La Bahía* crossing on the Brazos. He dubbed it Washington in honor of his old home in Washington, Georgia.

War! The *ad interim* government of Texas ordered the formation of the first company of those who would one day be known as Texas Rangers and named Three-Legged-Willie as its leader. Indian skirmishes as far away as today's Marlin and Groesbeck were temporarily forgotten, as with only 22 riders he screened the northern flank of Sam Houston's retreat from Gonzales and protected settlers as they crossed the Colorado in the "Run-Away Scrape." Then, a wild ride through the night took the company to the bloody charge at San Jacinto.

Independence! With it, there was a position as judge for the new Republic of Texas. In the first year, he rode a circuit of over 1000 miles, convening courts and talking of the new Constitution and its guarantees of rights for citizens. At last he arrived in Columbus, to an ancient spreading oak on the east side of the village square. Under the branches a simple monument reads, "Beneath this tree, the First Court of the Third Judicial District of the Republic of Texas was held in April, 1837, by Judge Robert McAlpin Williamson— 'Three-Legged-Willie.'"

According to legend, a litigant once slammed a knife into the table in front of the new judge with the statement that, *"The knife is the law in this county."*

To which Three-Legged-Willie drew a pistol in response and stated, *"This is our new Constitution which overrides your law."*

Three-Legged-Willie rode on to a seat in the Republic's Congress, then to his last home in Wharton, and later he was carried to his final resting place in the State Cemetery in Austin. The old oak in Columbus is also gone, but the roots are deep and the stump and monument remain.

1829—James Coryell, Frontiersman

There are 254 counties in Texas, many of them bigger than states up in New England. Each county has a name, and, each name has a story. Among these names are those representing physical features, historic designations, one woman, and many men. The men received recognition for many things. Among those is one who loved, explored, and fought for Texas, and then died for honey.

James Coryell was fiddle-footed. That is to say that his feet couldn't stay still. He, like many others before and since, had that insatiable desire to see what was on the other side of the next hill. His feet took him to the buffalo plains and to the fur trade in the Rockies when he was little more than a boy. In about 1829, they brought him to Texas.

You've got to understand that, during the 1820s, things were not so good in the United States. Back in 1819 the bottom fell out of the economy that was going pretty well after the War of 1812. They called it "The Panic of 1819" and a lot of folks in the United States lost everything they had. There were no economic laws to protect you back then. If you owed anyone money for anything they could take your land, stock, tools, home, and the clothes off of your back and leave you standing in the road. The "Panic" played the tune for the fiddle-footed, and they just naturally headed for the West. In 1830 Texas was full of men and women just like James Coryell. They came for land, and they came for a new start. They came for adventure, and they came to get away from some things and to find others. James Coryell found James Bowie.

James Coryell
by Nathan Smith

Now, we've all heard and read about James Bowie, who was a legend even back then. He came from Louisiana and Arkansas, was a farmer, a slave dealer and smuggler, and a partner with Jean Lafitte in a variety of shady deals. He was also both fearless and a charming fellow, who married Ursula de Veramendi, the daughter of the Mexican vice-governor of Texas. What many of us haven't heard is that on November 2,

1831, he left San Antonio with his brother, Rezin P. Bowie, and ten other handpicked adventurers, including James Coryell, to locate a silver mine in the San Saba and Leon River country. History records that the group successfully fought off the attack of several hundred Lipan Apache for three days before limping back to San Antonio. The group split up, but Coryell had seen the country, with its clear, cool streams. He liked it and wanted to go back.

After his return from the silver mine expedition, Coryell moved in with the family of a fellow adventurer, Arnold Cavitt, and, together, they developed a frontier farm near today's Marlin. This gave him ample opportunity to further his explorations. In 1835, he located his "headright" of one fourth of a league of land on a small creek near the Leon

Sterling C. Robertson
by Sam Woodfin

River, a creek which today bears his name. There, not far southwest from where Waco later grew, he proudly built a cabin and cleared land for his first crop. Then he went back to fighting Indians.

During the spring and summer of 1836, while Texas fought for Independence, Coryell was a part of Captain Sterling C. Robertson's Ranging Company, shielding the northern flank of the settlements and later protecting the new Republic. When that enlistment was up, he checked his cabin and crops and immediately re-enrolled as a member of Captain T.H. Barron's company of Rangers.

One of Sam Houston's first acts as president of the new Republic of Texas was to dismiss most of the regular army as an unnecessary expense and to reinforce the ranging companies. The Texas Rangers were born as an official arm of the Republic, and, with his company, Coryell camped at the three forks of Little River, never far from his new home, which he checked from time to time to be sure that all was well.

In the spring of 1837, the Rangers abandoned their camp at the three forks of the Little River and concentrated their forces at the Falls of the Brazos. Still not far from his chosen home, Coryell frequently made unofficial scouting expeditions on his own.

Then one day, Jim's fiddling feet carried him too far. Desire of one kind or another has been the downfall of many men. Jim, along with fellow Rangers Castleman and Webb, slipped away from camp to cut a bee tree. Unfortunately, they were neither the first nor the last to let a sweet tooth get them into trouble. While they concentrated on the bees, they were killed in an Indian ambush.

Texas remembers her heroes, even those who unwisely die for honey. James Coryell was typical of many at that time. He loved adventure and was bold in seeking it. He loved Texas and died defending her frontier. When, in 1854, enough settlers had entered the region around Coryell Creek, a grateful state named its newest county in his honor.

1830—*Los Ciboleros*

In 1830, Belva Lockwood became the first woman to argue a case before the U.S. Supreme Court. She was also the first woman nominated for President of the United States. In Fayette, New York, Joseph Smith founded the Church of Jesus Christ of Latter Day Saints. Closer to home, the Mexican government, under Anastasio Bustamente, passed the Law of April 6, which prohibited any further immigration of colonists to Texas from the United States. All of these actions created quite a stir in their respective areas.

Meanwhile, in what we now call the Texas Panhandle, a way of life continued as it had for over 200 years.

They were a special breed of people. For over 200 years they followed ancient Indian trails from the *pueblos* along the Rio Grande in New Mexico onto the *Llano Estacado*, the "High Plains" of the Texas Panhandle. They came to hunt the American Bison that we call the buffalo and that the Spanish called *cibolo*. The goal was meat, hides, and sport. They were *Los Ciboleros*, men of the buffalo. It is possible that, of all of the European cultural derivatives in the New World, they adjusted best to the environment and to the Native American way of life.

Los Ciboleros were the hard-riding descendants of the first Spaniards to follow Don Juan de Oñate into his "promised land" of New Mexico. There they intermarried with Puebloans of the Rio Grande Valley. The

Los Ciboleros
by Gary Manthei

Puebloans hunted buffalo for thousands of years on foot until the Pueblo Revolt of 1680 gave them the horse. By 1700 the hunting continued, adding the new twist of hunting from horseback.

They hunted from horseback using the lance and the bow and arrow of the Apache and Comanche. In fact, authors have suggested that the Comanche, Lipan, and Cheyenne first learned their horsemanship by watching Los Ciboleros weave their way through running herds in search of the best kill. Since there was competition for the buffalo between Los Ciboleros and the Plains Indians, it was natural for friction to develop. This brought about the policy of bringing trade goods from New Mexico to buy a certain amount of protection. This, in turn, led to regular trade between the New Mexican settlements and the plains that ultimately produced *Los Comancheros*, or those men who went to the plains with the primary goal of trading with the Comanche.

But, back to Los Ciboleros. Old Josiah Gregg, that trail blazer whose book *The Commerce of the Prairies* became required reading for the Santa Fe Trail, described them as follows:

> They *"usually wear leathern trousers and jackets, and flat straw hats; while, swung upon the shoulders of each hangs his* carsage, *or quiver of bow and arrows. The long handle of their lance being set in a case, and suspended by the side with a strap from the pommel of the saddle, leaves the point waving high over the head,*

65

with a tassel of gay parti-colored stuffs dangling at the tip of the scabbard. Their fusil, if they happen to have one, is suspended in a like manner at the other side, with a stopper in the muzzle fantastically tasseled."

They went to the plains in October, after the crops of corn, melons, beans, and peppers were harvested from each *pueblo's* small garden plots, and when the buffalo were moving to the South on their annual fall migration. With them they carried fresh-baked bread, trinkets, and other trade goods, and they returned with their two-wheeled *carretas* (carts) loaded with hides for the Chihuahua trade, meat for the long winter, tallow for candles, and the sheared buffalo wool for blankets and mattress packing. Like the Indians, Los Ciboleros wasted little of the buffalo. The horns were carved into spoons, combs, and other trinkets. The hooves were rendered into gelatin, the eyes pickled, and the tongues smoked for sale in Mexico City, where they brought about $2.00 each—a princely sum at that time.

As the years went by and the pressure of encroaching civilization on the Plains Indians increased, the competition between the Indians and Los Ciboleros also increased, resulting in several fierce battles that are unrecorded in most histories. By 1860, government policy excluded Los Ciboleros from the Panhandle because their trade goods supported the Comanche in their attacks on Anglo settlements in Central Texas and made travel on the Santa Fe Trail difficult.

The final bell tolled for these brave and gaudy horsemen with the coming of the railroad and the repeating rifles of eastern buffalo hunters. The plains were littered with rotting carcasses; the buffalo all but disappeared. Los Ciboleros, the colorful descendants of Spanish, Moorish and Indian cavalry, vanished into legend. We will see their like no more.

1830—Three-Time Loser

Back in 1829, Andrew Jackson was inaugurated as the seventh President of the United States and began his attacks on Nicholas Biddle, who controlled the Second Bank of the U.S. That same year, Edgar Allen Poe published a bunch of his poems, a fellow named Bill Burt patented the first American typewriter, and Sir Charles Wheatstone patented a little, octagonal musical squeezebox called a concertina. Down in Mexico, the government changed to a Centralist dictatorship under Anistacio Busta-mente, slavery was abolished to be replaced with peonage, and General Mier Y Terán reported that there were about five times as many Anglo-Americans living in Texas as there were supposed to be. All of these folks had problems of one kind or another. So do we.

illustration by Lillian Cowden

So, you think you've got problems? Well, you probably do. We all do, but please consider those of Sarah. She had a few, too. Sarah was born in 1809 up in Illinois, and she came to Texas as the new bride of Johnny McSherry twenty years later, in 1829. The Illinois frontier wasn't exactly a picnic at that time, and the winters were somewhat bitter. The McSherrys had survived and looked like good candidates for making a successful home on the Texas frontier, so together, they settled on a grant of land in Green C. DeWitt's colony on the Guadalupe River, just above where it crosses the current Victoria County line.

Things looked pretty good. General Mier y Terán's report led to the Mexican Law of April 6, 1830, which prohibited any further entrance into Texas by colonists from the United States, but the McSherry family had just squeezed under the wire. Johnny was a strong worker and Sarah was described by contemporaries as *"very handsome in person, yet without any formal education, being unable to read or write."* This was common on the frontier, but in this case, it was important, as we shall see.

In 1832, Johnny was carrying water from the spring to their cabin when he was killed and scalped by a wandering band of Indians. Sarah, with their new son John (named for his father), witnessed the whole affair before barring the cabin door and praying for help. Sometimes prayers are answered in the affirmative. This time help came in the person of another John, this one another Scotsman named McCrabb, who was armed and had a strong horse that easily carried the three to the nearest neighbor for safety.

Johnny McSherry's estate wasn't large, but Sarah just didn't know how to handle it. She was unable to read the will and file the necessary papers. Despite what some books say, folks often took advantage of widows on the frontier, and she needed help. She was still young and still attractive, whether she could read and write or not.

Enter John number three, who was willing to help and protect the new widow from fraud. Sarah and John Hibbins, a prominent landowner and stock raiser in the area, were married sometime between 1832 and 1834. The McSherry estate was added to the Hibbins holdings and things began to look better. Another son was born, and, in 1835, Sarah took both children back to Illinois for a visit to her parents. She returned in February 1836 with her children and her half-brother, George Creath. John Hibbins met them with an ox cart down at Columbia on the Brazos River.

Now, you've got to remember what else was going on in February of 1836. Troops of a provisional state government in Texas, determined to uphold the Mexican Constitution of 1824, had captured San Antonio and sent Mexican General Martín Perfecto de Cos back across the Rio Grande. His brother-in-law, Antonio López de Santa Anna, who had recently proclaimed himself *"President for life, for the good of the people,"* and who had abolished the Constitution of 1824, was on his way back to Texas to punish the Texans who, by then, occupied the abandoned chapel of the *San Antonio de Valero* mission, also known as "The Alamo." A new convention was meeting at Washington-On-The-Brazos to discuss independence. The entire Texas frontier was in turmoil. If that were not enough, that winter and spring turned out to be the wettest on record since the beginning of weather observations by Franciscan missionaries over a hundred years earlier. Travel of any kind was difficult.

The route home to the Guadalupe took the Hibbins family through what is now Lavaca County, and they camped one night on the banks of Rocky Creek, near the present town of Sweet Home. The creek was flooded and they couldn't cross with the ox cart until the waters went down. History repeated itself. Thirteen wandering Comanche attacked the camp. Husband John and brother George were killed and scalped while Sarah and the two children were captured. The Indians tied them on horses and headed for the broken country along the Colorado River above today's Austin. During the first day the baby cried constantly, and, to minimize the sound of their passing, one of the Indians knocked its brains out against a tree trunk and left the baby where it fell. The next night Sarah managed to slip away and make her way to the river. Accounts differ as to who actually found her, but she turned up the next day at Reuben Hornsby's little settlement at Hornsby's Bend on the Colorado—barefoot, ragged, raped, and bloody—but alive.

It was time for Sarah to have a little good luck. A "ranging company," those forerunners of the Texas Rangers, was camped at Hornsby's, and all were under the command of John Tumlinson. In one of the more successful rescue operations of the time, they not only recovered the other McSherry boy and killed some of the attackers, but also collected all of the horses and mules and assorted plunder from other attacks *in the settlements.*

While all of this was going on, Texas declared its independence on March 2. But then came the fall of the Alamo on March 6.

During the War for Texas Independence, Sarah and her son joined the Hornsby women in the Run-Away Scrape. After victory at San Jacinto, she came back. Now she really needed help. Estates were beginning to pile up with assorted debts, claims, and privileges. She needed help in sorting them out, and, so far, "Johns" had not been particularly lucky in her life. So, in June of 1836, Sarah McSherry Hibbins married Claiborne Stinnett, the newly elected sheriff of Gonzales County. While the sheriff was busy trying to sort out Sarah's affairs, Sarah was busy at home, and, in 1838, a daughter was born.

By now, you've probably guessed what happened. Claiborne was killed by Indians, or, as some people said, by escaped slaves, just after the birth of his daughter. The baby died a month later from some childhood disease, and, on May 30, 1839, Sarah, a three-time loser at age thirty, married Phillip Howard in Gonzales.

Things were tough. Husband number four was not the estate manager Sarah needed, but he did manage to keep his hair safe from Indians. Most of the land was lost in one way or another to folks who claimed debts from the old estates, but at least Sarah had someone around the place. The last 30 years of Sara McSherry Hibbins Stinnett Howard were spent in relative domestic tranquility.

1831—Lorenzo the Magnificent

From time to time there are men and women who, somehow, slip through the cracks of memory, although their contribution to the human endeavor is more important than that of others. Sometimes time rectifies the situation and they receive their just accolades. Sometimes they are forgotten.

When fifty-nine delegates signed the Texas Declaration of Independence at Washington-On-The-Brazos on March 3, 1836, only three of them were natives of Mexico. All of the rest were relative newcomers to the Mexican Province of Texas.

Yes, I know, you think Texas Independence Day is March 2. It is. On March 2 the delegates approved the Declaration. That makes March 2 Texas Independence Day. But they didn't sign a copy until March 3.

Two of these natives of Mexico came from San Antonio and one from the Mexican State of Yucatan. Many signers served their governments in an official capacity before coming to Texas. Sam Houston, for instance, had served two terms in the U.S. House of Representatives and, briefly, as the governor of Tennessee. But when you get right down to length and breadth of government service, no other delegate surpassed Lorenzo "The Magnificent."

Manuel Lorenzo Justiniano de Zavala
by Suzy Keller

Manuel Lorenzo Justiniano de Zavala was born in the little village of Tecoh, near the town of Merída in the Mexican Yucatan, on October 3, 1789. His family was both rich and influential, and young Lorenzo was sent to school at the Seminary of Ildefonso in Spain. The United States had won its independence and the French Revolution was demonstrating the power of an aroused public when Lorenzo became an ardent supporter of liberalism and democratic reforms in 1807.

Back home in Merída, young Lorenzo served as the secretary for several elective councils before he was thrown into prison in 1814 because of his revolutionary beliefs. He was 25 years old. During the three years he spent in prison, he studied medicine and the English language and was prepared for a new profession when he was released, but his countrymen instead elected him to the Yucatan Provincial Assembly in 1820 and, in 1821, as the representative of Yucatan to the Spanish Cordes in Madrid.

He was in Madrid when he learned of Mexican independence from Spain. He hurried home to take a part in the new government. As a member of the first Mexican Constitutional Congress and, later, the Mexican Senate, he helped to create the Mexican Constitution of 1824, which, among other things, provided for the settling in Texas of immigrants from the United States who would swear allegiance to that Constitution.

Please allow a recess from this story. You must understand something about Mexico and Mexican politics that very few Texans care to understand. Thousands of people have died because of this misunderstanding. You *need* to understand.

Under Spanish rule, social distinctions were *very* important and were controlled by law. The most powerful and richest people in the government, business, the Church, and the military, were known as *Península res*, that is, people who were born in Spain or Portugal on the Iberian Peninsula. This distinction was so great that families sent mothers-to-be back to Spain so that their children would be born there.

Those in the second most important and powerful group were known as *Criollos*. These were people with pure European blood, but they had the misfortune to be born in the New World, not in Spain. Together, these two social groups controlled over 90% of the wealth, land, and political power in Spanish Mexico. And yet, together, they represented far less than 10% of the total population.

Below a boundary, which could be crossed only in one direction, was the next social group. These people were recognized as *Mestizos*, people of mixed blood. The law recognized over two-dozen degrees of blood mixture, depending on what the mix was and where it was in your family tree. A mestizo could never aspire to a position of power, wealth, or land ownership.

At the bottom of the social scale were the *Indígenes*, those indigenous Americans with pure Indian bloodlines. These were not even considered to be human, unless they were communing members of the Spanish version of the Roman Catholic Church. Non-Christians were *"savage beasts, some in the shapes of men."* These last two social classes controlled less than 10% of the wealth, land, and power, but they represented well over 90% of the total population. In the Spanish feudal system they owned no land and owed allegiance, and taxes, to those whose land they occupied.

71

On September 16, 1810 (*Diez Y Seis de Septiembre*), Father Miguel Hidalgo Y Castilla, a mestizo priest in the little town of Dolores, nailed the *Grito de Dolores*, the "cry or shout from Dolores," on the front door of his church. This Grito became the Mexican Declaration of Independence from Spain and began the Mexican War for Independence. The Grito called for a social revolution in which all social groups would be equal and in which there would be a complete redistribution of the land base. The ownership of land was recognized as true freedom—freedom to own and control one's home and one's livelihood. If successful, the War for Independence would mean the loss of power by that controlling, less than 10%, of the population.

After many starts and stops, Mexico won its independence in 1821, eleven years later, but it didn't realize the goals of the Grito. In some ways it made things worse. Spain, as a controlling influence, was gone. That put even more power in the hands of a very few people who began to call themselves *Centralistas*, or Centralists, who believed that all power in Mexico should be controlled by one central authority. Agustíne de Iturbide declared himself Agustíne I, Emperor of Mexico.

The Empire of Mexico didn't last long. The people rose up in righteous indignation and ousted the Centralist government. The people called themselves *Federalistas*, or Federalists. They wanted "power to the people," a representative form of government like that in the United States, an elected presidency, and semi-autonomous states and municipalities which could elect their own officials, make their own laws, collect their own taxes, and spend them the way they wanted.

Those in power, whether they are groups or individuals, rarely relinquish that power willingly. In the first ten years of Mexican independence, mini-revolutions shifted power between Federalists and Centralists eleven times. Every time there was a change of government, people died and laws changed.

Now, back to the story.

Lorenzo, even though he was of a Criollo family, became a Federalist, that is, one who believed in democratic power to the people and a limited central government. In 1827 he was elected governor of the State of Mexico, but, in a military move by the Centralist Army, was forced to flee to Mexico City, where a Federalist coup placed Vicente Guerrero as President and Lorenzo as the Minister of the Treasury. He still retained his governorship and, in that capacity, received an empresarial contract to settle five hundred families in Texas near the Louisiana border.

During another internal revolution in Mexico, the Centralists again took over the government and removed Lorenzo from his governorship in 1830. He took that opportunity to travel through Texas and the United

States. He entered into an agreement with David G. Burnet and others to organize the Galveston Bay and Texas Land Company, which would attract settlers from the United States to the forests of Southeast Texas. Back in Mexico in 1832, he was again elected to the governorship of his state; he also served in the Mexican Chamber of Deputies in 1833. Then he was appointed as the Mexican Ambassador to France.

When Mexican President Antonio López de Santa Anna was elected, he promised many liberal reforms and a pure Federalist form of government. He promised that there would be land reform so that everyone would be able to own a piece of the pie. He promised that the power of the military would be lessened. He promised lower taxes and greater freedom for individuals.

Then he changed his mind, abolished Federalism in 1835, and declared the Constitution of 1824 null and void. Elected to serve the people, he became a dictator. A distressed Lorenzo hurried home from France and joined with his new friends in Texas to oppose Santa Anna and support the old Constitution. He built a home on Buffalo Bayou near where the San Jacinto River joins it and installed his family there, while he participated in the events that led to the Texas Revolution. He signed the Declaration of Independence at Washington-On-The-Brazos, and, because of his wealth of experience, was appointed vice-president of the ad interim government of the new republic.

Then came the war. It did not begin as a war for independence. In September of 1835, Texans voted *not* to seek independence, but, as Federalists, to willingly fight to support the Mexican Constitution of 1824. The battles at Gonzales, Concepción, and Béxar changed all that, and a new convention met at the end of February, which led to the Texas Declaration of Independence.

In one of the least understood and greatest ironies of the war, those who fought and died at the Alamo on March 6, Anglo and Tejano alike, were fighting as Federalists and for the Federalist Constitution of 1824. That was the Constitution that guaranteed them their land. They never knew that Texas had declared independence. Despite what many generations of Texans and Mexicans have been taught, the war was *not* between Anglo-American Texans and the Mexican people.

Many Mexicans fought for Texas. It was a part of a larger war between the Federalist majority of the Mexican people and a dictatorial Centralist government. In many ways, that war continues in Mexico today as "the people" still seek land reforms promised over 150 years ago.

The Battle of San Jacinto took place just across the bayou from the de Zavala home. After the battle, Lorenzo, in his capacity as a medical practitioner, treated both Texan and Mexican wounded, and his home became a hospital. The years of conflict had taken their toll. Lorenzo relinquished his office in October of 1836 and died at his home a month later.

It is a shame that he never really got to see what he helped to create.

1832—Mike Muldoon, the Friar Tuck of Texas

Frontier Texas probably saw the widest assortment of strong-willed and outspoken "characters" ever assembled. They came from around the known world and for as many reasons as there were people. And they, each and every one, left a mark on our heritage.

Texas, in 1832, was filled with unhappy people. The Mexican "Law of April 6, 1830" prohibited any further colonization of Texas from the United States. It also prohibited the importation of slaves or even crossing "the northern frontier" without a passport "under any pretense whatsoever." People responded in a variety of ways, none of them friendly to the Mexican government. Throughout 1832 and 1833 there were "disturbances" recorded in blood, and a variety of folks became outlaws in the eyes of the Bustamente Centralist government.

Father Mike
by Nathan Smith

Legend tells us that when Robin Hood and his merry men took residence in old Sherwood Forest they had with them an ecclesiastical gentleman known as "Friar Tuck," who not only saw to the spiritual needs of the band, but who could also out-drink, out-sing, and out-fight almost any man there. That's why we call Father Miguel Muldoon the Friar Tuck of Texas.

According to family tradition, Michael Muldoon was born about 1790 in County Caven, Ireland, the son of an Irish father and a Spanish mother. Such unions were quite common at the time. Life was hard in Ireland then, as it almost always was. The English prohibited the practice of Roman Catholicism, and, at an early age, young Mike went to Spain, where he received his education and was ordained as a priest at the Irish College of Seville. A true son of Ireland, he looked for adventure and came to Mexico in 1821 as the personal chaplain to Don Juan O'Donoju (another Irish Spaniard), who was the last Viceroy of the Spanish Crown in New Spain.

Mexico gained her independence from Spain in 1821, and Father Muldoon appeared in Texas as the spiritual leader of the Irish colony of McMullen and McGloin at San Patricio. You see, under the colonization laws of Mexico, no one could acquire land or live in the province of Coahuila y Texas who was not a Catholic.

Father Muldoon met Stephen F. Austin on one of his many trips to Mexico City, and the two got along well. Tradition tells us that Muldoon taught Austin to speak Spanish, and Austin, in return, requested that Muldoon be sent to his colony as the officially sanctioned curate. Austin also promised Muldoon a grant of eleven leagues of land, about 48,610 acres.

Father Miguel "Mike" Muldoon arrived at Austin's seat of government in San Felipe in 1831. He immediately went to work. Since the law said everyone had to be Catholic, he pronounced the predominantly Protestant Anglo-Americans to be Catholic. Since the law said that all marriages had to be Catholic marriages, he performed them that way on a production-line basis. His record seems to have been thirty in one ceremony, after which the party lasted for two and one-half days—that is, until Father Muldoon managed to drink the rest of the men under the table.

If there was a dance, he was there. The frontier scout and early Texas Ranger, Noah Smithwick, remembered that Muldoon could "pat juba" (set the rhythm by slapping his thighs with his hands) better than most, and that he could continue to sing and drink in the process.

When it came to fighting or diplomacy, Father Mike was there. In one case he followed a band of Indians and brought back the captured wife of a settler. When Austin was sick in bed, he traveled with Mexican General Mier y Terán on his inspection tour of the Texas colonies as Austin's personal representative. When, during one of the "disturbances," angry citizens marched on the Mexican garrison at Anahauc to liberate some prisoners, he led the way and offered himself as a hostage in their place. In the summer of 1835 he helped to get Stephen F. Austin out of prison in Mexico City. After the Texas Revolution, he smuggled William H. Wharton out of prison in Matamoras dressed in a priest's robe. He told Wharton that if anyone stopped him he should extend his right hand with two fingers raised and intone *"Pax vobiscum,"* which was, probably, the only Latin that Wharton ever learned. The rescue allowed Wharton to get home in time to be elected to the Texas Senate.

75

As for "Father Mike," he became the Catholic vicar general for the Republic of Texas. In 1839, while serving as an interpreter for Col. Bernard E. Bee Sr., who was on a diplomatic mission to Mexico at the time, Muldoon was arrested for leaving Mexico illegally when he went to Texas.

We don't know for sure what happened to Miguel Muldoon. Some sources say that he was arrested by Santa Anna's troops in Mexico City and executed during the Mexican War in 1847. Other sources suggest that the Church recalled him to Spain, where he lived out the rest of his life in quiet happiness growing grapes and making wine.

Down where the Colorado River cuts its way through Fayette County and the heart of Austin's original colony there is the tiny town of Muldoon. A marker commemorates Father Miguel Muldoon and the role this "Friar Tuck" played in our history. It is located on the land he once received from Stephen F. Austin, but he isn't there—he has gone on into the legends.

1835—Henry, the Redheaded Ranger

Those who carved the first trails through the frontier wilderness are often described as "men with the bark on." Certainly, there were among them those with culture and a classical education. But the majority was what we, today, would call "functionally illiterate"— in pre-Civil War Mississippi, for instance, over 80% of the white population could neither read nor write.

They didn't let that stop them. They had a nation to build.

Most of his biographers agree that Henry Wax Karnes could neither read nor write. Although highly educated men and women shaped much of our destiny, there were certainly many whose contributions ran to deeds rather than words. Karnes was one of these. In retrospect, we named a county and a city for him in that important ranching and agricultural area just below San Antonio.

But that came later, in 1854. In the 1830s, when Henry first saw it, the country was mostly prairie, with trees along the streams, and crossed by two heavily traveled supply roads. One was from the old "French Way" crossing of the Rio Grande below today's Eagle Pass to San Antonio. The other was from "*Old Cópano*," a port on the northwest side of Cópano Bay, which also terminated in San Antonio.

Redheaded Henry Karnes was born in 1812, a native of Tennessee. The family moved to Arkansas when Henry was a child, and there Henry learned all about trapping and hunting from his father.

Even before the American Revolution, Tennessee contributed her share of men who went "yondering" to see what was on the other side of the next hill or down the next valley. At age 16, Henry joined their number and attached himself to a group of trappers operating in what are now parts of Arkansas, Oklahoma, and the Texas Panhandle. The group disbanded on the headwaters of the Red River out in what is now Collingsworth County. With three companions,

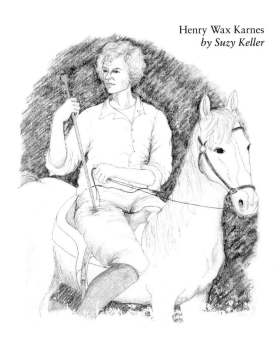

Henry Wax Karnes
by Suzy Keller

Henry made his way overland to the upper reaches of the Trinity. There, somewhere around today's Wise County, they ran into trouble and lost their horses, but not their hair, to Indians.

They weren't too sure just where they were, except that it was a long way from anywhere they wanted to be. So, they built a canoe and may have become the first European-descended Americans to follow the Trinity past where Dallas is today, and on to the more settled area at Robbins' Ferry at the *Paso Tomás* crossing of the old San Antonio and La Bahía roads in today's Madison County. From there Henry crossed over to the Brazos, and for some years he was an overseer on Jared Groce's Plantation near today's Hempstead.

He was there when the War for Texas Independence broke out, and his "yondering" spirit got the better of him. Leaving his job, he hotfooted it to Gonzales and arrived just in time to join the company of John York on its march to the Battle of Concepcíon and the Siege of Béxar.

The Texas Army at that time was without real organization, made up completely of companies of volunteers who elected their own officers. Stephen F. Austin was elected as the overall commander, but it was an honorary title and little else. There were few similarities between that army and the organized forces of established governments. Buckskins and bandannas rode and walked beside swallow-tailed coats and top hats. There were moccasins and riding boots flanking farmers' brogans and clerks' slippers. Horses, burros, and mules shared space with the two longhorn cows that pulled the one piece of artillery. Long-barreled squirrel rifles, smooth-bored muskets and shotguns loaded with "blue-whistlers" were in about equal distribution.

At the Siege of Béxar, today often referred to as the Battle of San Antonio, Henry took a leading role with the weapon of his choice, a crowbar, breaking down walls to allow the Texans to advance from house to house without coming under fire from the Mexican Army.

Then, on March 20, 1836, he formed a company of his own at Goliad—a volunteer company of cavalry that went to join Sam Houston rather than stay under the command of the inept Col. James Fannin. That decision saved his life. When Fannin surrendered his command, Henry was scouting for Houston and brought him verification of the fall of the Alamo. Before San Jacinto he rode with Erastus "Deaf" Smith on scouting expeditions, and, during the battle, was a captain and second in command of Lamar's cavalry. After Santa Anna's capture, Sam Houston sent Henry to Matamoros to arrange an exchange of prisoners. Instead of honoring the agreement for the exchange, the Mexican army threw Henry into the local prison. He managed to break through the wall and escape.

Back in the new Republic in 1838, he was authorized to form eight "ranging companies" to guard the frontier from Comanche attack. He fought with one of these companies in a battle on the *Arroyo Seco* (dry gully) in 1839. Later, he became an Indian Agent and was instrumental in arranging the meeting in San Antonio between Comanche leaders and the government, which ended in the Council House Fight.

This was a life too tame for Henry. He became a full-time Ranger and gathered around him many, including Jack Hays, Sam Walker, and Ben McCulloch, who later played important roles in the history of the West. In one engagement, he was captured by Indians, but they unexpectedly released him after their efforts to wash the red out of his hair failed. Finally, in an episode that we've seen recreated a hundred times by Hollywood, he offered to settle an Indian confrontation with a one-on-one fight with the war chief of the band. He won the fight and the battle was averted, but he received a wound that ultimately led to his death. Weakened by the wound, he contracted yellow fever. Old wounds and disease weren't enough to keep him down, so he decided to travel from San Antonio to Houston on business before he fully recovered. On the way, he suffered a relapse and died on August 16, 1840. He was only 28.

Henry Karnes, the redheaded Ranger, could neither read nor write, but he made his mark on history.

1835—The Price of Poker

People came to Texas for a variety of reasons. Most came for land. Many came for economic reasons. Some came for a new start, and some came because they had to. I had hoped to learn more about this story before I told it, but I have been unable to trace it in any of the readily available records. Those who took the census in the days before Texas became a republic were sometimes lax in their duties. With the flood of immigrants to the Republic, the job got more difficult. Even today, we miss a lot of people who move from place to place and have no established residence.

illustration by Gary Manthei

Johann Friedrich Ernst, who had once been a postmaster for the Duke of Oldenburg in what we, today, call Germany, came to Texas about 1831. He built a home near today's Cat Spring in the beautiful rolling country of Austin County, and from there he wrote glowing letters back to Germany about the beauty of Texas, the availability of land and its productivity, and about the ease of living. Among those who received his letters were members of the von Roeder family.

Lieutenant Ludwig Sigismund Anton von Roeder was the head of a large family of minor nobility in Prussia. The von Roeders had fifteen sons and daughters, and, like many families, they had a few problems with one of their children, a tempestuous young man named Sigismund, after his father. Although dueling was illegal in Prussia, "fencing" with sharpened sabers as a sport was deemed a necessary part of a young man's education and a tradition of the nobility. The fact that some "fencing" matches were more than that was understood, and members of the Prussian Army's officer corps wore dueling scars as a badge of honor well into the 20th century. Young Sigismund had the combined skill and bad luck that caused him to kill the Prince of Prussia in a "fencing" match in 1833. As a condition of a pardon for young Sigismund, several families of von Roeders, and many of their friends, were banished from Prussia. They came to Texas to be near Friedrich Ernst in 1834.

79

In Texas, things went well, except for the fact that the von Roeders got homesick and young Sigismund refused to give up the Prussian habits of the nobility which caused him to clank around the frontier with his riding boots and sword. The result is best told in the words of the older von Roeder in a letter that he sent to a sister back in Prussia:

> *"And that brings me to the bittersweet wedding of our wild son Sigismund, whose duel with the Prince of Prussia, and conditional pardon from prison, brought us all to Mexico.*
>
> *"He had a precipitous marriage at San Felipe, after he killed a man with the same sword that killed the Prince of Prussia. Louis Kleberg was present and saw both the killing and the wedding in a succession of 20 minutes. He gave us the following account:*
>
>> *"It seems that a dozen or so young blades met at the house of Benjamin Buckingham, on the Brazos. This young Kentuckian had only recently brought his beautiful young bride to his plantation. They were all celebrating—dancing, drinking, singing, and laughing until finally—as usual in this new world— for lack of other entertainment, the men drifted into cards. At first, it was a social game; the stakes were small. Soon, the losers dropped out. Sigismund was most favored by the Goddess Fortuna; she slighted Buckingham. The game narrowed to these two. My son proposed a restriction of stakes. His adversary, the scion of Blue Grass wealth, demanded removal of any limit. They played and drank into the night—and through it.*
>>
>> *"Fortune swayed back and forth, liquor lending its aid to keep excitement at a high pitch among the onlookers; but Sigismund was gradually forging ahead. When Buckingham's cash was gone, he put up his bills of sale for his mules, work-horses, yokes of oxen. With but a slight interruption the stream trickled over to Sigismund. Then, one by one, Buckingham's slaves came into the game; out in the hall they stood— poor black chattels--old and young, men, women, and children.*
>>
>> *"Sigismund raked the bills of sale for everyone from the middle of a long table, stacked them neatly and weighted them down with a large, red Brazos River*

bottom brick. *The game went on. At noon the onlookers ate juicy beef and wild turkey sandwiches brought from the kitchen outside. The players ate nothing—they played.*

"When his personal property—wagons, buggies, saddles, plows, planters, race horses, and all other animals with their feed and harnesses—was gone, Buckingham sent for the title papers to the various plots on his plantation. His friends begged him to stop. 'I will not stop,' he shouted back with a gambler's frenzy, as the cards were dealt again. 'My luck will come back—you wait and see.'

"Of course, Sigismund couldn't quit when he was the winner—he had to play. 'I'll quit when he calls it off—not before.'

"The title papers came. Buckingham laid the deed to the big farm in the bend of the Brazos River on the table. Sigismund followed with all of the stuff under the brick. They played.

"Buckingham lost, but not without a dreadful oath. Deed after deed followed the first, until the big brick, symbolic of the deep rich, red soil of the Brazos River bottom, rode and hugged them all.

"Buckingham looked around the room. Every eye evaded his search. Not a word was spoken. Light thickened, infiltration of the gloom of night worked gray upon the window frames. An old, white haired Negro shuffled up to the table and put candles before the players. As he went out, he opened wide the big heavy doors. Every man rose to his feet. There stood the bride—like a February dogwood in bloom among the drab and wintry trees of the Brazos River bottom! She stepped forward and laid her hand on her husband's arm. 'Come on, honey. Let's go. You're tired.'

"'And that ain't all,' said some young fellow with a snigger.

"' You mean I'm broke?' snorted Buckingham, 'but I'm not!' His fist struck the table with a profanity, as he drew his marriage certificate from his pocket, and threw it between the candles. 'We'll play for that!' Instantly, Sigismund pushed his winnings—brick, deeds, and all—into the middle of the table.

81

> "'Certainly we will.' And then arising, and with a
> cavalier's sweep of his hat and a deep bow to the bride,
> 'but not without the consent of the lady.' She smiled;
> they played; Buckingham lost. And, as Sigismund raised
> the brick to consolidate the marriage certificate with his
> other winnings, Buckingham fired, but missed, and as he
> reached for another pistol, Sigismund flashed his sword
> and ran him through.
>
> "The coroner came, saw, found self-defense; and as
> the body on a stretcher passed out the double doors, the
> same official in a loud, ringing voice was heard: 'Will
> you, Barbara Buckingham, take this man … ?
>
> "Oh, my dear, dear sister: was ever woman in this
> humor wooed? Was ever woman in this manner won?"

As I said, I tried to find out what happened to the young couple after that, but I failed. Several of the von Roeder and Kleberg men fought in the Texas Revolution while the women moved their cattle to Louisiana. The house at Cat Spring burned during the Run-Away Scrape, and other members of the family appear in the census records. But, of young Sigismund and his bride, I know no more.

1835—The "First to Fall"

Here is a good question for argument: "When did the Texas Revolution begin?"

There are those folks up in East Texas who might claim that the Fredonia Rebellion of Hayden Edwards back in 1826 was the starting point. Certainly, people died in the encounter, and, today, they fly the flag, but they forget that the Fredonia Rebellion was an illegal attempt to steal land from people who had occupied it for many generations. Militia formed in Stephen F. Austin's colony terminated that "rebellion."

Some might choose "The Disturbance of 1831" down at Anahuac. More than a few shots were fired. No one was killed that I am aware of, but the "Turtle Bayou Resolutions," which supported Antonio López de Santa Anna for president of Mexico, were a result. Folks seem to forget that this particular "disturbance" had two causes. It involved people who didn't want to pay their taxes and those who tried to free William B. Travis and Patrick Jack from jail, where they were locked up for "inciting to riot."

Or, there was "The Disturbance" down at Velasco in 1832. A bunch of folks died in that one, which was started, again, by folks who didn't want to pay their taxes.

My personal favorite for a beginning is the battle between the Brazos River steamboat Laura, *the "cotton bale battleship," and the* Corréo de Mexico *in September of 1835. One reason I like that one so much is because it is the first use in world history of steam power to determine the outcome of a naval battle, and the Texans won. Folks died in that one too, but they were mostly English sailors on the Mexican ship, and few people today even know anything about it.*

Although shots were fired and people died, most historians, for some reason, don't call these "disturbances" war, or even battles in a war. I guess they feel that they must wait for some politician to call it a war before they will accept the idea.

Richard Andrews
by Gary Manthei

On September 19, 1835, Stephen F. Austin spoke before the convention at San Felipe:

"We must seek peace, if it can be attained on constitutional grounds, but we must prepare for war ... War is our only recourse. There is no other remedy. We must defend our rights, ourselves, and our country by force of arms." A few weeks earlier he'd written to friends in the United States, *"I have no doubt but that American long rifles will ultimately determine the issue."*

It is depressingly strange that so many people today feel it is "un-American" to think of personally defending the rights of the people, ourselves, our homes, or our country "by force of arms." They learn little from world history. Thomas Jefferson wrote, "The tree of liberty must be refreshed from time to time with the blood of patriots and tyrants." Government is not always right, and it does not always represent "the people."

Although that convention voted against declaring independence and instead chose to fight to defend the Mexican Constitution of 1824, historians choose it as a starting place because the "Come and Take It" encounter at Gonzales followed shortly thereafter, and that started the ball rolling down the hill. If that is the case, then, despite earlier deaths, the "honor" of being "The First to Fall" for Texas Independence must go to Richard Andrews.

Richard (usually called "Big Dick" because of his size and strength) Andrews came to Texas with his family sometime in the mid-1820s and settled near Fort Bend on the Brazos River, where the city of Richmond is today. He and his brother, Micah, joined one of Austin's Ranging Companies and fought several skirmishes with Indians before they answered the call for volunteers from Gonzales at the end of September 1835. Someone suggested that "Big Dick" was as strong as an ox—and moved like one, too. In any event, he was among the wounded at the "Come and Take It" fracas on October 2, but he was well enough to march with the fledgling Texas Army on its march from Gonzales toward San Antonio a week later.

Perhaps the most readable account of that march comes from Noah Smithwick, whose book, *The Evolution of a State*, should be "must" reading for anyone interested in Texas history. He described what the "army" looked like, how it was armed and led, and how it became involved in the Battle of Concepcíon on the pastures of the old and abandoned *Misíon Concepcíon*. According to Smithwick, Texas troops were strung out below the bank of a winding gully behind a fringe of brush and trees, while the Mexican Army, using European tactics, marched shoulder-to-shoulder across the open field.

I must digress. Bear with me; we'll come back to the subject in a minute. Ever since the dawn of warfare, organized armies have been slow to adopt change—unless they are forced into it. The legions of the Roman Empire gained their great strength by fighting from behind a moving wall of shields. As long as the shoulder-to-shoulder "shield wall" held, the troops won battles. Even though "barbarian hordes" on horseback broke the "wall" and ultimately defeated the Roman Empire, they were, well, *barbarians*. "Civilized" men fought shoulder-to-shoulder. That tactic, as far as organized armies were concerned, did not change with the coming of firearms. Companies, battalions, and whole regiments marched into battle shoulder-to-shoulder. On the order of an officer, the first rank would either kneel or continue to stand upright, point their weapons in the same general direction, and all fire at the same time. Then, while they reloaded, the second rank would pass through their line, take position, and, on order, fire. This system was devastating, as long as the other side played by the same rules. Both North and South used this system during the Civil War and slaughtered three entire generations of humanity on both sides.

Like I said, armies are slow to change. On the frontier, however, people learned to take advantage of concealment, and, except in a few instances, each rifleman picked his own target and fired at will. To an organized army, they didn't play fair. They were barbarians because they didn't fight like civilized, slow-to-change armies. What was worse, or better, the concealed frontiersmen usually won.

Now, back to the topic. That is what happened at the Battle of Concepción. The Mexican Army, led for the most part by officers trained in the European tradition, marched shoulder-to-shoulder and fired their volleys even when they couldn't see the enemy. The Texans were ordered to stay in the gully and stick their heads up only long enough to pick a target and fire. Then they would drop below the level of the bank and reload. It was almost impossible for the Mexican Army to hit any enemy target. It was almost impossible for the Texas Army to miss. For all practical purposes, the Texans won the battle almost before it started.

Near the end of the battle, however, when Mexican dead littered the field and their ranks were retreating, one lone Texan got so excited that he forgot his orders, climbed out of the gully, and ran out into the field. Out of the entire next volley fired by the Mexican Army only one bullet found its mark.

You've guessed it already. "Big Dick" Andrews became "The First to Fall." There is a marker for him on the Concepción battlefield, and we have a city and a county named for him.

1836—Nine Lives

The myths of many cultures tell of those who seem to be untouchable by death. Through the fires of battle and ordinary hardships, they move unscathed. They are mortals who, for a time, become immortal. Texas has had a few of these. There were men, women, and children who survived when others fell.

It may be that Bill Scurlock carried a rabbit's foot ... or a four leaf clover ... or a tobacco sack full of bats' wings, gopher fur, and lizard teeth ... or some such. Lots of the old timers did. Some do today. But, it could be that he was extremely good at the game of survival, or just plain lucky. You be the judge.

William Scurlock was born in 1807 over in North Carolina. Like many at that time, the family moved west, arriving in Texas in 1834. Bill and his younger brother Mial were living in old San Augustine when the sabers started rattling for the War for Texas Independence. After the "Come-And-Take-It" battle at Gonzales, they headed together down the Old Spanish Road to join Henry Augustine's Volunteer Company on the march to San Antonio.

On November 26, 1835, Bill fought beside Jim Bowie in the Battle of Concepcíon. The Mexicans lost about 50 men, while the Texans lost only one. It wasn't Bill. That's one life we can count.

That action started the Siege of Béxar, which ended on December 5, 1835, when about 300 Texans followed "Old Ben Milam" into San An-

William Scurlock
by Gary Manthei

tonio, and, after bitter house-to-house fighting against 1200 Mexican soldiers, won the victory. Against odds of 4 to 1, only four Texans—including Ben Milam—were killed. Chalk up another life for Bill.

After San Antonio, brother Mial stayed with a few others at the Alamo. On March 6, he died there. Bill, however, joined Dr. James Grant, the English agent gadfly, on the ill-fated expedition to attack Matamoros. The "Matamoros Expedition" didn't pan out. There was dissention among the men and about half of them decided it would be more profitable for them to trap wild horses and take them back home to sell. On March 2, 1836, they were attacked by a vastly superior Mexican force on the banks of Agua Dulce Creek about 26 miles west of the Irish colony at San Patricio. Only six of the Texans escaped. Bill was one of them. That's three.

The closest Texan force that offered protection was Colonel James Fannin's command up at Goliad. That was a long way through the brush, and the six survivors couldn't use the roads because they were patrolled by Mexican troops under General José Urréa. Still, they made it in time to join Fannin in his retreat. At the Battle of Coleto Creek, near today's little town of Fannin, Bill served as a captain in command of a company of volunteers. Again outnumbered by about three to one, the Texans put up a good fight. The final score was 250 Mexican soldiers killed to seven Texans. Bill wasn't one of the seven. Chalk up life number four for him.

When the Mexican Army brought up artillery, Fannin surrendered his command, and they were marched back to Goliad. On Palm Sunday, at Santa Anna's orders, they were all herded out and shot in what is known as the "Goliad Massacre." All of them were killed, that is, except for a few who escaped and some who had been chosen as hospital attendants to care for the Mexican wounded. That's our Bill. Make that life number five.

In May, Bill escaped from Refugio, where he was being held, and made his way on foot back to East Texas. Along the way he crossed the Mexican Army's retreat following the Battle of San Jacinto, eluded a troop of Mexican lancers, and survived a run-in with Indians. Let's lump those three encounters into two and call them lives six and seven.

Back in San Augustine, he recruited another company, the San Augustine Volunteers, and served with General Thomas J. Rusk from July 4 to October 4, 1836, while they mopped up remnants of the Mexican Army and began a campaign to pacify the Indians. There were at least half a dozen dangerous encounters during this time, but we'll call them all life eight.

Released from service, Bill married and moved his bride to Red River County, which he represented in the House of Representatives during the Fourth Congress of the Republic of Texas in 1839-1840. Just staying out of trouble during his political career, the US-Mexican War, the Regulator-Moderator Feud that raged through East Texas, the Civil War, and conflict with Governor E. J. Davis's reconstruction State Police has got to count for at least one more life. That makes nine.

Bill finally died in bed in 1889 with the reputation of having a charmed life. Maybe he did carry a rabbit's foot, but I think he was just very good at doing what he did best—surviving.

1836—The Paul Revere of the Brasada

By the end of 1835, the United States had 1,098 miles of railroad. Halley's Comet had reappeared, but the world had not ended as some had feared. Up in New York, a fellow by the name of Phineas T. Barnum began his career of showmanship by exhibiting a black woman named Joyce Heth who claimed that she was 160 years old and had been George Washington's nurse.

Here, in Texas, another revolution was underway—one that bore many similarities to the American Revolution. It even had its own Paul Revere.

If you have ever hunted, lived, or even traveled through the *brasada*, you have some special feelings about that part of Texas that stretches south from a line drawn roughly between Victoria and Eagle Pass. You probably won't find the word *brasada* in a dictionary. It is derived from a word for wood that is still hot, even after the fire has gone out. This is what the Spanish called the *Llano Mesteños* or the "wild horse prairie." Most Texans call it the brush country, and to many generations of the men and women who lived there it was, simply, the *brasada*—a sun-baked expanse of sand and caliche, covered by thorns on almost every plant that grew. It was, and is, a place of wild cattle, wild horses, and people appropriate to the conditions.

Plácido Benavides was born in Reynosa, below the Rio Grande, across from today's McAllen. There the *brasada* recognizes no international boundaries and sweeps south into the Mexican state of Tamaulipas.

Round Top House
*by Thom Ricks
courtesy of UTSA's Institute of
Texan Cultures at San Antonio*

No doubt his parents planned for him a calm life, in tune with his name. He was the god-son of Capt. Henrique Villareal who paid for his education. As a clerk, Plácido came to Texas in 1828 as secretary to Don Francisco DeLeón, land commissioner and son of *empresario* Martín DeLeón, the founder of Victoria and the DeLeón Colony. In a few years Plácido was eligible for a grant of his own, married Augustina DeLeón, the daughter of the *empresario*, and became both very important and very rich.

Placido Benavides
by Gary Manthei

In the heart of Victoria he built a home called the Round Top House. It served as a fort for the Mexican and Anglo population, and from it he led frequent battles against both Comanche and Tonkawa. In 1832 he succeeded his father-in-law as the *alcalde*, or governor, of the colony, and he was re-elected in 1834.

Plácido was a Federalist and a supporter of the Mexican Constitution of 1824. This document, prepared when Federalists were in control of the government, provided power to state and local governments to elect their own representatives, to make their own laws, to administer their own court systems, and to collect their own taxes. As a Federalist, Plácido had little liking for Antonio López de Santa Anna, who became a Centralist dictator. When Santa Anna scrapped the Constitution of 1824 and replaced it with his own set of laws, Plácido chose to side with the Texans.

With George M. Collinsworth's Matagorda Volunteers, Plácido led *rancheros Tejanos* to capture Goliad from *"Santanistas."* When Santa Anna's brother-in-law, General Cos, occupied San Antonio in 1835, it was Plácido who formed another volunteer company of *rancheros Tejanos* and fought beside the Anglo Texans in the Siege of Béxar. In the rag-tag Texas Army, Plácido's hard riding *vaqueros* formed disciplined troops who were born to the saddle and gun and fought well for the Constitution of 1824 that guaranteed them their homes and their rights.

With the defeat of Cos, there were those among the Anglo settlers who wanted to carry the war into Mexico. Major Robert Morris, Colonel Frank Johnson, and Lt. Colonel James Grant stripped San Antonio of military supplies and set out with about 500 men to raid Matamoros down below the Rio Grande. Now, you've got to understand that our first "provisional state government" really didn't work too well. The provisional governor, Henry Smith, favored creating a defensive line along the Guadalupe River and appointed Sam Houston to do just that. His "council," however, favored an attack on Mexico, and, encouraged by Dr. James Grant (an agent of the English government sent here to keep Texas out of the hands of the United States), ordered the Matamoros Expedition and attempted to impeach Smith. Intercepting these troops at Goliad, General Sam Houston convinced all but about 150 of them to stay in Texas to defend their homes. Grant and Johnson refused to recognize Houston's authority, and, with their small group, set out for the Rio Grande. With them as a guide through the *brasada* went Plácido Benavides, not because he wanted to attack Matamoros, but because he wanted *Los Diablos Yanquí* out of his territory.

At the Nueces River, there was an argument over horse hunting. Plácido suggested that, instead of attacking Matamoros, the group should capture a herd of the wild horses in the area and return to the colonies to sell them. Since Johnson and Grant had been arguing over who was in command anyway, the little force split. Small to begin with and split by dissention, these two splinter groups were the first to meet the cavalry of General José Urréa in his sweep up the coast as the right flank of Santa Anna's invasion. On the night of February 27, 1836, Urrea's troops surprised Johnson's men at San Patricio, and, on March 2, they found the remainder with Grant on Agua Dulce Creek 20 miles away.

Legends are funny things. They are hard to pin down. Urréa reported that he had killed "the traitor" Plácido Benavides, but there is other evidence. Wounded in the attack by lancers but still mounted and able to ride, Plácido reported to Grant, who told him, "Plácido, fly with the news to Colonel Fannin at Goliad."

Through the Irish settlements of McMullen's and McGloin's San Patricio Colony, to Refugio, and through the *brasada,* to every settlement on the way to Goliad, Plácido carried the word of the invasion. At Goliad, Fannin refused to believe him because he was a Mexican, and, in his indecision, was later trapped on open prairie. Plácido rode on to Victoria to warn the town and his family.

Most history books mention Plácido only in regard to his official position at Victoria and accept Urrea's report of his death. However, the Mexican-Americans of the brush country remember his ride to warn Victoria, and Lt. Colonel José Enrique de la Peña reported that Plácido was alive and well in Victoria after the Battle of San Jacinto. Other reports and a will filed for probate indicate that, after the war when new-comer Anglos took away their property, Plácido, with his wife and three daughters, moved with other survivors of the DeLeón family to Louisiana, and that the Paul Revere of the *brasada* finally died of his wounds at Opalousas, Louisiana, a pauper, one year after his legendary ride.

1836—The Alamo Rose

Legend tells us that during his wars in Europe, Napoleon often called meetings of his officers. While they argued what they thought best to do, he slept, with his eyes open. When they were through arguing he woke up and told them what he planned to do in the first place. Is it truth, or fiction?

Madame Candelaria tends to an ailing James Bowie *by Gary Manthei*

Have you ever wondered how legends get started? A large part of the job assumed by revisionist historians is to seek out and destroy legends that cannot be proven. I guess they perform a valuable service. I've done it myself on occasion, but that doesn't get to the question, "How do legends get started?" Let's try an example.

The date is March 3, 1836, and a hardy mixed bag of about 180 frontiersmen and patriots are bottled up in the old Spanish mission of *San Antonio de Valero* that we now call the Alamo. John W. Smith, later to

Suzanna Dickinson comforts her child in the Alamo chapel *by Gary Manthei*

become a member of the First Congress of the Republic of Texas, slips through the south wall with William B. Travis's last communication to the outside world. The stage is set. Before dawn on March 6, while the Mexican trumpets play the *Deguello*, Santa Anna's forces overwhelm the defenders. You've read it a dozen times and you've seen it in movies. Now come the questions. What happened in the Alamo between the time that Smith left on March 3 and the defenders died on March 6? How do we know?

Well, of course, 18-year-old Suzanna Dickinson can tell us. She was the wife of

Almeron Dickinson, a blacksmith by trade, who commanded one of the cannons. She was there and she survived. Well, she did tell us, but then again, she didn't. You see, when the Mexican artillery started lobbing shells into the mission, Suzanna and a handful of other non-combatants were herded into an enclosed room, and they didn't come out until it was all over. According to Suzanna, she could hear the battle but could not see it. To make matters worse, she later changed her story many times.

Then there are the stories of Andrea Castañón Villanueva, usually known as Madam Candelaria. She was also in the Alamo, along with the wives and families of other loyal Federalist Tejanos who were fighting to regain their Constitution of 1824. Although you rarely hear of her today, people once beat a path to the door of her little house on South Laredo Street in San Antonio to hear her tell of the Alamo defenders' last hours. She was there. She was not herded into an enclosed room with others. She nursed the sick and injured James Bowie, and said that he died in her arms. Of course, over time, her stories also tended to change somewhat, and they frequently disagreed with those of Suzanna. The two were simply not in the same place at the same time, so they didn't see the same things.

What about the citizens of San Antonio? No, they couldn't see it either. The old mission wasn't in the middle of town like it is today. What there was of San Antonio was on the other side of the river, and, in any case, its citizens wouldn't have been able to see inside the walls.

So, we are left with a puzzle surrounding that legendary episode in which Travis made a patriotic plea to his troops, drew a line on the ground with his saber, and asked all who would stand by him to cross the line. It is a memorable point in most stories of the Alamo and is rarely left out of the movies. Suzanna doesn't mention it. Madam Candelaria does. We cherish that legend of heroism. To believe it though, we must also believe the legend of Louis "Moses" Rose, and a lot of folks prefer to leave that out. You see, he also could have told the story.

Louis "Moses" Rose goes over the wall
by Gary Manthei

Rose was a veteran of Napoleon's defeat in Russia and the bitter retreat from Moscow. He served Napoleon well, becoming an officer and receiving the award of the Legion of Honor. He came to Texas seeking peace in about 1827. In the Nacogdoches area he worked as a timber cutter until he was involved in the Fredonia Rebellion. Somewhere along the way he met, and became friends with, Jim Bowie, and went to join him in the Siege of Bexar. Apparently he was a valiant soldier, but not a foolish one. Later, when folks asked him why he left the Alamo, he simply said that he saw no benefit in dying.

According to the legend, when Travis drew the line in the sand, all crossed over except Rose. Madam Candelaria mentions the incident, but she doesn't mention Rose by name. She said that all crossed over except two—James Bowie, who couldn't because he was too sick and weak to leave his bed and so asked to be carried over, and "another," who jumped over the wall. She may have been in a good position to know all about it. If she were Bowie's nurse, she would not have been far away, and would have taken a great interest in the proceedings. Since Rose was in the Alamo because of his friendship with Bowie, it stands to reason that he stayed with him until Bowie made his choice.

According to the legend, on the night of March 3rd, Rose dropped out of a window, made his way west, through San Antonio, then south, to circle around the Mexican troops, and then east. He avoided the roads and saw no one until, crippled and starving, he reached the Colorado River. A family that we'll never know took him in and fed him, but then threw him out—not because he left the Alamo (surprisingly few Texans cared about it then), but because two traveling hucksters from Nacogdoches wanted his bed and convinced his hosts that they could pay for it. Rose went on to the home of the parents of Captain W. P. Zuber in Washington County, and there he told his story about Travis, the line in the sand, and his departure from the Alamo.

Rose was no youngster. He was over 50 at the Alamo, and they called him "Moses" because of his age. He almost died there in Washington County, but the Zubers cared for him and removed festered cactus spines from his legs. When he was finally able to travel, Rose moved on in search of the peace he wanted.

He lived in Nacogdoches for many years, working as a butcher, and was very helpful to the heirs of those who died at the Alamo, helping them to receive land offered by the Republic. But, we have no record that he ever told that particular story again. The Zubers in turn told the story to their son, and, in Richardson's *Texas Almanac* for 1873, he passed the story on to the public. Zuber later corrected a few details, and the result appeared in Pennybacker's *History For Schools*, but not before a baker's dozen of self-appointed historians got their hands on it and began to publish their own "true" accounts—although they hadn't been there to see it.

Zuber was still defending his story in the July 1901 issue of the *Quarterly* of the Texas State Historical Association. Most textbooks now offer only an edited version, or leave it out altogether. We are left with the problem that surrounds all legends: *"Is it true, partially true, or false?"* We may never know.

1836—The Forgotten Saga of Greenbury Logan

There ought to be a county named for Greenbury Logan. Or, at least there should be a school or two, and maybe a few streets. Texas has a way of recognizing her heroes that way. But, as far as I can tell, the powers that be decided to forget all about Greenbury. You see, he was different.

Greenbury Logan was a blacksmith and a good one. Blacksmiths were in short supply on the Texas frontier, and every community needed at least one. Stephen F. Austin recognized the need and enlisted Greenbury as one of his colonists in 1831. Greenbury was also a fighter and a good leader. That made him three times valuable. His craft helped to build the farms and ranches of the Gulf Coast, and, when called on, he provided both arms and leadership in protecting them. Although he had intended, like many others, to make his fortune in Texas and return to the United States, he came to love both the land and the people. While the representatives of the colonies debated independence, he put down his hammers and tongs, took up his rifle, and headed for the fight at Gonzales.

On the road from Gonzales to the siege of San Antonio, there were those who wouldn't go until Greenbury agreed to lead them. On October 28, 1835, he fought beside James Bowie at the Battle of Concepcíon. During the battle that defeated Mexican General Cos at San Antonio on December 5, he was in the lead and

Greenbury Logan
by Suzy Keller

94

was the third man to fall, his right arm shattered beyond repair. Greenbury Logan was 38 years old and a blacksmith who could no longer handle hammer and tongs when he was discharged from the army.

San Jacinto brought Texas independence and freedom, but, under the leadership of Vice-President Mirabeau Lamar, the Congress passed a law saying that Greenbury Logan could not live here. You see, Greenbury was a free African-American, at that time called "a free man of color," and Lamar felt that there was no place in Texas for a free black man. Without a special act of the Congress passed in their names, no African-Americans could live in Texas unless they were slaves. This is ironic since, before the coming of the Anglo settlers, the Spanish census of 1792 recorded that of the 1,600 non-Indian residents of the area, 449 were of African descent, not Mexican or Spanish. But then, that's the sort of fellow Lamar was.

In 1837, twenty-three prominent Texans, including Henry Austin, signed a petition requesting that Greenbury Logan be allowed to stay in Texas as a free citizen. The petition was granted, but, as a disabled craftsman, he could no longer make a living at his trade and, as a black man, free or not, he was denied civil rights. True, because he was a veteran, the government did add to the one-quarter league of land he had by right of early citizenship, but no sooner was the land granted, than the problems of paying taxes arose. Document 2582 of the Sixth Congress contained his request. In part, it reads:

> *"... every privilege dear to a freeman is taken away—*
> *no chance to collect a debt with out a witness, no vote or*
> *say in any way, yet liable for taxes. It is out of my power*
> *to either settle on my lands or to sell them or to labour for*
> *money to pay expenses on them. If my debts was payd I*
> *would be willing to leave the land though my blood has*
> *nearly all been shed for its rights. I know I have friends.*
> *The Congress would not refuse to exempt my lands from*
> *tax or otherwise restoure what it has taken from me in the*
> *constitution.*
>
> *yours with respect,*
> *G. Logan"*

There is more to the story, but we don't know it all. We know that Greenbury and his wife operated a little hotel down in Brazoria and that he received title to some lands in Callahan and Brown counties because of his service, but we know little or nothing about his life. Although many similar petitions were passed for tax abatement for Anglo-Americans who had

95

fallen on hard times, Greenbury Logan's request never reached the floor for debate in Lamar's Congress. We know he served with honor, suffered through hard times, and died in 1881.

Like I said, there should, at the very least, be a Greenbury Logan Street.

1836—The "Father" Without A Home

For some reason, most of the original founders of what became the Republic of Texas fell on hard times. Colonization was expensive and both emotionally and physically draining. There were numerous suicides and a few murders. Many who were responsible for bringing thousands of colonists to new homes died early and penniless.

Stephen F. Austin is usually considered to be the "Father" of Anglo-American Texas. His was the first official colony, and, for over ten years, he expended all of his resources of funds and personal health to make sure that it worked. Certainly, he was the most successful of the *empresarios*. Today, there are cities, streets, schools, lakes, and universities named for him but, in 1836, he was in disfavor and personally believed that he was a

Stephen F. Austin, the "Father of Texas"
courtesy of the Texas State Library and Archives Commission

failure. You see, Austin was an honorable man who believed in playing the game by the rules. A lot of people don't like those with a fine sense of personal integrity. They make them aware of their own shortcomings by comparison. Before Texas Independence, Austin insisted that his colonists follow the laws of Mexico. After all, Texas *was* a part of Mexico, and Mexico gave the colonists land in return for their promise to obey Mexican law. Newcomers didn't see it that way. Many of them saw Texas as rightfully belonging to the United States and a part of the Louisiana Purchase.

This is, of course, another story—and one that is frequently forgotten. In summary: When Thomas Jefferson bought the Louisiana Purchase from

Austin's Cabin
by Gary Manthei

France in 1803, he was convinced that he bought everything between the Rio Grande and the Mississippi. At first, Spain refused to recognize any claim to land west of the Arroyo Hondo and the Calcasieu River, which enters the Gulf of Mexico east of Sabine Pass. Finally, as a result of the continuing Mexican War for Independence from Spain, the Spanish government drafted and ratified a treaty with the United States granting all lands north and east of the Rio Grande as a part of the Louisiana Purchase. Times had changed in the United States, and so the secretary of state, John Quincy Adams, refused to accept what is today Texas, the eastern half of New Mexico, a large chunk of Colorado, and parts of Oklahoma, Kansas, and Wyoming. He was afraid that the increased land would increase the power of the South and upset the balance of power in the United States Congress. It was an extremely controversial decision and wasn't finally ratified by the United States until 1823. Southerners, in particular, never forgave John Quincy Adams because they felt that their taxes had bought and paid for Texas, and that it was given away by a Yankee from Massachusetts.

History would have been a lot different if the United States had accepted the Spanish offer. You'll find a lot of "professional" historians who have never heard of this controversy.

Other folks in the United States simply didn't care. They saw empty land and decided to occupy it. By 1828 there were roughly ten times as many Anglo-Americans in Texas as were allowed by the contracts of all of the *empresarios*. The best thing you could call them, as far as the laws of Mexico are concerned, would be "illegal aliens." The majority of them probably never heard of Stephen F. Austin. Most of those who had didn't like him. As I said, he tried to play by the rules. Despite all that he did for

Texas and its colonists, and despite the fact that his health was completely shattered by the time he spent in prison in Mexico because of his attempts to guarantee colonists titles to the land they occupied, many saw his weakened condition as an opportunity to take away from him that to which he was entitled.

Very few of his original colonists paid Austin the fees for his services. The land he was entitled to under his contract with Mexico never materialized because of the war. His home and office in San Felipe were destroyed during the "Runaway Scrape," and he was sick. In a letter to a friend, he expressed his feelings. Please note the date—it is six months after the Battle of San Jacinto and only a few months after his return to Texas from the United States, where he had arranged loans to finance the Texas Revolution and represented its *ad interim* government. That was just after Sam Houston took office as the first elected president of The Republic of Texas.

> *"Peach Point, Near Brazoria*
> *October 30, 1836*
>
> *Mr. Joseph Ficklin,*
>
> *My Dear Sir:*
>
> *"I have received several letters from you, and I fear that you have accused me of neglect in not answering them sooner. As an apology, I have to say, that on my arrival at Velasco on June 29* [remember that Austin had been sent to the United States during the Texas Revolution to gather support for the cause] *I was called up the country on important business, and was in motion during the whole of July and August. The last of August I was taken sick with fever at the headquarters of the army, and with difficulty reached this place (the residence of my brother-in-law, Mr. James F. Perry). I have had a severe attack, but am now convalescent, though dyspeptic to a great degree, and so debilitated that I am barely able to get about.*
>
> *"I have been told that I have been accused of not treating* [the volunteers from Lexington, Kentucky] *with sufficient attention. This has mortified me very*

much, for I do not merit it. I have no house, not a roof in all Texas, that I can call my own. The only one I had was burnt at San Felipe during the late invasion of the enemy. I make my home where the business of the country calls me. There is none here at the farm of my brother-in-law. He only began to open up the place three years ago, and is still in the primitive log cabins and the shrubbery of the forest.

"I have no farm, no cotton plantation, no income, no money, no comforts. I have spent the prime of my life and worn out my constitution in trying to colonize this country. Many persons boast of their three or four hundred leagues [of land], acquired by speculation without labor or the sacrifice of years or even days. I shall be content to save twenty leagues—acquired very hardly and very dearly indeed.

"All of my wealth is prospective and contingent upon the events of the future. What I have been able from time to time to realize in active means has gone as fast as realized, and much faster, for I am still in debt for the expenses of my trip to Mexico in 1833, 1834, and 1835 (when I was imprisoned). My health and strength and time have gone in the service of Texas, and I am therefore not ashamed of my present poverty.

"In this situation what attentions could I have offered to any one? I held no office, and was then unpopular with the army and many others, on account of the Santa Anna excitement. I mention these things to you—they are not for publication; my only object is to inform my old and esteemed and dearly cherished friends in Lexington of the facts so far as they relate to myself.

"I deeply, most deeply, regret that any difficulty or dissatisfaction should have occurred with the volunteers. It is a misfortune, but it ought not and certainly cannot injure the cause of this country.

"Please to remember me to my old friends. I hope before March the United States flag will wave all over Texas. God grant it may.

Yours most truly,
S.F. Austin"

Alas, it was not to be. It was ten years before Texas was able to join the United States. Stephen F. Austin, the "Father of Texas," died in a borrowed room two months after writing this letter.

The Republic of Texas: 1836–1846

1837—Captain Burton's "Horse Marines"

According to Walter Prescott Webb, who wrote the somewhat dated but still definitive history of the Texas Rangers back in 1935, there is no great body of evidence to suggest that the Texas Rangers, as an organization, distinguished themselves during the Texas Revolution. In fact, they didn't even exist as a unified service until the establishment of the Republic. There were, of course, several "ranging companies" in the field—three in fact—and they contributed screening operations for the army and civilian population from as far north as Groesbeck to the Gulf Coast. But, they were not an organized part of the Army itself.

To say that they failed to distinguish themselves is, however, to forget the activities of Captain Isaac Burton and his men.

A long time ago I learned the first verse of a little song about a "Captain Jinks of the Horse Marines," who, apparently, fed his horse "on corn and beans" and had a variety of amorous adventures with young ladies. It

Isacc Burton at Cópano Bay
by Gary Manthei

all sounded rather exciting to a ten-year-old, and, being both young and impressionable, I wanted to know just what a "horse marine" was. According to my dictionary, the "Horse Marines" were "a mythical body of marine cavalry." That didn't satisfy me too much, and I imagine that Captain Burton's men would find that "mythical" part downright insulting.

Isaac Burton was a captain in the ranging companies by order of the General Council of Texas in 1835. At San Jacinto he was a private in red-headed Henry Wax Karnes's cavalry, and, after Santa Anna's defeat there, was dispatched with twenty men to patrol the Gulf Coast below Matagorda in search of Mexican activity.

Now, there were not a great number of ports on the Texas coast at that time. Matagorda, at the mouth of the Colorado River, was one, but the Colorado led inland to the Anglo-American colonies and was not likely to be used by the Mexican army. Besides, the river was blocked near its mouth by an extensive logjam that made navigation inland directly from Matagorda Bay impossible.

The port of Powderhorn, which would eventually become Karlshafen and then Indianola before being destroyed by two hurricanes within about ten years, was not yet important. The port most used by the Mexican government to supply its troops in San Antonio and beyond was Cópano.

Don't spend too much time looking for it on a map. It isn't there. The Mexican port of Cópano was located just north of where Bayside is on the west end of today's Copano Bay, north of Rockport. A *cópano* is a small boat, and the word is derived from a *cópa*, or cup. Copano Bay is quite shallow with very tricky passages between sand bars and oyster reefs, but shallow-draft sailing ships could enter Aransas Bay from the Gulf by passing between Mustang and St. Joseph's islands. By several days' worth of tricky sailing through Aransas Pass and Copano Bay, they could finally make their way to the port of Cópano. It was not an easy trip, but it beat trying to haul freight in ox carts across sixty or seventy miles of salt-grass marsh. Cópano was a popular point for landing supplies, and a road led directly from there to Refugio, Goliad, and San Antonio.

So it was that on June 2, 1836, Captain Burton and his motley band were watching the port of Cópano when the Mexican supply vessel *Watchman* dropped anchor off shore. The *Watchman* was an American vessel under contract to the Mexican government to deliver supplies to the Mexican army. Two of the Rangers ran down the beach, waving frantically and making signs of dire distress, whereupon, a boat set out from the ship carrying the ship's captain and four members of the crew. These five were quickly captured, their clothes donned by several of the Rangers. A total of 16 Rangers piled into the boat for the return trip to the ship. They took the *Watchman* without a shot being fired, and they found that their prize was loaded with supplies for General Cos and the Mexican army at San Antonio.

This was a good haul for the supply-starved Texans, and Captain Burton and his men made ready to sail the ship to Velasco at the mouth of the Brazos, where the supplies could be used. Before they could weigh anchor, however, two more ships came in sight. With a certain amount of encouragement, the captain of the *Watchman* signaled the captains of the other two ships, the *Comanche* and the *Fanny Butler*, to come aboard for a party. One by one, the two new arrivals were captured, and their ships were found to contain more of the same supplies. When Captain Burton finally set sail for Velasco, it was with three shiploads of military supplies for the Texas army.

Henderson Yoakum wrote in his multi-volume *History of Texas* that this activity earned for Captain Burton and his ranging company the title of "Horse Marines." Mythical, my eye!

1837—Standing Alone

We are saddled in our society with many unfortunate stereotypes. I guess that it has always been that way, and we are chipping away at them when we can. One of the more unfortunate misconceptions is the idea that women are naturally weaker than men and need men to care for them. That feeling was especially strong in the nineteenth century during the peak of emphasis on "The Cult of True Womanhood." Conditions on the frontier, however, didn't always allow such distinctions.

"Stand By Your Man" was, and is, a very popular song, but we sometimes forget that women are perfectly able to stand by themselves in the absence of men. They've proven it many times. Take Margaret Hallett, for instance. After her husband died, she packed up all of her goods, moved, and opened a combination trading post, hotel, and bar near the Lavaca River, where Hal-

illustration by Gary Manthei

lettsville is today. Her place, being the only one around, was quite popular with the pioneer settlers and Indians alike.

One day a bunch of young braves came looking for something of an alcoholic nature to drink. Now, Maggie wasn't above sealing a bargain with a sip or two, but she didn't plan to serve the whole tribe. When one of the group got a bit frisky and decided to help himself, she raised a

Mother Jane Long & Margaret Hallet
by Lillian Cowden

"knowledge knot" on the Indian's head, laying him out with a hatchet. Turned out it was the chief's son, and it wasn't long before the father came around to see what had happened to his boy. Maggie offered to raise a knot on his head too, but it wasn't necessary. The chief declared her to be *"Bold Squaw"* and from then on she got all of their business. Everywhere she went, she carried a heavy drawstring bag. Nobody ever had courage enough to ask what was in it, but one man reportedly said, *"Whatever it is, I sure bet it ain't powder puffs."*

illustration by Gary Manthei

Or, you might think of Sophia Auginbaugh. Sophia came from Indiana and was married to a schoolteacher up in Nacogdoches. The reports were that he had been a Prussian army officer and that his sympathies were with Mexico during the Texas Revolution. Colonel Juan Almonte reported that a Prussian fitting the description of Sophia's husband joined the Mexican troops at their camp on the Brazos. In any event, Sophia and her husband were separated when she decided that, rather than run away to Louisiana like most folks, she was going to stay and fight. With a borrowed rifle and "borrowed" horse she headed south and arrived at San Jacinto a day late for the battle, but in time to nurse the wounded Sam Houston.

Old Sam had another female visitor about that time. Peggy McCormick was a 50-something Irish widow whose son was a courier for Houston's army. She also happened to own that prairie in the bend of Buffalo Bayou where the San Jacinto Monument now stands. In fact, there was a good-sized, but shallow, lake named for her on the premises. Private Washington Winters of the Texas Army reported that at Peggy Lake "occurred the greatest slaughter." The Mexican soldiers and horses killed made a bridge across the swampy lake. Peggy didn't like that at all. She stormed into the Texas camp demanding that Sam Houston get all of the dead bodies out of her lake. He didn't do it, and years later she was still fighting to get the Republic to pay her damages.

Then there was Pamela Mann. She, too, was a widow of a rather emphatic disposition. After crossing the Brazos River during the Run-Away Scrape, she loaned her team of two oxen to Sam Houston to pull his two cannons, the "Twin Sisters," as long as he and the army were headed for Louisiana. When the Texas Army turned south at New Kentucky on its way to San Jacinto, Pamela demanded the return of her oxen. Houston refused on the grounds that they were needed to pull the artillery. There was an argument. Pamela pulled out a bowie knife and cut the oxen out of their harness. Although Houston sent men to bring them back, no one was willing to challenge "Widow Mann" to a fight, and the Twin Sisters made their way to San Jacinto by manpower.

Reuben Hornsby's place was the first settlement above Bastrop on the Colorado River. There were Reuben and his wife Sallie, six sons, one daughter, and all of their families. When the men were away, "Aunt" Sallie was the boss, and she did a good job. One time when all of the men were off on a hunting expedition, a large band of Indians decided the place would be easy pickings. After all, the men were gone, weren't they? Sallie made the women put on men's clothes and hats. Then they marched out carrying broomsticks and hoe handles. Faced by more "armed men" than they expected, the Indians *"lit a shuck,"* and Aunt Sallie went back to the more difficult job of taking care of a large family.

You'll also want to remember Jane Long, who held the fort on the Bolivar Peninsula; Kate Anderson, who was a professional cougar hunter at age 13; Mabel Doss Day, who was the "Cattle Queen of Coleman County"; Margaret Hefferman Dunbar Hardy Borland, who buried four husbands; and Jane Maria McManus Storms Cazeneau, who, among other things, was a secret agent for the United States during the Mexican War. You will read about these and many others before you're through. All in all, our women stand just as tall in history as our men.

1838—"Honest Bob"

I don't know who invented politicians. At times I hope that his, or her, subsequent death was slow and lingering. There are even times when I support the bumper sticker that proclaims, "There is something to be said for anarchy." However, I realize that, like fire ants, politicians sometimes find a valued place in the scheme of things. One such occasion occurred in 1838.

Robert "Honest Bob" Wilson
courtesy Jeff Carroll

It was three o'clock on the afternoon of December 24, 1838. After gaining independence from Mexico, the Republic of Texas faced severe financial difficulties. The United States was reluctant to annex as a new state an area whose primary assets were lands mostly controlled by Indians, whose existence was contested by Mexico, and whose debts far exceeded its current ability to pay. The situation was bad and getting worse rapidly. Sam Houston's first administration had tried to hold the line against increasing the debt incurred by the Revolution, but the new Lamar Administration, which was not interested in annexation to the United States, was printing currency as fast as it could. The rate of inflation had doubled. In the United States some banks discounted Texas "paper" by as much as fifty to one.

The Texas Senate was meeting at the capitol of the Republic in Houston, and the first order of business on that Christmas Eve was to disband the Texas Navy as an unnecessary expense. Then, Vice-President David G. Burnet, who had taken office fourteen days before, took an unprecedented step. Ordering the doors of the meeting room locked, he called the Senate into secret session. Once secrecy was assured, Burnet revealed that President Mirabeau B. Lamar, he, and a few other investors had a plan to replenish the treasury. They had made a deal with bankers in Mississippi. The bankers would pay the debt and fill the Texas treasury in return for notes that gave the bank control of all unoccupied lands and resources in the Republic. But, said Burnet, the public must never know that Texas lands now belonged to a bank in Mississippi.

There was violent objection from the floor. Robert Wilson, representing his constituency in Harrisburg and Houston, stated that he personally knew the bankers involved. They were unscrupulous, the plan was unsound and unethical, and to even consider such a scheme in secret was a crime against the people of Texas. The resources belonged to the people, not to a few officials who stood to gain personal fortunes.

Robert Wilson was a staunch supporter of Texas and its people. His arrival with a schooner of supplies saved Austin's first colony. His mills, wheelwright's shop, and warehouses were the nucleus of Harrisburg. He had served in the provisional army in the Siege of Bexar. It was he who gave the Republic's first elected president a series of building lots in return for the use of his name for the town built by the Allen brothers on Buffalo Bayou, Houston. And, after Lamar's two strongest opponents for the presidency mysteriously "committed suicide" just before the election, he had made an unsuccessful bid for the presidency himself. Throughout Texas he was known as "Honest Bob" because of his contention that he was "always as honest as the circumstances of the case and the condition of the country will allow."

Faced with opposition, Burnet ordered him to "sit down and shut up." During the heated argument that followed, "Honest Bob" swore that no power but God's could keep him silent about this or any other measure calculated to injure Texas. With that, he marched out onto Main Street where he publicly announced what the vice-president was trying to do. This resulted in a riot during which the irate citizens surrounded the Capitol.

After much debate, supporters of Burnet tabled the proposed action but demanded, and got, the expulsion of "Honest Bob" from his seat in the Senate on the grounds of misconduct. They set January 11 for a special election to refill the position.

"Honest Bob's" faith in his constituents was well founded. He was re-elected almost unanimously, and a mob of his supporters mounted him on a makeshift throne, marched him up Main Street, broke open the doors of the Senate, and replaced him in his seat, telling him to stay there

Political reprisals by the Lamar Administration were many. Wilson never again held public office. Lamar moved the capital from Houston to Austin, and financial claims by Wilson and his supporters for payment due from the government were never paid. But, the plan to sell the Republic was crushed, and when Texas entered the Union, it did so with its lands intact and unencumbered.

1839—What If He Had Stayed In Bed?

Every morning faces us with the same problem. "Do I, or do I not, want to get up and do what I am supposed to do today?" The choice isn't always an easy one. We forget that each day offers new and unique opportunities. Even at the end of the day, we often wonder if it might have been better to have stayed in bed. Often the value of the day doesn't appear until later.

What may have been the most important Indian battle in Texas was quite small and certainly didn't appear important when it began. In the long run, it not only led to a reversal of our national policy, but also cemented a feeling of mistrust between Anglos and Mexican citizens that is, unfortunately, felt to a certain extent today.

It all might have been different if one Ranger had decided to stay in bed.

Remember that Mexico, during the years of the Texas Republic, was in political upheaval and did not recognize Texas independence. Instead, for ten years, Mexico considered Texas "a province in rebellion." Federalists who wanted a representative form of government like the United States were opposed by Centralists who wanted all power vested in one central authority, such as that found in a modern military dictatorship. There were plots and counter-plots. Santa Anna, a Centralist, was in and out of power, and France was pressing claims that would culminate twenty years later in the advent of Maximilian as Emperor. Mexico still claimed Texas, and although San Antonio was attacked twice, there was no well-planned military campaign to make up for the defeat at San Jacinto. The upstart Texans were much on the minds of those below the Rio Grande.

At this time, very early on the morning of May 18, 1839, the seventeen men of Lt. James Rice's Ranging Company stumbled upon a mixed party of Indians and Mexicans on the San Gabriel fork of the Little River north of Austin. It was a surprise to both sides. Neither party expected the other to be there that early in the morning. In the

illustration by Gary Manthei

short fight that followed, the Rangers killed three men and captured 600 pounds of gunpowder, lead for bullets, a lot of camp supplies, as well as over 100 horses and mules—a very good and totally unexpected haul.

Then came the important part. One of those killed was a fellow named Juan Flores, who once lived both in Mexico and in Nacogdoches. In his pockets were some very important papers. These included the plans, complete with prepared treaties, to unite all of the Indians on the Texas frontier in a concerted attack on outlying settlements, to coincide with an attack by a large army from Mexico. The powder, lead, and horses were to seal the bargain. In return for their assistance, the Indians were to be guaranteed the possession of their hunting grounds in Texas, where they would also serve as a buffer between Mexico and the United States. The documents implicated Mexican agents living throughout Texas and detailed meetings with Indians over a period of several years.

When the Flores papers reached Secretary of War for the Republic Albert Sidney Johnston, he set in motion a mobilization of the entire army and all of the Ranging Companies to strike at Indian strongholds before the Mexican plan could be carried out.

The Cherokee, who during Sam Houston's term as President had enjoyed peaceful relations with the settlers, were pushed out of East Texas into Oklahoma. The Delaware, Shawnee, Caddo, Kickapoo, Boloxie, Creek, Muscogee, and Seminole were driven either north across the Red River or west, out of the timber of East Texas to the plains, where they were crushed between the Texans and those lords of the plains, the Comanche and Kiowa. In the anti-Indian administration of Mirabeau B. Lamar, it never entered anyone's mind that, if Texas had offered citizenship to the civilized tribes in East Texas, as Houston had promised he would try to do, they would have become productive members of society.

In the contrived Council House Fight in San Antonio, 30 of the Comanche tribal leaders were killed, and so for the next 40 years there was no peace between the Comanche and the Texans.

As far as Mexico was concerned, the feelings of Texans, fed on stories of the Alamo and Goliad, were fanned to a fever pitch at the thought of anyone encouraging and supporting Indian raids. Many peaceful Mexican families, who had supported Texas independence, were forced from their homes into Mexico, where their own people treated them as traitors.

In history, great events often depend on simple things and often do not make it into the textbooks. Our entire future might have been different, if, on May 18, Lt. Rice had stayed in a nice, warm bed.

1840—The Truest Texan

What is it that makes someone a Texan? Must one be born here to share in the pride? Must one be of Native American ancestry? (Remember, they were here first.) What does one's ethnic proclivity have to do with it at all? Robert Ardrey's book, The Territorial Imperative, *might offer some insight, but the fact remains that we all have a claim to being "Texan" if we want it. Just remember that being Texan has more to do with how we feel and how we act than who we are.*

We can be both loyal to Texas and loyal to our own heritage at the same time.

José Antonio Navarro was a native-born Texan, perhaps the truest Texan of them all. We have a county named for him and the county seat, Corsicana, is named in honor of the island of Corsica, the birthplace of his father. José was born in San Antonio on February 27, 1795, as the eighth child (his six other brothers were also named José and his five sisters were all named Maria) of Angel Navarro, and his wife, Josépha Ruiz. When, on *Diez y Seis de Septiembre* 1810, Father Miguel Hidalgo y Costilla (we also have a county named for him) issued his *Grito de Dolores* and began the war which would ultimately free Mexico from Spain, young José joined others of his family to fight for Mexican independence. After Hidalgo's execution in March of 1811, the Navarros sided with the Gutiérrez-Magee expedition's "Republican Army of The North" and again supported independence from Spain. The Spanish counter attack, the Battle of the Medina River, and the brutal aftermath of Spanish General Joaquín de Arredondo's retribution left Texas so under-populated that it could no longer be considered a separate state. The Navarro family fled to Louisiana for protection.

With Mexican independence in 1821, the family returned to San Antonio, where José became an attorney and a member of the legislature of the Mexican state of *Coahuila y Texas*. There, he became a strong supporter of the Federalist Party and the newly created Mexican Constitution of 1824. There also, he met Stephen F. Austin, and helped pass laws favorable to the new Texas colonists' interests. Further encouraging colonization, he became the land commissioner for Green C. DeWitt's empresarial grant down around Gonzales and later for the entire Béxar area.

The people of Mexico elected General Antonio López de Santa Anna to the office of president as a Federalist. His platform stressed a return to the principles of Father Hidalgo's War for Independence, the strict enforcement of the Constitution of 1824, and a representative, "power to the

José Antonio Navarro *by Dee Hernandez,*
courtesy UTSA's Institute of Texan Cultures at San Antonio
(Navarro Elemendtary School, San Antonio, Texas)

111

people," Federalist administration, complete with land ownership reform. They tried it for awhile, but the entrenched power structure wouldn't have it, and so Santa Anna did a complete political flip-flop, became a Centralist, declared himself—for the good of the people, of course—as "president for life," abolished the Constitution of 1824, disbanded the National Congress and all state legislatures, and, for all practical purposes, destroyed the Mexican state of *Zacatecas*. That was what caused Texans to meet in September and October of 1835 to form a provisional state government and to pledge themselves to support the Mexican Constitution of 1824.

While Centralist Mexican troops under General Santa Anna looted the Navarro family store in San Antonio and defeated Travis at the Alamo, José and his uncle, Francisco Ruiz, represented their people by signing the Texas Declaration of Independence. Shortly thereafter, José helped draft the new Texas Constitution, making sure that it included the prohibition against the forced sale of a family's homestead in debt actions. During his term in the Mexican Congress, he had sponsored a similar law to protect the poor, or anyone else, from greedy bankers and the government. He wanted to be certain that Texans got the same protection. Later, as a member of the Third and Fourth Congresses of the Republic of Texas, Navarro made sure that the rights of individual citizens were upheld, and he defeated legislation proposed by Mirabeau B. Lamar that denied citizenship to ethnic Mexicans.

Navarro was appointed civil commissioner of the ill-fated Santa Fe Expedition and was captured by the Mexican Army, along with the rest of the adventurers. Although he'd been crippled by an accident in his youth, he was forced to walk from Santa Fe to Mexico City, where he was imprisoned separately. Santa Anna did not like Navarro because of his family's unfailing support for Federalism, for the Mexican Constitution of 1824, and for Texas.

One of Jack Hays' Texas Rangers reported later, "The [Mexican] authorities offered him his liberty if he would cut the Lone Star buttons off of his coat. He said he would die in prison before he would disgrace the cause of Texas." Santa Anna was agreeable to that and sentenced him to death, but later commuted the sentence and imprisoned him in solitary confinement in the old dungeon of the Holy Inquisition under the castle of San Juan de Ulloa at Vera Cruz.

In December 1844, the Mexican public kicked Santa Anna out of the country, and a new Federalist government took control. (Antonio López de Santa Anna was in and out of power in Mexico eleven times.) After four years in prison, Navarro escaped to Havana and then to New Orleans. In February of 1845, he returned to Texas and took his place in the convention that voted to join Texas with the United States. Again, his sharp legal mind went to work on a new constitution, this time the Constitution of the State of Texas. This first state constitution again contained Navarro's protection of the "homestead." In fact, many of the protections we now take for granted are the result of his work—not just debtor protection, but the legal rights of women to sign contracts, inherit property, seek divorce under the terms of community property, and, in general, manage their own affairs. They exist because Navarro brought them from Spanish Colonial Law to the Mexican Constitution of 1824, through the Constitution of The Republic of Texas, and, finally, into the Constitution of The State of Texas. Texas was the first state to grant these rights.

In the new state government, he served his people and Texas twice in the Senate and continued his support of growth and settlement. A firm believer in "states' rights," he supported secession. Although he was too old to serve, his three sons fought for the Confederacy; and his grandson, Antonio Victor Navarro, continued the family traditions during the 20th century by becoming first the sheriff and later county judge of Zapata County, as well as a leader in the Democratic Party.

José Antonio Navarro, statesman and supporter of the rights of the people, never learned to speak English. He was proud of his heritage. His speeches in the Legislature were delivered in Spanish and interpreted for a public that respected his words. When he died on January 14, 1871, he died as a Mexican in heritage, a Texan by birth, and a citizen of the United States by choice. You can find his restored home on Laredo Street in San Antonio.

1843—The Red Texian

A current trend in arts and literature pictures all Native Americans living in peaceful harmony with nature and with each other. It isn't true. Some groups, mainly agriculturists, were relatively peaceful, but they fought long and hard if their territories were invaded. For others, violence was a long-established and respected way of life. In their own way, they were and are just like we are. Some fought because, "it is the right thing to do." Others were pacifists for the same reason. It is a matter of perspective. Many of the movies we see would have us believe that all Indians on the frontier waited with eager anticipation for the opportunity to kill every settler, trader, or casual traveler. Certainly, there were those who fought to the death to protect their way of life and the country that they considered to be theirs, but there were also those who stood beside the newcomers in everything they did.

A major difference between Sam Houston and Mirabeau B. Lamar was their attitude toward Native Americans. Houston, having lived with the Cherokee for many years, saw them as a people at least as "civilized" as their Anglo-American counterparts, and tried to provide them with citizenship in the Republic and titles to their land. Lamar did not.

Lamar saw all Indians as *"vermin on the skirts of humanity"* who would not make good slaves and so should either be removed or exterminated to allow room for the Anglo-American advance. Actually, he felt much the same way about Mexicans, but agreed that a few should be kept as servants because *"they work well with horses."* During the Lamar Administration, his troops initiated the Cherokee War in East Texas.

The Cherokee were among the so-called "Five Civilized Tribes." Forced from their ancestral homes in the Southern Appalachians, they made their homes in Arkansas, Louisiana, Oklahoma, and Texas. They had their own written language and newspaper. They built Christian churches where sermons were delivered in their own tongue, and most of them lived in the same style houses as their white neighbors. They even had representation as a nation in the Congress of the United States.

This wasn't good enough for Lamar and, in the Battle of the Neches River, those who didn't leave were killed. That was OK by Lamar and his followers, because, to them, Indians really were not human. Despite this, the Indians knew they had a trusted friend in Sam Houston and many of these so-called *"vermin"* fought and died for Texas beside their more tolerant white neighbors.

Flaco, or Flacco, was a chief among the *Lipan* Indians. The name is not particularly complimentary. It roughly translates as "Skinny." Actually, there were two Flacos, father and son—who both served as chief

Captain Flaco, Texas
Ranger of the Republic
by Jason Carranza

at different times, and who both accepted with gusto the advance of the Anglo-American culture, especially the friendship of Sam Houston. When the Mexican Army attacked San Antonio in one of the hit-and-run raids of the days of the Republic, the younger Flaco volunteered a band of Lipans to serve as scouts for the Texas Militia. There was great fear that the Mexican Army would attack Austin as it had San Antonio, and, for a while, the new capital was deserted. Only when Flaco and his men returned with word that there was no Mexican military presence to the south and west of the town did people return.

Later, in 1842, when Captain Ephraim McLean found it impossible to recruit volunteers who would serve without pay to protect the frontier, it was Flaco who brought 52 Lipans to join John Coffee "Jack" Hays' first group of Rangers. Once, Flaco was quoted as saying of Hays, *"Me and Red Wing are not afraid to go to hell together. Captain Jack is too mucho bravo; he's not afraid to go to hell all by himself."* In June of that year, Flaco received a commission from the Republic as captain in command of a company of Lipans. He declared, *"Flaco will not fight like Indians any longer and steal horses. Flaco is a Texian officer and will fight like Texians."* So it was that Flaco, War Chief of the Lipan, went to war with his Texian comrades and acquitted himself well, earning not only personal glory, but also respect for his people from those who fought beside them.

Not everyone saw it that way. On orders from General Somerville, Flaco was bringing horses to the Texian camp, when he was murdered by two of Lamar's followers from the Trinity River. These men, who saw him only as *"another dirty Indian,"* appropriated the horses for themselves. An East Texas court acquitted them, suggesting that no one could tell one Indian from another.

"Sam Houston wrote to the Lipan people:

EXECUTIVE DEPARTMENT,
Washington, March 8, 1843

"*My Brothers: My heart is sad. A dark cloud rests upon your nation. Grief has sounded in your camp. The voice of Flaco is silent. His words are not heard in council. The chief is no more. His life has fled to the Great Spirit. His eyes are closed. His heart no longer leaps at the sight of the buffalo! The voices of your camp are no longer heard to cry, 'Flaco has returned from the chase.' Your chiefs look down on the earth and groan in trouble. Your warriors weep. The loud voice of grief is heard from your women and children. The song of birds is silent. The ear of your people hears no pleasant sound. Sorrow whispers in the winds. The noise of the tempest passes— it is not heard. Your hearts are heavy.*

"*The name of Flaco brought joy to all hearts. Joy was on every face! Your people were happy. Flaco is no longer seen in the fight; his voice is no longer heard in battle; the enemy no longer makes a path for his glory; his valor is no longer a guard for your people; the right arm of your nation is broken. Flaco was a friend to his white brothers. They will not forget him. They will remember the red warrior. His father will not be forgotten. We will be kind to the Lipans. Grass will not grow in the path between us. Let your wise men give the council of peace. Let your young men walk in the white path.' The gray-headed men of your nation will teach wisdom. I will hold my red brothers by the hand.*

> *Thy brother,*
> *Sam Houston"*

1843—The Strange Case of John Hill

Despite the defeat and capture of President General Antonio López de Santa Anna at San Jacinto, the Mexican government refused to recognize Texas independence. As far as Mexico was concerned, the Treaty of Velasco wasn't worth the paper it was written on. For ten years, as Federalists and Centralists exchanged power in Mexico City, there was a seesaw of military action between Mexican forces and those of the Republic of Texas in the area between San Antonio and the Rio Grande. On two occasions San Antonio was re-captured by Mexican forces, and then vacated as Texas militia units began to assemble. It was a time of great turmoil. Embedded in this chaos lies the story of John Christopher Columbus Hill. It illustrates the bravery, compassion, and honor that rises in places we don't always expect to find it.

On November 15, 1828, John Christopher Columbus Hill was the first white child born in Columbus, Georgia. That made him seven years old when he came to Texas with his family in 1835. He was only nine when his brother fought at San Jacinto and when Sam Houston ordered his father, Asa, to carry warnings of the "Run-Away Scrape" to East Texas. John was impatient because he, too, wanted to fight.

In 1842, the Mexican Army made three attacks on Texas. Antonio Canales descended on the area below San Patricio, while Rafael Vasquez and Adrian Woll captured San Antonio. President San Houston called out the militia, because the army, as a full-

John Hill
by Gary Manthei

117

time entity, had been abolished in 1837 because of its expense.

The militia was similar to our National Guard, but kept two distinctions handed down from English common law. The "regular militia" drilled on a regular basis and was issued supplies and equipment by the government. The "volunteer militia" consisted of whoever wanted to come. They mustered only when

The Lottery
by Gary Manthei

needed, and they supplied their own weapons, etc. Ever since the signing of the Magna Charta, it is from this second, much larger, body of volunteer troops that we inherit the Second Amendment to the Constitution, the right to keep and bear arms for the defense of home, family, and the nation.

On October 3, 1842, Houston commanded Alexander Somervell to organize a punitive expedition against Mexico, made up of members of both the regular militia and volunteers. Flaco, from the previous story, was murdered while bringing horses for this expedition.

Having one hero in a family is dangerous business. It sets a precedent. Partly to uphold family honor, partly for adventure, partly because it is the responsibility of citizens to defend their country—the volunteer force that assembled held three Hills: father Asa, brother Jeffery B., and John Christopher Columbus Hill. John was thirteen.

The Somervell Expedition was a disaster. Poorly planned and poorly executed, and, sad to say, poorly led, it fell apart after the capture of the little town of Guerrero. Finally, on December 19, Somervell ordered the men to disband and make their ways to their respective homes. Unfortunately, some 308 men, commanded by W.S. Fisher, chose to stay in Mexico, to continue the fight and to attack the city of Mier. Textbooks call this the Mier Expedition. It, too, was a disaster. In the battles that followed, the Texans fought bravely and well, but were outnumbered and finally surrendered. Among those who distinguished themselves by their bravery in battle was John Hill. His captors could not believe that he was only thirteen.

The aftermath of the Mier Expedition became known as the "black bean episode." There was an attempt to escape. Guards were killed. General Santa Anna ordered that one out of every ten men would be executed. Black and white beans were placed in a covered container and each man drew a bean. A black bean meant death. A white bean meant life. All three Hills drew white beans.

The recognition of bravery knows no geographic or cultural boundaries. General Pedro Ampudia offered to adopt John, and, in that way, keep him out of prison. John agreed, but on one condition—John would stay in Mexico with Ampudia only if his father and brother were released and allowed to return home. Ampudia agreed, released the two Hills, and adopted John. He sent him to school at Matamoros to see if his mental abilities were as strong as those he evidenced on the battlefield. They were. He excelled, and, in a demonstration of honor, Ampudia sent John to Mexico City for a special audience with Santa Anna himself.

You've got to remember, John was still only fourteen. Today, at that age, they play video games and ride skateboards. John so impressed Santa Anna that he placed him under his own protection. John promised that, in return, he would serve Mexico.

General José María Tornel, the Mexican Secretary of War, became John's second foster father and took him into his home. In September 1843, (check that age again) Tornel enrolled John in the prestigious College of Mines of Mexico. He graduated in 1851 as a civil and mining engineer. While living in Mexico, John adopted the name Juan Cristobel Gil. During the time John spent in school, Mexico fought and lost a war against the United States and lost about half of its total land base. John could have gone home. However, he had made a deal in good faith.

John kept in touch with his Texas family but also served his adopted country well. During the early 1860s, while the United States was involved in a bloody Civil War, Mexico, too, had its problems. Ever since independence in 1821, Mexico had feared foreign intervention. In the 1860s this came true, with the establishment of the Austrian-French "protectorate" under the Emperor Maximilian. John was among those who resisted, and later he managed to free his benefactor General Ampudia from prison, after the old man was charged with collaboration. John built railroads and opened mines. He also studied medicine and became a practicing physician. Through it all he found time to marry and rear a family. One of his sons attended Swarthmore College here in the United States.

During his life John made many visits to his home in Texas and maintained close contact with the governments of both countries. After his wife died in 1891, he returned to Texas with the intention of making Austin his home while he worked for the General Land Office. While in Austin, he was among those who created the Texas State Historical Association, and he became an honorary life member in 1897. Mining interests, however, drew him back to Mexico where, with a new wife, Mary Ann, the girl he'd left behind when he went to war at age 13, he established a new home. Having served both countries well as a debt of honor, John Christopher Columbus Hill, citizen of two nations, died at age 76 and is buried in Monterrey, Mexico.

1844—Two-Gun Sallie Scull

According to the "Cult of True Womanhood," women of the nineteenth century were supposed to stay at home, mind the children, submit to their husbands, and devote themselves to "good works." Many folks, even today, feel that this is the proper role for women in society. However, there have always been those who refused to accept what society dictated and so led their own lives. In 1846, George Sand, whose real name was Aurore Dupin, wrote one of her best-known novels, The Haunted Pool, *and championed the rights of women in France. In 1849, Amelia Bloomer began her campaigns for women's dress reform in New York, and, in Texas ...*

During the years between the annexation of Texas as a state and its secession to join the Confederacy, our western frontier stretched in a giant crescent from the Red River north of Dallas down to a point near Kerrville and Bandera and on west to El Paso. The primary concerns there were the Comanche, Kiowa, and Apache, who often offered hair-raising experiences to those who traveled through the country or tried to live there.

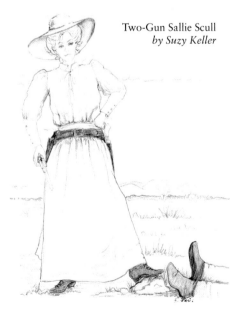

Two-Gun Sallie Scull
by Suzy Keller

Combined actions by the U.S. Army and the Texas Rangers made this area somewhat more secure than it had ever been before, and the tide of farms and ranches pushed farther west each year.

There was, however, another Texas frontier. Between the Nueces and the Rio Grande in South Texas stretched what the early Spaniards had called the *Llanos Mesteños*, or wild horse plains, but which the Texans came to call the "Nueces Strip." Most of the land had belonged to Spanish families who fled to Mexico during the Mexican War. In the wake of their departure came the bandits and Jayhawkers from both sides of the border. Along the Rio Grande, the "Cortina War" shuffled men and cattle back and forth across the border with little restriction, and even the new town of Brownsville was once held for ransom. Only Richard King and his private army of *Kineños* dared to establish and maintain operations in the Nueces Strip. John Salmon "RIP" Ford and his Rangers cut a wide swath through the "bandit" population, while other travelers and traders to and from Mexico moved in armed groups for protection.

To the edge of this frontier came Sarah Jane Newman Robinson Scull. She didn't like the name Sarah Jane and preferred "Sallie." People said that she was almost, but not quite, beautiful. Sallie, born in 1817, was the daughter of Rachel Rabb and John Newman; she arrived in Texas with the extended Rabb clan as part of Stephen F. Austin's "Old 300" colonists. Her first husband—she married when she was 16—was Jesse Robinson, who, at twice her age, was one of Austin's Ranging Company captains. They made their home together near Gonzales, but Jesse was rarely there. After the birth of a daughter, Sallie moved to her family land near Columbus, where she could be closer to the much larger Rabb clan. Jesse didn't come home until long after San Jacinto, and, although Sallie had another child, a son, things just weren't the same. While Jesse wandered the country looking for excitement and couldn't settle down, Sallie found that she could do rather well on her own. They divorced in Colorado County in 1843.

Eleven days later Sallie married George Scull. When she married George, they sold 400 acres of her land and moved south to the Nueces Strip. They settled in the tiny community of Banquete and started capturing and taming the wild horses that infested the area. Then, in 1849, George Scull either died or disappeared. Many women would have pulled up stakes and headed east, but not Sallie. She became a living legend. In what was basically a man's world, she accepted a man's responsibility—and outdid the men. She became a horse and mule trader on a large scale.

She bought horses and mules in Mexico or nearer, if the questionable residents between her ranch and the Rio Grande had any to spare. She trail-drove them, just as cattle were, to markets in New Orleans. Cash was the medium of exchange, and she carried it in her belt and in saddle pockets. She dressed like a man and rode astride. Also, she carried two of Sam Colt's .36 caliber Navy revolvers.

In 1852, Sallie married John Doyle, husband number three. Sallie's third husband couldn't stand up to her pace and he, too, disappeared. In 1854, on one of her solitary buying trips to Mexico, she was waylaid on the trail by one of the area's questionable residents, who, at gunpoint, suggested that she hand over her money belt.

Old RIP Ford and a few of his Rangers were nearby. In his memoirs, RIP wrote:

> *"The last incident attracting the writer's attention occurred while he was at Kenney's Tank and wending his way homeward. He heard the report of a pistol, and raising his eyes, saw a man falling to the ground and a woman not far away from him in the act of lowering a six-shooter. She was called Sallie Scull and famed as a rough fighter, and prudent men did not wittingly provoke her into a row."*

On another occasion, she treated a man who made some uncomplimentary remarks to a frontier lesson in manners, making him "dance" on the street until her pistols were empty. He was lucky. A traveler through the area reported that she had killed several other men who chose to insult her. Business was booming, and Sallie married again in 1855. Husband number four was Isaiah Wadkins, and he may also have been lucky. He neither died nor disappeared, and Sallie divorced him in 1858. In 1860, at age 43, Sallie married Christoff Horsdorff, husband number five, who was 18 years younger than she.

During the Civil War, while Union warships blockaded the Texas coast, Sallie organized and led wagon trains loaded with cotton to Matamoros and to the Mexican port of Baghdad at the mouth of the Rio Grande. Later in the war, when Brownsville was occupied by Union troops, her wagons crossed farther upstream as she led them to Tampico. Sallie Newman Robinson Scull Doyle Wadkins Horsdorff became very rich indeed.

Sallie may have made a fatal mistake when she married Chris Horsdorff. He was something of a "hardcase" himself. Some folks say that while Sallie hauled cotton, Chris rode along as a guard. Others suggest that he hid in the brush country to keep out of the war. Others say he rode with RIP Ford's irregular "Cavalry of the West." Still others suggest that he joined with the Emperor Maximilian's forces in Mexico.

Sallie always said that she took better care of herself when she was alone, but, after the war, Chris tagged along wherever she went. Maybe she lowered her guard. Maybe she trusted him too much, or not enough. Maybe the two of them together weren't quite good enough in a pinch. Maybe they just wanted to start over somewhere else. We'll never know. Sallie and Chris left with a great deal of money for a buying trip to Mexico and never returned.

We may not know the final chapter of her story, but we won't forget Two-Gun Sallie.

1844—The Barebacked Riders and Those Who Walked

In 1762, Franciscan missionaries founded the mission of San Lorenzo de la Santa Cruz near the Nueces River in today's Real County. Originally built to preach to the Lipan-Apache and to protect the workings of a series of silver mines a short distance away, the mission was abandoned in 1769 as a part of Spain's cost-cutting "Bourbon Reforms." The rugged Nueces and Frio canyons and the fringes of the Edwards Plateau remained a refuge for both the Lipan-Apache and Comanche well into the latter half of the nineteenth century. The last recorded Indian raid in the area was in 1881, near today's Leakey, when Mrs. Kate McLauren and a 15-year old neighbor, Allen Lease, were killed by Indians passing through on their way to Mexico. In 1844, the area was both rugged and desolate.

The four men weren't the best, and they probably weren't the worst, but they were Texas Rangers, and that said a lot back in 1844. Some of our modern western writers are criticized for painting their characters "bigger than life" and "tougher than possible," but believe me, these four put modern book heroes to shame.

In 1844, Texas was a republic, seeking admission to the United States, but still fighting its own battles on the frontier. President Sam Houston had effectively disbanded most of the army shortly after independence; it was troublesome and far too expensive for the Republic to maintain. Instead, the new nation relied on "ranging companies." The president would ap-

illustration by Gary Manthei

123

point a captain, and he, in turn, would select citizens to solve certain problems.

Ranger Captain John Coffee "Jack" Hays picked his men in San Antonio and sent them west. Kit Ackland, Rufus Perry, James Dunn, and John Carlin were instructed to scout the area west of San Antonio for about a hundred miles to where Uvalde is today, and to then turn north into the canyons of the Nueces. It was August, and there were rumors that the Comanche were on the move.

Now, that part of Texas is rough. It always has been and always will be. US 90 will take you through there today in a couple of hours, but in 1844 it meant several days of dry rocks, brush, and thorns—and in August, it was H-O-T.

Without incident, the four rangers reached the canyons of the Nueces one day about noon. So far, there had been no sign of the reported Comanche. The cottonwoods were shady, and the water was cool. After lunch, Ackland decided to take a nap, and, while Perry stood guard, Dunn and Carlin left behind the saddles and all of their gear (including their clothes), and took the horses for a swim in the river. No one saw the Comanche until they came out of a gully next to the camp.

In the first flight of arrows, Perry fell with two through his body and one in his face. Ackland, roused from his nap, returned fire but also fell with two arrows in his body and one through his mouth, which knocked out several teeth and tore through a part of his tongue. Dunn and Carlin didn't have a chance. They were stuck in the middle of the river with the horses. Seeing their comrades filled with arrows and with nothing between them and the Indians but a wet skin, they jumped on one horse and headed into the brush in the general direction of San Antonio, some 120 miles away. The Comanche followed in hot pursuit.

Today, those who ride those limestone and cedar-covered ridges wear heavy jackets and chaps. They don't call them "brush poppers" for nothing. Dunn and Carlin didn't have a stitch of clothes, much less a saddle. Now folks, that is *real* bareback riding. They couldn't move into open country. Only the thickets would hide them from the Comanche. And they had to keep moving. Ride through the brush, and you leave a trail. But, stick to the brush they did, all 120 miles of it. By the time they reached San Antonio they looked like slightly underdone hamburger. There, in San Antonio, they reported that the first rumors were true—the Comanche were on the move. They also reported that their comrades were dead.

As the stories say, "meanwhile, back at the camp," Perry and Ackland looked like a pair of road-killed porcupines. The Comanche were off playing hide-and-seek with Dunn and Carlin in the brush. Perry was too weak to move, so Ackland, arrows and all, picked him up and carried him to the river. They knew that the Indians would soon be back, so their only chance was to hide well enough so that they wouldn't be found. Since both were leaving a blood trail, that wouldn't be easy. The water revived them some-what, and as they drifted downstream, they came to an area where flash floods over the years had deposited several acres of dead trees and brush. Places like this are prime habitat for snakes and other assorted unfriendly wildlife. Normally neither man, being naturally prudent about such things, would have ventured into it. But, in a choice between a possible snake and the surety of losing your hair, the possible snake wins every time.

Although it was hard for him to talk, Ackland let Perry know that he would try to hide him in this mess and then hide himself. After the Comanche left, he said, they would come out of hiding and decide what to do. With a strength and fortitude that some folks only imagine when they write, Ackland was as good as his word. He hid Perry deep under a collection of branches and tree trunks, then disappeared to find his own hole.

The Comanche came back and stayed for two days searching. Both men later reported that they heard them walking above their hiding places, but the Indians never found them.

Loss of blood from their wounds, exposure, shock, and lack of food and water took their toll. Perry woke up in the dark, unable to see because of the blood dried over his eyes. Navigating by sound, he pulled himself out of his hiding place and crawled to the river where he drank the first water in two and a half days and washed the blood from his face so he could see. Not know-ing where Ackland had hidden or whether or not he had been found by the Comanche, and afraid to call out for fear of attracting unwanted attention, he began his long dry trip back to San Antonio—sometimes walking, sometimes crawling.

Ackland emerged like a battered gopher from his hiding place a little later. He was certainly in no better shape than Perry, and his swollen tongue made it difficult to breathe. When he found Perry gone, he assumed the worst, and he, too, started for San Antonio afoot.

They never saw each other, nor did they see their brother Rangers who were dispatched to find and bury their bodies. Six dry, hot days and 120 miles later, they both walked into San Antonio within two hours of each other—Perry first and Ackland second. Their wounds were festered, and their faces so swollen and disfigured that their messmates didn't recognize them, but they were alive and they had their hair.

Now, the next time you question the exploits of some fictional character, remember the barebacked riders, and those who walked and crawled. All four lived to fight other battles and serve under other flags—but, in 1844, they served Texas.

1846—"Dutchallover"

Newcomers to the United States often do not speak English. During the 19th century, when the flood of immigrants from Europe made cities like New York a modern "Tower of Babel," we felt the impact here in Texas as well. Every ethnic group brought its own language, foodways, dress, church, and customs. Often they brought the names of the towns and villages that they'd called home in the Old World. Living together in almost pure ethnic enclaves, they saw no need to change their ways; many communities remained that way up through the middle of the 20th century. Today, there are new enclaves as new folks come en masse to take advantage of our standard of living. Various organizations offer English as a second language classes on a regular basis. As always, folks on their own, without benefit of "community," must get by as best they can. Sometimes they even lose their names.

Back in 1842, a young man named Anton Diedrick, who lived in Antwerp, Belgium, had the misfortune to witness an impromptu duel between two young men of noble standing. It ended in death for one of the eager, but somewhat overzealous, participants. Although the *code duello* was a frequent, and popular, way to settle personal differences, it was usually illegal, and deaths under these circumstances were treated as murder. Anton not only saw, but also was seen. To protect the surviving young nobleman involved, he was immediately "Shanghaied" and placed on an outward-bound sailing ship.

Anton Diedrick
by Gary Manthei

For several years, the ship and its reluctant passenger visited the ports of the world, until one day it docked in Galveston. There, in 1846, with Texas just annexed to the United States, Anton jumped ship and began looking for a job. He did not speak or understand English, and his Belgian was just as incomprehensible to prospective employers. Soon, there was a war with Mexico, and Anton enlisted in the United States Army as a private soldier. According to family tradition, the recruiting sergeant didn't speak Dutch or Belgian, and Anton didn't speak either English or Spanish. Part of his name came through the ordeal, but the rest didn't. The sergeant commented to the corporal, *"Well, it's obvious that he's some kind of Dutch all over, so we'll call him that."* Anton Diedrick became Diedrick Dutchallover and served his adopted country by that name throughout the remaining period of the Mexican War. With peace and the signing of the Treaty of Guadalupe Hidalgo, Diedrick moved to the frontier. Years later he dropped the "all" and simply became Diedrick Dutchover.

In the 1850s, the powers that be in the U.S. Post Office contracted with Henry Skillman to haul the United States Mail from San Antonio to El Paso. This was a long route and a dangerous one. Stage stands were established every fifteen to thirty miles and were fortified against Apache attack. The first commercial run of the 693-mile route was made in a Concord stage pulled by six mules, along with an armed escort of eighteen riders, a driver, and a shotgun guard on the seat. The driver was no less than "Bigfoot" Wallace, the legendary Ranger and Indian fighter, and the shotgun guard was Diedrick Dutchover.

Diedrick liked West Texas. Although he continued to ride as a guard for the mail company for many years, he also acquired land and built a small ranch near the newly established Fort Davis, at the mouth of Limpia Canyon. According to the records, Diedrick Dutchover and E.P. Webster, who had accompanied that first stage run as one of the armed riders, were the first non-Hispanic, non-Indian civilian residents of Fort Davis.

Then came the Civil War. For a while, soldiers in gray, instead of blue, occupied Fort Davis. When peace and the United States Army returned, there was Diedrick to welcome them back and to provide them with milk in big cans from the cattle on his ranch. During his career as a stage guard and driver, Diedrick spent a lot of time in El Paso. Since he had come almost immediately from Europe to Texas and then quickly to the frontier, he didn't have that inherited animosity toward Mexico found in most Texans of that era. In El Paso he married a Mexican woman, and, together, they reared a family of at least six—this in a wild country where Apaches occasionally took shots at the house, and missing stock was more common than not.

Anton Diedrick, who was "Dutchallover," but who became a Texan, died in 1904. The name, however, lives on. By 1942 there were forty-two Dutchovers living in Jeff Davis County, along with others in Marfa, Balmorhea, El Paso, and in New Mexico. Today, there are even more. Sometimes a name, like a spirit, never dies.

1846—The Marvelous Meat Biscuit

Seventy-four men, women, and children, in twenty wagons from Sangoman County, Illinois, left the main wagon train in 1846 to try a new shortcut to their promised land in California. They didn't realize that history would record their names on geographic features and in books describing epic adventures and great tragedies. Today, Donner Pass hosts a variety of winter sports and the Donner Party is best remembered as a story of survival. All across the world, the story of the forty-seven survivors made headlines, even here in Texas. Trapped in the snow, some starved, some froze, and some ate their friends and relatives.

Gale Borden
by Suzy Keller

Down here in Texas, one man read the story of the Donner Party with particular interest. Gail Borden, Jr., was born up in Norwich, New York, back in 1801, and he learned the practice of surveying from his father before he was 16. Although he had only about a year and a half of formal education, he loved to read and, later, to write. After following a circuitous route from New York to Indiana and to Mississippi, he arrived in Galveston in 1829, where he began farming and surveying for a living in Stephen F. Austin's colony. Then came politics, and, in 1835, he began publishing the Telegraph and Texas Register. Then came the Texas War for Independence. As a surveyor, newspaper editor, and veteran of the Texas War for Independence, Gail Borden was familiar with both frontier hardships and the news.

"*What if,*" he thought, upon reading of the Donner Party's fate, "*I can invent something that will make such a tragedy obsolete?*"

You see, Borden was also an inventor. His "Locomotive Bath House" was a privy-like structure on wagon wheels that you could roll into the waves at Galveston so that ladies could feel the sand between their toes in privacy without having to deal with sun, surf, and curious on-lookers. The trouble with that invention was that it kept floating away, carrying the hapless occupant either up on the beach or out to sea. Then there was his "Terraqueous Machine." It was a boat designed with wheels so that

128

DIRECTIONS FOR COOKING

BORDEN'S

MEAT BISCUIT

OR THE

EXTRACT OF BEEF

DRIED IN FLOUR,

Invented and Manufactured in Galveston, Texas,

By GAIL BORDEN, Jr.

J. H. BROWER & Co. General Agents, 45 South-st. New-York.

PATENT SECURED IN THE UNITED STATES FEB. 5, 1850—
PATENTED IN ENGLAND SEPT. 5, 1851,

NEW-YORK.

D. Fanshaw, Printer, 35 Ann-street, corner of Nassau.

....

1855.

it could sail either on land or sea. That one didn't work too well either, although it scared the bejabbers out of a bunch of horses. Anyway, Gail Borden was ripe for a new invention.

The "Marvelous Meat Biscuit" was the result. After six years of chopping, cooking, grinding, mixing, squeezing and baking, Borden developed what he called: *"... an improved process of preserving the nutritious properties of meat, or animal flesh, of any kind, by obtaining the concentrated extract of it, and combining it with flour or vegetable meal, and drying or baking the mixture in an oven, in the form of a biscuit or a cracker."* He felt that it would benefit all of the seamen of the world, colonists *"... on long journeys through destitute regions ..."*, and those faced by hostile Indians and so dared not build a fire, geologists, surveyors, explorers, patients in hospitals, and any family that didn't want to cook, 'especially in warm weather.'"

Now folks, that sounds like a good idea—sort of a cross between a dog biscuit and those dry soups that you pump up with water. Others thought it sounded good, too. In fact, for several thousand years, Indians had been doing about the same thing by mixing grease, berries, nuts, and cornmeal. Borden offered a full partnership in the venture to Dr. Ashbel Smith, the Yale graduate who became the Surgeon-General of the Republic of Texas. Smith, in turn, wrote an article for the prestigious *De Bow's Review*, explaining that the new invention would revolutionize industry throughout the South and raise the standards of living throughout the world. He then attended the Crystal Palace Exhibition in London in May of 1851 where, as the only American on the international panel of judges, he gave his partner the highest award for a contribution to the food industry. He said that it was the responsibility of America to provide for, "the poor of those countries who never taste good meat."

But, all was not sweetness, light, and good taste. Elisha Kent Kane, who carried a supply of Borden's meat biscuits on his first polar expedition, reported that even starving sled dogs wouldn't eat them. Frederick Law Olmstead, in his often-quoted *Journey Through Texas*, fed his biscuits to the birds and reported that, for himself, he would, *"... decidedly undergo a very near approach to the traveler's last bourne ..."* (perish of starvation) before he would eat them. Others simply said they were*"unsightly."* The Army preferred real beef.

So, after he spent $60,000 to build a beef processing plant in western Colorado County and to promote, for a decade, the "Marvelous Meat Biscuit," Borden concluded that his project had failed. In a way though, that failure led to a success.

On his way back from receiving his award at the London exposition, Borden became interested in the problems encountered when milking seasick cows. When he saw how first-class passengers on the ship faced the trauma of coffee without cream, a new idea was born. In May 1858, a new advertisement appeared in the New York edition of *Leslie's Illustrated Newspaper*:

> *"BORDEN'S CONDENSED MILK - - is hitherto unequaled in the annals of the milk trade. For Sale at 173 Canal Street, or delivered at dwellings in New York and Brooklyn at 25 CENTS per quart."*

Unlike the meat biscuit, this idea for canned milk worked. The Civil War guaranteed the success of Borden's Milk. He adapted to the research he'd used to extract the *"essence"* from beef into a method for preserving milk. "Canned Cow" became a staple of the Army, and laced the coffee of Union officers and that of the more affluent enlisted men. With that success under his belt, Borden bragged that, in the future, he could condense anything.

He never went back, however, to making the "Marvelous Meat Biscuit."

Early Statehood and the Civil War: 1846-1866

1847—"On Leaving"

Education in the Western World became a function of the Roman Church during the Dark Ages. Centers of learning were restricted to either members of the clergy or those of the nobility who were willing to pay large sums and confine their learning to those topics deemed suitable for the masses. The 12th century brought a change, and soon, schools sprang up in many places. Many of these were called "universities" because they attempted to impart a universal learning. As worldwide trade began, more and more people needed learning beyond the basics. In North America, the Massachusetts Bay Colony opened a nonsectarian school for men in 1636 and, three years later, named it for educator John Harvard. In 1702, the Collegiate School of Connecticut opened in Killingworth. After two moves it settled in New Haven in 1716, and in 1718 it was renamed in honor of its primary benefactor, Elihu Yale. Despite the fact that other colleges and universities sprang up on the Atlantic Coast, the American frontier expanded much faster than educational facilities. Along the frontier, many families were functionally illiterate. Those who could, sent their children to the East for an education.

We have always valued education in Texas. In many ways, we probably valued it more when the Republic was young than we do today. We didn't take educational opportunities for granted—we worked for them.

Today, when students finish school at home, they may say, *"Bye, Mom, Dad. See ya Friday night!"* They jump in their new car and rush off to college. This hasn't changed much except for the mode of travel and destination. Another thing that hasn't changed is the fact that parents can't resist this last opportunity to express their love in the form of instructions.

Joseph Cone was born on August 8, 1831, on the muddy banks of Buffalo Bayou. Throughout childhood, he grew along with our infant Republic and dreamed of someday following in

illustration by Gary Manthei

the footsteps of his father, Henry Hale Cone, who was a respected physician and surgeon. In 1847, not quite 16 years old, he was ready for college. But, colleges were rare in frontier Texas, and none taught medicine. It was much farther then from backwoods Houston to Yale University than it is today. There could be no weekends at home, or Christmas either. A student might not return home for several years. There was a need for last-minute encouragement and instruction. But, let Joseph's mother tell the story in her own way, as she did on the opening pages of her parting gift, a small diary:

"Houston, Texas
May 20, 1847

"My dear and only Son living. It is your Mother's wish you should attend to some important rules I shall give you on leaving our Humble Cottage for Yale College.

"First, every night when you retire let your petitions ascend to God for protection over yourself and all that's dear to you. Ask forgiveness for past offenses and quietly lay down trusting in God who is mighty to save.

"Second, let it be your first duty in the morning to render thanks to the power that has preserved you. Always attend to evening and morning prayers on your knees when you can. If you should have anything to hinder your morning devotions make use of the first opportunity you have, as I think Secret Prayer is worth more than all other.

"Third, on rising in the morning put on your stockings, then your pants, say your prayers, then wash. Clean your teeth and fingernails, brush your hair, then the rest of your clothes, look in your mirror and put on a pleasing countenance to meet your associates.

"Fourth, be subject to the powers that be. Obey all in authority. Be kind, be courteous and remember 'that from a child thou hast known the scriptures, which are able to make thee wise unto salvation through faith which is in Christ Jesus.' Study them daily and the God of peace be with you and return you to your Mother if it is his will.

"Fifth, always ask the price of an article or anything you wish to purchase or bargain for. Have a written agree-

ment with your best friends for any bargain or contract understood. Both assign the writing and others if necessary as such you will be guarded to do all you agree to as well as bind them to the same. "Sixth, in changing your clothes be sure you never put any away damp. They will mildew if damp — clean or dirty.

"Seventh, be careful with your wash woman to number every piece and specify the articles when you give them to her and when returned. "My son, there are many more important duties that you are not ignorant of and will be reminded of daily. Attend to all that is pleasing in the sight of God and you will have the prayers of your Father, Mother, and Sisters.

S.E. Cone"

Words of wisdom, then, and now. The little book was never used as a diary, but it was kept and treasured by many generations.

1850—The Grindstone Chariot

Anthropologists tell us that civilization began when our ancestors stopped roaming the countryside, searching for food like wild animals and settled down to plant crops. A settled society meant that there had to be laws so that folks wouldn't keep harvesting their neighbor's crops and running off with his domesticated animals. Laws meant lawyers, and that led to the Spanish curse "May your life be filled with lawyers," but that's another story. This one deals with crops and how we process them before we sit down at the table.

illustration by Gary Manthei

Grain has been with us from the beginning. There were stone-age tools obviously designed to cut grain like a sickle. No doubt, early folks

135

ate the grain not only raw, but also whole. Their teeth didn't last long, and chewing whole grain without teeth is a problem. So, long before the beginning of the Christian era, folks learned to grind their grain before cooking it. Some of them pounded it, while others crushed it and rubbed it into powder between two rocks. Circular grindstones for grain became state-of-the-art machinery several thousand years ago, and you still can buy "stone-ground" meal at the grocery. Some folks say that stone-ground meal is supposed to be better for you because the stones don't heat up the way that steel mills do, and they also add valuable trace minerals to your diet as the stones gradually wear away. I don't really know about that, but I have ground quite a bit of corn.

Grinding grain, especially corn, by hand is a labor-intensive process. You either pour some out on a *metaté*, rubbing it with another rock (which is great for the shoulders, but hard on the back), or you drop it in a hopper and turn a crank. To produce enough corn meal for a large family takes one person a big part of the day, every day. Consequently, anyone who would set up a water-powered gristmill was considered a benefactor to any new community. The Mexican government recognized this and, in the early days of Texas colonization, granted extra land to anyone who would set up a mill.

James Barnes came to Texas in 1836 and settled over in today's Tyler County near Mount Hope. He got along pretty well with most folks, and even his grave marker in the old Mount Hope cemetery says that he was *"a friend of the Indians."* Tyler County has a lot of relatively flat land, but there are also some hills and a few streams that once had enough flow to operate a small mill. James Barnes didn't build a mill, but his son, Sam, saw the need and made his plans.

Time crept by. Texas relinquished her independence and became the 28th state in the Union. Tyler County was organized in 1846, and folks began to cut and haul the timber and plant cotton and corn between the stumps. Still, there was no public mill to grind the corn. It had to be done by hand. Finally, Sam Barnes had enough money to realize his dream and sent an order over to Germany for two of the finest grindstones made.

Now grindstones, by their very function, grind against each other. There is a lot of friction and weight involved. You can make one out of almost any rock, but the harder the rock is, the longer the grindstone will last and the less grit you get in your meal. German grindstones, made from particularly hard granite, were considered the best in the world, and, if Sam was betting his life's savings on the project, he wanted the best. He designed his mill and ordered stones three feet in diameter. The larger of the two was fourteen inches thick and would go on the bottom. The smaller was only seven inches thick, and it would go on top, revolving against the other to grind the grain. The mill on Russell's Creek, which took Sam about a year to build, had a sluice to direct the water against an undershot wheel. All was in readiness when word came that the stones had arrived in Galveston.

Now, stones that size are heavy, and there was not a wagon in the community that could carry them. Roads were still little more than mud holes between stumps, and it was a long way to Galveston. To find a freighter who would carry the stones would have cost Sam more than the rest of the mill and the stones put together. He simply didn't have that kind of money. But, you see, Sam was a thinking man, and he left for Galveston with two yokes of oxen and a strange contraption he created in his blacksmith shop.

You see, each of the stones had a hole in the center where it could be connected to the mill, so what Sam carried with him was an axle with a seat. Oxen, moving right along, still only average about ten miles a day. They are dependable, but slow. Today, by highway, the distance from old Mount Hope to Galveston is about 270 miles. Back then there were no direct routes, so the trip down took a couple of months. The trip back, because of the heavy load, took about twice that. At last, Sam came rolling into Mount Hope, perched on top of the axle with the two grindstones as wheels, and with the oxen plodding stolidly along. The grindstone chariot made its way to Russell's Creek, the wheels were dismounted and attached in place, and, for four generations, the mill provided meal for families who brought their corn as much as thirty miles. You could, indeed, say that Sam's chariot enriched the community.

1851—The Boss of Boonville

As the population of Texas grew in its early years of statehood, a need arose for an expansion of local governments. Travel was still difficult over almost non-existent roads, and people who needed a spot to transact official business regularly petitioned for the creation of new counties and county seats of government. By Texas law, a county seat must be within ten miles of the geographic center of the county involved. Sometimes there was bitter rivalry between existing towns for the honor and business advantages associated with being the seat of county government. Sometimes counties were formed where no town existed within the ten-mile limit, and so, to meet the need, a new town was brought to life.

If you go to Boonville today, the only thing you'll find easily is a well-kept cemetery. If you know where to look and don't mind crawling through a fence, you can see a big oak tree that once grew on the courthouse square. Part of the old town is a relatively new subdivision and part is covered by a proliferation of new and used auto dealerships strung out along the Texas Highway 6 bypass around Bryan and College Station. Today they call it the Earl Rudder Freeway. Two highways actually cross the area, and, in the middle, is a 40 some-odd acre pasture, including the tree, where someone is planning to build a massive movie theater. A map of the original town and the compass used to lay it out are in the Brazos Valley Museum of Natural History. That's all that is left of Boonville, the first county seat of Brazos County.

Harvey Mitchell
by Nathan Smith

There is more than a passing association between Boonville and both Texas and American history. Daniel Boone, who led settlers into the "Dark and Bloody Ground" we now call Kentucky, and then on to Missouri, had a large family. When he was 22 years old he married 17 year-old Rebecca Bryan. That tied the Bryans and the Boones together. Moses Austin had three children: Stephen F., Emily, and James. Emily Austin married James Bryan, connected in that way with the Boones, and so a large and connected clan of families came to Texas by way of Kentucky, Missouri, Mississippi, and Arkansas. Each one of these states, plus California, has a Boonville in honor of Daniel and other members of the family. Here in Texas there were four Boone names on the petition that led to the creation of Brazos County, and the new county seat took a name in honor of Mordecai Boone, Sr. Few people actually lived there.

But Boones, Austins, and Bryans weren't alone in making the new town. In 1839, at the age of eighteen, Harvey Mitchell came to Texas with his family. While some of his brothers fought Indians and the Mexican Army, Harvey taught school. It's not that Harvey was afraid of duty—he had once served with the local "Minute Men"—he just wasn't the woodsman that his brothers were, so he spent most of his time building the community. His one attempt at deer hunting was a fiasco in which he got lost and lost his new hat. He vowed *never* to try to do *that* again. His attempt to join a bear hunt was even more disastrous in that he lost large portions of his clothing. But, when the new county was formed in 1842, Harvey was there. Since the newly elected county clerk lacked certain refinements in penmanship, Harvey became the deputy clerk and kept all of the books and records.

Although Boonville was the county seat, it lacked population. Most county residents lived on surrounding farms and plantations. Town lots were auctioned, but less than twenty were sold, and few buyers occupied them. Harvey bought more town lots than anyone else—six, for a grand total of $30. The county jail, called "The Dungeon" because it was mostly located under ground, was the county's first official structure. It took a year to build, and during its 25-year life span, it housed mostly fleas and lice. The county courthouse was next. Twenty men built the one-room, floorless and windowless log structure in one day in order for it to be ready for the first sitting of the county court. This magnificent edifice left a bit to be desired and was abandoned after three or four court sessions in favor of the open air and, later, for a building built for a store but never occupied.

Since Boonville residents were few, most of the official duties fell to one man, Harvey Mitchell. He was Chief Justice of the county and also Justice of the Peace. He served as County Clerk, County Treasurer, and Sheriff. Most of the time he also acted as postmaster and, in addition, operated the blacksmith shop, the only store, the gristmill, and the only hotel. At times he convened a one-man commissioner's court and was said to argue both sides of any question. Although others came and went, for all practical purposes, Harvey Mitchell was both Boonville and Brazos County, and the rest of the folks were happy to leave it that way.

An old family story indicates the extent of Harvey's activities. It seems that in 1852, there were only two families living in Boonville when a young couple arrived one evening at Harvey's store and asked for lodging. Harvey said, *"I can handle that,"* and took them to his home where his wife operated a boarding house to meet the needs of folks who came to the county seat on business. One of the young couple's horses needed a new shoe, and Harvey said, *"I can handle that,"* and led the horse to his blacksmith shop and fired-up the forge. When Harvey returned, the young man asked for the County Clerk, and Harvey said, *"I am your man,"* and took him back to the store, which also served as the Clerk's office. Then it transpired that the couple wasn't married but wanted to change the situation. So, Harvey, in his role as County Clerk, sold them a license. Then, in the role of Justice of the Peace, he took their affidavits and conducted the ceremony with the two families of Boonville as witnesses. Then the wedding dinner was held in Harvey's hotel. After the departure of the newly-weds the next day, Harvey, in the role of Deputy Sheriff, reported on the proceedings and en-couraged an irate father-of-the-bride to take his armed band of friends and neighbors back home.

When the railroad right-of-way bypassed Boonville in the late 1850s, William Joel Bryan, nephew of Stephen F. Austin, donated a tract of land for a new town about three miles away, and Bryan officially became the new county seat. Harvey Mitchell kept right on going, however, and through his efforts as a contractor, he built the first courthouse in Bryan. Then, in 1872, Harvey led the delegation that was instrumental in bringing Texas A&M College to the Bryan area. For a while, there was a Harvey Mitchell Hall on the A&M campus, but it is gone now, and there is a marker in its place. There is a Harvey Road that once led to a community with his name, and Farm Road 2818 around the west and south sides of Bryan and College Station was recently renamed the Harvey Mitchell Parkway in his honor. All in all, a lot of folks called Harvey not only "The Boss of Boonville" but also "The Father of Brazos County."

If you stop by the Boonville Cemetery, pay a visit to old Harvey, "The Boss of Boonville." He could sure tell you a thing or two.

1852—The Hermit and the Bear(s)

Bears once roamed the entire United States. They came in a variety of species, sizes, and degrees of irritability. In some parts of the Old South they were so thick that farmers joined forces to hire bear hunters to clean them out. Pigs, almost immune from other harassment on the frontier, found themselves the lunch of choice for wandering bruins, and anyone who raised pigs considered these ursine gourmands to be their natural enemies. Since almost everyone owned pigs, this made bears of any persuasion "personae non grata."

There was, at one time, a popular song entitled "The Preacher and the Bear." Basically, the story involved the encounter between a preacher who, playing hooky from church on a Sunday, had a disagreement with a bear that carried the two of them down a road, up a tree, and into a creek. There were prayers, a razor, and a pair of snapped sus-

illustration by Gary Manthei

141

penders. A "good" time was had by all. No doubt stranger things have happened.

Of all of the assorted wildlife on the frontier, none gave pioneers more trouble than bears. From backwoods Appalachia to the California coast, bears in a variety of species raided pigpens and chicken houses, destroyed crops, and were direct competitors with people for honey. In some parts of the country, bears were about the only natural enemies that pigs had. Indians wouldn't touch them. Even cougars thought twice before mixing it up with a fierce boar or sow. Snakes didn't bother them. In fact, the easiest way to rid your property of snakes was to stock it with a few pigs—they loved to eat snakes. The point is, with pigs a staple of frontier diet, farmers often hired hunters to rid the vicinity of bears.

Frederick Law Olmsted was the architect who designed the Biltmore Mansion in North Carolina and Central Park in New York City. He also wrote a journal of a trip he made to Texas during the days of its early statehood. The book was published in 1857 and was called *A Journey Through Texas*. He was not favorably impressed with most of what he saw. However, the book was not without humor and included, among other things, the story of a bear hunt in the hills above San Antonio.

The hero of the story was an elderly hermit of German extraction who had a "personal difficulty" with a certain bear near his pigpen. The wounded bear left in a hurry and, with the hermit in hot pursuit, disappeared into a hole in the rocky hillside. The hermit could neither see into the hole nor hear anything, so he rolled a rock over the entrance and went for help.

Help arrived in the person of another Teutonic gentleman of the local community who brought advice and a jug of liquid courage. They soon cleared away the rock at the entrance. It was still dark in the hole, but the hermit wiggled his way, head first, into the entrance and, after fumbling around in the dark, found a warm but dead carcass, attached a rope, and with the help of his neighbor, pulled a five foot bear to the surface.

It seems, though, that while he was in the hole, the hermit heard a growl that did not emanate from his already dead bear. So, loading his Colt revolver and taking his knife in his teeth, he went back down the hole. Sure enough, way down in the dark hole, he came to the realization that he was not alone. He heard the bear but couldn't see it. Taking a few deep breaths he aimed in the general direction of the sound, fired a couple of shots, and backed out as fast as he could. On the surface he and his friend had a drink and built a fire at the entrance of the hole to see what they could smoke out. Nothing. That called for another drink and another headfirst trip down the hole. This time our intrepid hero took a torch made out of beeswax. There, at the end of his trip, was another dead bear. Attach the rope, drag out the bear, have another drink. By now there was a pretty good assemblage of locals who had come to watch the fun.

Where there were two, there might be three! Back down the hole! At the bottom was a narrow passage and, wedged in it, another bear— already dead, probably suffocated from the smoke. This was getting easy. More rope! Another bear! Another drink! Back down the hole.

This time he squeezed through the crack where the last bear had been and came nose to nose with an extremely unhappy and irritated fourth bear. He dropped the torch and, discretion being the better part of valor, tried to squeeze back through the crack, only to get tangled up with one of his neighbors who had come down to see the show. About that time there was a whole lot of growling and hollering in a variety of languages going on. In what was left of the light from the torch, he aimed between the red glowing eyes and fired a shot. The eyes disappeared only to reappear a few feet away, and he took another shot. By then the guy in the rear had extracted himself, and our hero beat a hasty retreat to the surface.

After a few more drinks to celebrate his escape (and, no doubt, a few choice words for the gentleman who had been in the way), the hermit took another headlong dive down the hole. There it, no, *they* were—two more dead bears, shot right between the eyes.

The cave may have gone farther. There may have been more bears. Five seemed to be enough—especially since after all the celebrating they'd done, the hermit and his friends couldn't find the entrance to the cave.

1853—Bride's Secret Recipes

During the 18th and 19th centuries, Anglo-Celtic Americans from the South recognized a "holy trinity" of foodways: corn, pork, and something sweet. In many parts of the country this is still the norm. I freely confess that when I eat cornbread, sausage, and molasses, it somehow makes me feel closer to my roots.

Throughout the world, brides have always looked for new recipes with which to impress their new husbands. If you put these two facts together, you may find an interesting result.

Mary Adeline Cornelia Cone
by Nathan Smith

At the close of December 1853, Mary Adeline Cornelia Cone married James Theodore Dudley Wilson in Houston, Texas. Mr. Wilson, a veteran of several battles of the Texas Revolution fought while he was still a teen-ager, was the son of Robert Wilson, one of the founders of the town of Harrisburg, another veteran of the Texas War for Independence, and a member of the First and Second Senates of the Republic of Texas. "J.T.D.," as the younger Wilson was called, became a real estate broker in Houston and served during the Civil War as an agent of the Texas War Board, with the responsibility of shipping state-owned cotton into Mexico to by-pass the Union blockade of Texas ports. During the 1870s, he served two terms as the home-elected mayor of Houston following "Reconstruction." Miss Cone was the daughter of Dr. Henry Hale Cone, who came to Texas in 1835, was a surgeon in the Army of the Republic of Texas, and who was an early resident of Houston, bringing his family from Georgia when there were only eight houses in the town.

Like many brides, Miss Cone searched diligently for new recipes with which to brighten her new home. Cookbooks were rare on the Texas frontier. In fact, many years later, Miss

Louisa Cunningham
courtesy Jeff Carroll

Cone (Mrs. J.T.D. Wilson) was instrumental in publishing the first cookbook "written by and for Texans" when she was a leader in Houston's First Presbyterian Church. The collected "Wilson Papers" contain the following letter from a friend of Miss Cone's, one Mrs. Louisa Cunningham of Galveston. Don't worry about the spelling. The "receipts" are primarily desserts and leave a bit to both the imagination and to an understanding of cooking on and in a wood stove.

"Galveston, December 15, 1853

Dear Miss Cone,

Agreeable to your request, and to make good my promise, I embrace the opportunity to give you these Receipts. I have been much engaged since my return, trying to get fixed so as to be comfortable for the winter. I found the place my husband had removed, during my absence, much out of repairs, but considered it would be much pleasanter than boarding—as to me there is no place like Home be it ever so humble. I hope you found your parents and friends all well. I received a long letter to day from my sister Lissie, all well and of course miss me very much. Give my kind regards to your sister and with much love for yourself, I remain respectfully yours—
Louisa Cunningham*

Cocunut Pie
1 cocunut grated, 2 soda crackers, rolled, 4 eggs, 1 quart milk, 2 table spoon fulls sugar, half table spoon nutmeg and salt. Crust on bottom of dish.

Soda Cake
1 egg, half teacup butter, half tea cup sour milk, 2 tea cup flour, 1 tea spoon cream tarter, half tea spoon full soda. Mix Cream Tarter and Soda in the flour. Add egg, butter and milk. Consistancy of pound cake.

Custard Pudding
Pint of milk, 3 spoonfuls of flour, 6 eggs, salt to taste, Sugar.

Apple Custard
Take apples, pared, cored and slightly stewed, sufficient to cover a dish, 6 eggs, 1 quart milk, Spice to the taste, Bake it one third of an hour.

Cream Pudding
3 eggs beaten very light, stir in it a pint and a half of flour, salt to taste, mix a little milk, then put in 6 ounces of sugar. Just before you put it in the oven add a pint of thick cream. Bake three quarters of an hour.

Transparent Pudding
Beat up 8 eggs, Put them in a stew pan with a half pound of sugar, the same of butter, and some grated nutmeg, and set it on the fire, stirring it until it thickens. Then pour it in a basin to cool. Set a thick paste [crust] around the edge of a dish. Pour in the pudding and bake in a moderate oven. A delicious and elegant article.

Macaroons
Blanch 4 ounces of almonds, and pound them with 4 spoonfuls of orange flower water. Beat the whites of four eggs to a froth, mix it with a pound of sugar, sift the almonds into a paste and lay it in different cakes on paper to bake.

Calves-foot Jelly
Take four calves feet, well boiled, half pound of sugar, one pint of wine, two lemons, the whites of four eggs and shells, boil all together about five minutes, then pour through a flannel bag to strain.

Orange Pudding
Take one pound of butter creamed, one pound of sugar, 10 eggs, the juice of two oranges. Boil the peel, then pound it fine and mix with the juice, add the juice of one lemon, a wine glass of brandy and rose water.

Vermicelli Pudding
Boil a pint of milk with lemon peel and cinnamon, sweeten with loaf sugar, strain through a sieve and add a quarter of a pound of vermicelli. Boil ten minutes, then put

in the yolks of five and whites of three eggs. Mix well together, and steam it one hour and a quarter, or bake half an hour.

Custard Without Eggs
One quart of new milk, four tablespoonfulls of flour, two of sugar, season with nutmeg and cinnamon and add salt to your liking. The milk should be placed over a quick fire and when at the boiling point, the flour should be added, being previously stirred up in cold milk. As soon as thoroughly scalded, add the sugar, spice and salt. It may be baked either in cups or crust.

Plain Pudding Without Eggs
1 pound of flour, 1 cup of raisins, 1 cup of currents, 1 cup suet, salt, boil 1 1/2 hours, mix up with cold water and tie the pudding bag tight. Boil one and one half or two hours.

Nottingham Pudding
Peel six good apples, take out the cores. Be sure to leave the apples whole. Fill up where the core was taken from with sugar. Place them in a pie dish and pour over them a nice light batter prepared as for batter pudding and bake an hour in a moderate oven.

Batter Pudding
Take six ounces of flour, a little salt, and three eggs. Beat up well with a little milk, added by degrees til the batter is smoothe. Make it the thickness of cream. Put in a buttered pie dish and bake three quarters of an hour.

I have selected some of my receipts, which I hope you will like. Please, when convenient, let me know how you like some of them. I have several more, but presume this will answer for the present. Excuse the blots and all mistakes, as I have written by candle light and not taken much pains, as I was fearful you had begun to think I had forgotten my promise.

L."

1855—The Strange Case of "Wandering John"

There is a Spanish curse that is a fearsome thing to wish on anyone: "Que tu vida sea llena de abogados," or, "May your life be filled with lawyers." Such a curse is enough to sober even the most dedicated alcoholic and cause women to flee in fright, their arms filled with wailing children. The elderly tremble. Small, defenseless animals curl up and expire, and rain falls on a flooded land.

However, all is not dark and dismal. Some lawyers are welcome.

During the days of the Republic of Texas and its early statehood there was probably a greater percentage of lawyers in the Texas population than ever before or since, at least until the recent explosion of membership in the legal profession. We owe a lot to those early practitioners of the law. Although some were scoundrels, others designed and maintained an entire judiciary system, a new nation, and a new state. Generally, they were a gregarious lot. County and district court sessions brought them in from far and wide. Residents also came from the towns and from the forks of the creeks because "Court Day" was the best, and sometimes only, excite-

"Wandering John" Taylor
by Gary Manthei

ment and entertainment around. Legal minds of various persuasions took over local inns, ardent spirits flowed freely, and a good time was had by all. Strangers shared beds as a matter of course, and the crowded accommodations appealed to most, but not to everyone.

Nobody seems to know where John Taylor was before he came to Texas, or even if that was his real name. Some questions you just didn't ask on the frontier. He may have been here all along, but no one seemed to notice, and census records are mute. He just appeared out of nowhere at the spring of 1852 meeting of the district court in Centreville, up in Leon County. He was tall, about six feet, slender and well proportioned, with a pleasant face and manner and the graceful carriage of a dancer or an actor. He arrived on horseback, with three other horses tied nose-to-tail carrying supplies. Forsaking the comradeship of fellow lawyers and, for that matter, everyone else, he pitched his camp on the edge of town, won a few cases for puzzled but thankful customers, and disappeared.

People began to ask about him. He was good. In a day when the most successful lawyers were the best speakers, he had the power to charm the bark off of a post. His clients knew no more than the rest of the people. He was kind and available, and he won their cases, accepting as payment anything they offered, from cash to a horse or a sack of coffee or side of bacon. No one knew where he came from or where he went when he left.

Then, as if by magic, he appeared again, and again, at court sessions in Cherokee, Anderson, Houston, Leon, Madison, Robertson, Limestone, and Freestone counties. The pattern was the same. He would appear as if conjured up by a wand-waver, be kind and courteous and eloquent to the point of witchery, and disappear with his horses laden with whatever he collected in fees. People began calling him "Wandering John" and looked forward to his appearances in court as the high point of the session's entertainment. Slowly, in the absence of fact, legends began to grow.

Some folks said he was from New York or Philadelphia, but others thought Baltimore or Richmond or Savannah or even New Orleans. Some said he wasn't a lawyer at all, but an actor who had left the stage because of a tragic love affair. Some said he was a wanted criminal in Louisiana, that he had killed many men in arranged duels. Then it was rumored that he and a son shared a fortress-like building designed as a sawmill, near where Clear Creek joins the Navasota River. Visitors, it was said, were not welcome.

He had a way of appearing at some troubled farmer's cabin as a stranger, asking to sleep in the barn but not in the house, and then offering his legal services to the owner who invariably needed help. Children remembered him, and the legend grew that whenever someone was in desperate need, he would appear.

For about ten years "Wandering John" made regular appearances at the crossroads courts of East Texas. He didn't always win, but he always put on a good show and, when necessary, accepted defeat in the same gracious manner in which he accepted victory. If your interest is aroused, you can review the dusty court records of the period in any one of a dozen counties. You'll find him involved in disputes over stock, land boundaries, and marital infidelity. There are references to theft and even murder.

Then came the "War for Southern Independence," what some folks call the "Civil War" (although there was nothing "civil" about it). Some say he enlisted under another name and died at Shiloh or Manassas or in "the Wilderness." Some say that "Wandering John" wandered west into the mining camps of Colorado or California or Idaho. Some say he never left at all, that there was really no mystery attached to the man who simply liked his privacy. In any event, "Wandering John" seemed to disappear for good along with the death of the "Old South."

1859—*Cheno El Rojo*

Much of history is a matter of perspective—where you stand both physically and emotionally when you view an action. Any attorney will tell you that three witnesses will give you three different versions of what happened in an accident and swear that theirs is the correct one.

This happens all of the time, so we should not be surprised if people don't agree on what happened over one hundred years ago. This is especially true when we talk about what people think of other people.

Saint or sinner, hero or villain, it all depends on your perspective when you think about Juan Cortina, the Robin Hood of the Texas border. He was born on May 16, 1824, down in Camargo, two miles south of the Rio Grande, in the Mexican state of Tamaulipas. Juan Nepomuceno Cortina—*Cheno*, as he was called—was the son of a small rancher, whose wife, Estafana, was the heiress to about 44,000 acres of ranch land on the north side of the river in Texas. Now, Cheno's father was classed in Mexican society as a Criollo, which meant that he claimed pure Spanish blood, but was born in the New World. His mother, however, was somewhat different. She sprang from a very well-to-do family of *conversos*. This meant that her family had Jewish roots stretching back to about 1490 in Spain, when they "converted" to Roman Catholicism in order to save both their lives and their estates. Since Mexico was also officially Catholic, this connection was hidden, but the fact was that as Cheno grew up, he grew up in a home where many Jewish rituals and ceremonies were still honored. The family was well respected, and although Cheno was something of a bully, most local residents accepted his ways with grace. As he grew older, Cheno grew a full beard that became a bright, glowing red. Hence *"El Rojo"* (The Red One) was added to his name.

During the Mexican War, Cheno served with the forces of General Mariano Arista, who opposed Zachary Taylor in the battles of Palo Alto and Resaca de la Palma. There he became a natural leader, drawing around him a mixed bag of misfits who rejected strict military discipline.

The Mexican War settled the boundary of the United States at the Rio Grande. Many Mexicans living north of the river were either forced off of their land or killed outright by unscrupulous *gringos*. Others retaliated as they saw fit, and among the leaders of bands which raided north of the river was Cheno El Rojo. Then came 1859.

General David Twiggs withdrew most United States troops from the Mexican border and moved them to meet Indian strength along the western frontier. From the Gulf to Laredo, only locally elected officials remained. On July 13, 1859, Brownsville City Marshall Robert Shears arrested and treated brutally a Mexican who had once worked for Cortina at his mother's ranch. Cheno interfered, shot the marshal, and rescued the prisoner. The fat was in the fire. Cortina became an outlaw in the eyes of the Anglo-American community, and they banded together to bring him to justice, but to the Mexican community, he was the protector of the people.

On September 28, Cheno returned to Brownsville at the head of a 200-man personal army and began to "tree" the entire town, killing Anglos and their Mexican supporters with both glee and vigor. The Mexican flag was raised over the city, and many soldiers from the regular Mexican Army in Matamoros crossed the river to join in the fun. The city was held hostage for a ransom of $300,000. By early 1860, Cheno's force had grown to 800. The steamboat *Ranchero,*

General Juan Nepomuceno Cortina circa 1866
courtesy UTSA's Institute of Texan Cultures at San Antonio

151

owned by Captain Richard King of King Ranch fame and his partner Mifflin Kennedy, was dispatched with the money.

Cheno planned to capture the boat before it had a chance to consummate the deal to save the city, and he set out with 300 of his best mounted men. They didn't reckon on the interference of John S. "RIP" Ford's company of Texas Rangers, and in the battle that followed Cortina lost 69 men. Ford, however, paid him his highest compliment:

> *"Cortina was,"* he wrote, *"the last to leave the field. He faced his pursuers, emptied his revolver, and tried to halt his panic-stricken men ... One shot struck the cantle of his saddle, one cut a lock of hair from his head, a third cut his bridle rein, a fourth passed through his horse's ear and a fifth struck his belt buckle, He galloped away, unhurt."*

Although he was pursued back into Mexico by Rangers and freshly arrived U.S. Cavalry under Captain George Stoneman, Cheno El Rojo didn't give up. He became a general in the Mexican Army, served as governor of the Mexican State of Tamaulipas during the American Civil War, and was mayor of Matamoros in 1875. When Mexico's political wheel revolved and Diaz became president, Cheno was arrested by the army, tried, and sentenced to death. His old adversary, Ranger Captain "RIP" Ford, interceded in his behalf, and so he was allowed to live out the rest of his life in comfort in Mexico City.

Juan Cortina, alias Cheno El Rojo, the Robin Hood of the border, died peacefully on October 30, 1894, and he is forgotten by many Anglos who may have only heard his name.

1860—The Texas Lee

There is probably no single person in Southern history more revered than General Robert Edward Lee. We tend to picture "Marse Robert" in gray, on his horse, watching his tattered troops march by, cheering as they go. Or, we think of him sitting at Appomattox, pen in hand, writing the obituary of The South. Somehow, we forget that Robert E. Lee spent more time in the U.S. Army protecting the Texas frontier than he did in Confederate gray.

Robert Edward Lee, the son of General Henry Lee and his wife Ann Carter Lee, was born up in Westmoreland County, Virginia, in 1807. He grew up with the family's military tradition and graduated as second in his class from West Point in 1829. While he was stationed at Fortress Monroe in Virginia as a second lieutenant in charge of fortifications, he married Mary Custis in 1831, and the couple ultimately had seven children. Lee was a family man, loved children and cats, and, early in his military career, proved to be an excellent engineer. While Texas was fighting for independence, Lee was in the office of the chief engineer, planning harbor facilities along the Mississippi River.

Lee first came to Texas in 1846 after Texas was admitted to the Union, and he served with General Wool in his march from San Antonio to Buena Vista during the war with Mexico. Later in that war, he served as General Winfield Scott's chief of staff in his march from Veracruz to Mexico City and, in the process, won advancement to major, lieutenant colonel, and colonel because of conspicuous gallantry in action. These were only stepping-stones, because, after the war and a return to the building of forts, he served as the commandant of the United States Military Academy at West Point from 1852 to 1855.

Texas, however, was in his blood. When Congress, in 1855, authorized the formation of two new regiments of infantry and two of cavalry, Lee became second-in-command of the Second United States Cavalry and brought his troops to San Antonio. The frontier in Texas was over 1,200 miles long and had only 2,886 officers and men to defend it. These men were scattered along the line like beads on a string, in about twenty forts and camps. Robert E. Lee became the commander of two squadrons of cavalry stationed at Camp Cooper up in Shackleford County.

Camp Cooper wasn't much as far as military posts went. There were no amenities, and the men were sandwiched between Texans eager to move west and about 30,000 Comanche in dispersed raiding bands. On July 4th, 1856, Lee wrote to Mary that the only shelter from the sun was *"my blanket elevated on four sticks driven into the ground."* That summer, he

153

General Robert E. Lee
courtesy Brady-Handy Collection, Library of Congress

also led four squadrons of cavalry in a 1600-mile exploration of the upper reaches of the Brazos River and the Cap Rock up above today's Post.

Then followed his command of the regiment in San Antonio. Lee once wrote to Mary about not only the quality of the fighting men in Texas but also, saying of a particular woman in San Antonio, that she *represented "the kind of women—a man wants in the army."* He said that Texas women were *"strong minded"* and had the benefits of *"Texas habits."*

In 1859, Mary's father died, and Robert returned to Washington on leave to oversee the settling of his estate. While he was there, John Brown raided Harper's Ferry, and Lee was dispatched with a company of Marines to put down the insurrection. But, in early 1860, he returned to his regiment in San Antonio and moved regimental headquarters to Fort Mason in Mason County. Then came a dispatch to the Rio Grande in pursuit of Juan Cortina, the Mexican Robin Hood.

Secession and war were on the horizon. While Lee chased Juan Cortina, South Carolina seceded from the Union. Mississippi, Florida, Alabama, Georgia, and Louisiana followed. There were questions both in Texas and in Virginia, and Robert E. Lee damned both the issues of slavery and abolition. On December 3, 1860, a secession convention met in Austin to discuss whether or not Texas should also leave the Union, and, on February 13, 1861, while they debated, Robert E. Lee was relieved of his command and called to Washington, where he was offered the command of the Union Army. He knew the offer was coming and had known ever since early in that year. Evidence suggests that he made his decision before leaving San Antonio. As much as he loved the United States, he was a Virginian by birth. In the last hundred years or so we have forgotten that the Constitution recognizes us as citizens first of sovereign states and secondly of the United States. Unfortunately, most states today forget the 10th Amendment to the Constitution and give up their rights to sovereignty without a murmur. Lee knew that he owed allegiance to Virginia before he did to the United States. With the secession of Virginia, Lee resigned his commission ... and you know the rest of the story.

Robert E. Lee never returned to Texas, but he remembered with pride his time on the frontier and the men of Texas that he commanded. He wrote, *"They have fought grandly and nobly and we must have more of them."*

1861—The Bloodless Battle of Adams Hill

Back in the 1860 Presidential election, Abraham Lincoln, a Republican, received no votes in Texas. In fact, he was not even on the ballot—a situation that existed throughout the South. Ultimately, this election and the simmering differences between North and South on the issues of the Constitution, states' rights, economics, and slavery led to the Civil War and the bloodiest battles ever fought by American troops.

Not all of those battles, however, ended with rows of stones in graveyards.

The Texas frontier in 1860 was a stronghold of the United States Army. When Texas entered the Union in 1846, it turned over to the Army all of its fortifications, and, following the Mexican War, this string of western forts stretched from the Red River to the Rio Grande. By 1860, there were over twenty of these forts, and, within their commands, you could find over ten percent of the entire military force of the United States.

On January 28, 1861, in opposition to the wishes of Governor Sam Houston, a convention met in Austin and, on the second day, voted 152 to 6 in favor of a resolution stating, *"It is the deliberate sense of this convention that the State of Texas should separately secede from the Federal Union."* Actual secession was not completed until February 23, and Texas joined the Confederacy one month later, on March 23. Meanwhile, things were happening on the frontier.

While the convention was in session, someone raised the question of the U.S. Army and its 2,700 troops stationed at all of those forts on the frontier. It seemed inappropriate, and downright dangerous, to have the Army there when most folks expected war. Consequently, the convention sent Ben Mc-Culloch and 160 Texas volunteers to check it out. Now, it just so happened that the commander of all of those frontier forts was Major General David Emanuel Twiggs from Georgia. A month or so earlier Robert E. Lee had held that position; a confrontation between Lee and McCulloch might have been disastrous. Lee, however, was ordered to Washington, and Twiggs, at age 70, was in command.

Down in San Antonio, the Texans surrounded Twiggs' headquarters and pointed out the obvious—that the United States Army was in a position to be trapped between hostile Indians on one side and hostile Texans on the other. Twiggs supported the Southern cause but asked his superiors what to do. When he didn't get an answer from Washington, he surrendered all 2,700 men and the 21 forts in his command, resigned his commission, and went off to join the Confederate Army, becoming its oldest general. In one fell swoop, the Confederacy gained a great victory even before war was declared.

But, it wasn't quite that simple. You see, some of Twiggs' local commanders were more loyal to the Union than he was and didn't look with favor on the surrender. Among these was Colonel I.V.D. Reeves of the 8th United States Infantry. Col. Reeves commanded troops at Fort Bliss, Fort Davis, and Fort Quitman, all in far West Texas. He didn't have many men, only about 320 of them, including hospital stewards and the band, but they had not surrendered and were still under arms. Although they had abandoned their forts and were on their way to Indianola on the coast, they still represented a military threat. Reeves sent word that they were retreating but would not surrender.

By May, Ft. Sumter had been fired upon—the war was on. Reeves and his troops were still slowly moving east and

General David Emanuel Twiggs
courtesy Prints and Photography Collection, Center for American History, University of Texas at Austin

attempting to reach the coast. So far, there had been no confrontations, although Confederate scouts followed the progress of the little command. Colonel Earl Van Dorn, the Confederate commander of Texas, went to meet them.

On May 9, 1861, they met on Adams Hill near San Lucas Spring in western Bexar County. Reeves and his command, reduced to 270 by sickness and desertion, weary from the long march from the west, stood on Adams Hill, drawn up in line of battle. Half a mile away were over 1,200 Confederates commanded by Van Dorn, supported by a four-piece battery of artillery removed from Fort Sam Houston following Twiggs' surrender. Van Dorn demanded unconditional surrender. Reeves refused. Van Dorn again offered surrender with terms, and, again, Reeves refused. Then Van Dorn played his trump card. He invited Reeves to visit with him and see the odds he would have to face if he didn't surrender. They finally agreed that there was no reason to cause undue bloodshed, and the surrender was consummated. No shots were fired. No graves were dug. Since the war had already begun, the Union troops were considered prisoners of war, were imprisoned, and were later exchanged. Many, originally from the South, joined the Confederate Army.

Because there was no real battle, there is no cemetery on Adams Hill. Only a small historic marker identifies the spot.

1861—The Texas Boys and the Web-Footed Cattle

Any psychologist worth his sheepskin will tell you that we have some strange and very frightening problems in our society. Basically, we don't want to grow up. Growing up involves the acceptance of responsibility, and that is the last thing a lot of folks want. For quite some time, we've been told that the government is supposed to take care of us and solve all of our problems. We are told that a paternal government is supposed to protect us from outside danger and from our siblings who have a tendency to sometimes run rampant through our nursery, breaking things and killing people. We're also told that when our siblings do get out of hand, it is really our fault because we didn't give them what they wanted of ours in the first place and so damaged their fragile egos. Two things we should fear above all others in our society are those "children" of whatever age who refuse to accept adult responsibility for their actions and the idea that it is not their fault. On the frontier, children accepted adult responsibility at an early age.

W.D.H. Saunders—we'll call him Bill—came from Yalobusha County, Mississippi, in 1850, when he was five years old. You see, a lot of families were moving to Texas from the "Old South." Land in Mississippi was getting expensive at the same time that it was getting worn out. To make a living growing cotton on the less productive land, you needed a bigger plantation. That not only meant that you had to buy more land, but also you had to buy more slaves or hire more people to work. Altogether, it meant that if you had a small farm and limited resources, the best thing to do was to sell out to someone else and move to Texas where land was cheap and still fertile. The fact that more and more folks were doing that was reflected in the production of cotton in Texas, which rose from 58,072 bales in 1850 to 431,463 bales in 1860.

Anyway, that was why Bill and his family moved again, to Gonzales County, in 1859. Then came the Civil War.

On December 20, 1860, South Carolina seceded from the Union. Other Southern states followed suit, and finally, on February 23, Texas, with roughly 90% of its population from the Deep South, joined them. Although the first battle of the Civil War may have occurred here in Texas down in Laredo, the firing on Fort Sumter on April 12 is usually credited as the turning point.

The nation was involved in a big war. Bill Saunders had just turned sixteen.

Not everybody rushed to join the army. In the more western and southern counties of Texas, there were other things to consider—like Indians. Also, folks realized that the non-industrial South would need all the help it could get to feed and equip its army and population. South Texas didn't have any munitions factories, but it did have cattle. In October of 1862, Bill and two other boys, Jim Borroum and Monroe Choate, headed back toward Mississippi—just three teen-aged boys and a herd of 800 longhorn steers to feed the South.

When trail driving was perfected as a fine art during the late 1870's, it usually took a crew of eight riders, a trail boss, a cook, and a horse wrangler to handle a herd of one thousand cattle. Those three boys had their hands full.

They crossed the Guadalupe River down at Clinton. Near Sweet Home, in Lavaca County, the herd stampeded at the sight of a haystack, and after an eight-mile run it took most of a week to get them together again. They crossed the Lavaca below Hallettsville, the Colorado near Alleyton, and the Brazos at Richmond. Swinging northeast, they hit the Trinity at Liberty, the Neches at Beaumont, and crossed the Sabine into Louisiana near Orange. Over near Opelousas, two local men bought a half interest in the herd and added another 300 head, themselves, and a cook. Things were looking good. Then came trouble.

W. D. H. "Bill" Saunders, the "Scout on the Rio Grande"
courtesy UTSA's Institute of Texan Cultures at San Antonio (W. C. Duderstadt)

159

Somewhere near Alexandria a batch of hungry Confederate soldiers arrested them on the trumped-up charge of trying to take the cattle to the Yankees. The boys might not have weathered that one alone, but the two new men were pretty well known in the area, and they talked their way out of it.

By the time they reached the Mississippi, those cattle just about had webbed feet from crossing so many rivers and swamps. No problem. The first 1,000 head took to that mighty river like ducks. About 100 of the new cattle refused to swim and were sold on the western shore.

In Mississippi they were arrested again—same charge. A local bureaucrat wanted to "confiscate" the cattle as contraband. No one seemed willing to accept the idea that they had driven cattle all the way from South Texas. But Mississippi was where they were headed in the first place, and there were old family friends to help. At Woodville, the herd was divided. The boys from Texas sold their half as planned, and the two men from Louisiana took theirs on to Mobile.

That trip with the web-footed cattle took a little over three months. By the end of January 1863, the boys were back in South Texas, and in February, Bill enlisted in the Confederate Army at Corpus Christi. He was then only seventeen years old.

1863—Cinte and the "Paddle Roller"

Back during the Depression—I mean the "Big One" in the 1930's—one of FDR's plans for putting people to work was to take out-of-work teachers and give them a job working for the Federal Writers' Project. They collected data and wrote histories and tour guides and a whole bunch of other stuff. Some of it was quite good, and some was pretty bad. Most of it fell in the middle. One of their projects, however, had no parallel in history. For years they sought out, found, and interviewed those African Americans still living who remembered what it was like to be a slave. Thousands of these interviews fill 29 books called the "Slave Narratives." I've mentioned these before and will again. If you really want to know what slavery was like, don't ask a modern social scientist for his opinion, and be wary of new books that are edited versions. Those editors pick out only the parts they want to emphasize. Go to the source. The folks in those narratives are real people, and they were there when it happened.

Every county in the Slave States had what was called the County Slave Patrol. In some counties this was a function of the county commissioners. In others, it was a branch of the sheriff's department. In any event, the job was to patrol the lands of the county, sort of like today's game warden, and to be on the lookout for slaves who were not where they were supposed to be, or for any other activity by slaves that did not conform to state, county, or local law. This police function wasn't all bad. In most counties they also checked to be sure that slaves were well fed and sheltered and that folks followed laws against brutality on the part of owners and overseers. Some slave patrollers were conscientious, while some were political appointees who did nothing. Usually, the membership of these patrols was drawn from folks who had lost their land or who, for some reason, deserved a little extra money. Almost universally the slave population referred to these patrols as "Paddy Rollers," "Pattyrollers," "Pettyrollers," or something similar.

This brings us to the story of San Jacinto Lewis. San Jacinto "Cinte" Lewis was born near Richmond in Fort Bend County not long after the battle that gave him his name.

Although slaves usually worked from dawn to dark, they were expected to stay in their cabins at night. Not all of them did. Slaves frequently slipped away to meet slaves from other farms, to hunt, or just to experience a little solitude or a little taste of freedom. One night Cinte and several other slaves slipped away to visit another plantation where there was supposed to be a "hoe down" celebration. According to Cinte, *"We is slippin'*

The Escaped Slave
courtesy UTSA's Institute of Texan Cultures at San Antonio

'long quiet like and a Paddle Roller jump out from behin' a bush and say, 'Let's see your pass!' "

Well, without a pass from their master allowing them night travel—a pass they didn't have—their goose was cooked. They could expect at least 100 lashes each for leaving the plantation. Cinte was quick, though, and he remembered that in his pocket was a sheet of paper, a page torn from a songbook in a church the slaves were allowed to attend. He couldn't read, but he knew that the paper had something to do with God and the music he liked. Some day he hoped to be able to read it. It was all he had, so he pulled it out and handed it over to the Paddy Roller. Well, since about the only real qualification for joining the Slave Patrol was that the applicant be white, the Paddy Roller couldn't read any more than Cinte could. He took one look at it, told Cinte and his friends to be sure to be back by daylight, and let them go.

Cinte remembered, *"An' then we run, right through old burdock bushes with briers stickin' us an' everthin'."*

Well, Cinte is gone now, but if you'd like to meet him and those other black Americans who survived what some folks call the South's "peculiar institution," ask your library for the Texas copies of the Federal Writers' Project Slave Narratives. There you will find everything you've heard, along with a lot of stuff you've never heard about slavery—both good and bad.

1864—The Fighting Parson

During the three hundred years before Texas won her independence from Mexico, it was illegal to live in Texas unless one was a practicing member of the Roman Catholic Church. In fact, all of the settlers who came to the grants of the 25 or more legal empresarios after 1823 had to take an oath that they were Roman Catholic. Since most of them came from the Deep South, where Roman Catholics were about as rare at that time as hen lips, one must assume that there was a lot of finger-crossing going on when the oaths were taken. This regulation didn't keep Protestant preachers out, and many operated illegally in the years before independence. Once Texas became a republic, the doors were open wide, and preachers of whatever religious persuasion wrote an exciting chapter of frontier history.

There have been several movies made about preachers who conducted services with a Bible in one hand and a pistol in the other. They may all have been patterned after Jack Potter, the "Fighting Parson."

He had quite a reputation. When the U.S. Congress was considering the problems of frontier protection in 1872, one member spoke to the record, "*Remove your regulars from the garrison on the Texas border, commission Jack Potter, a reclaimed desperado and now a Methodist preacher and an Indian fighter, instruct him to choose and organize one hundred men, and Indian depredations along the Texas border will cease.*"

It all started when Andrew Jackson Potter was born in Missouri in 1830. He was about in the middle of seven children fathered by old Joshua Potter, who fought with Andy Jackson in the Battle of New Orleans. Jack was kind of small, but he survived an epidemic that left him an orphan without a home at the age of ten. He was small, but he was tough and could stick to a horse's back like a burr, so he became a jockey and for the next six years followed the frontier races from town to town.

Then came 1846 and the war with Mexico. Jack spent the next six years in the army as an ox-team driver, a mounted scout, and a sometimes nurse to the wounded in campaigns in New Mexico, Arizona, and Kansas. Finally, in 1852, at the ripe old age of 22, Jack came to Texas. He had already spent more than half of his life fighting for survival in one way or another, and he decided to settle down to the peaceful life of driving wagons of lumber from Bastrop County to the treeless regions west for $15 a month.

A big revival at Croft's Prairie in 1856 changed Jack's life. By 1859 he was licensed to preach and began a career that covered West Texas. In 1861 he hired on as a herder and carried the Word along with the cattle to the bloody Kansas-Missouri border region. In 1862 he found himself back in Texas and back in the army, this time in gray, as the chaplain of DeBray's Regiment of the 32nd Texas Cavalry. Down in Brownsville Jack publicly thrashed the editor of the local news-

Andrew Jackson Potter, the fighting parson of the Texas frontier
courtesy UTSA's Institute of Texan Cultures at San Antonio (H. A. Graves, 1881)

paper for printing defamatory statements about the regiment. In 1864 he found himself in the Red River Campaign in front of the troops.

Before a battle he would exhort, *"Boys, some of you may fall in this battle. In a few minutes you may be called to meet your Maker. Repent, NOW!!"* Then he would grab a rifle and lead the charge.

The war ended, and the fighting parson returned to riding the Methodist circuit of West Texas—first at Prairie Lea, then Kerrville, next Boerne, and then Uvalde, known at that time as one of the wickedest places along the Texas border. Wherever he went, he went armed and usually alone. More than once, he was attacked by Indians. Whenever he hit town, they'd make room for him in the biggest saloon, and the crowds, many of them former comrades-in-arms, would gather to hear the fighting parson preach. They said that he fought the Devil like he fought the Yankees, with the Word of God and a rifle.

In 1883, at the ripe old age of 53, the fighting parson began to feel the need for a change. He said that his strength was in the Lord and that Texas had become too tame. He needed, he said, a vacation from his spiritual flock and their constrained ways. So, he rode north as trail boss, blazing a new cattle trail all the way from Hebbronville, on the Rio Grande, up to Cheyenne, Wyoming. After fighting stampedes, blizzards, Indians, rustlers, and those who objected to Texas cattle, for almost a year, he felt refreshed enough to return to his pulpit.

As the frontier moved west, so did "Fighting Jack." There was Fort Concho at San Angelo and then the broad vistas of desert and mountain west of the "Pecos Barricade." Finally, in 1894, he was back on the Lockhart circuit near where he began, but things had changed. There were railroads where once there were trails, and the full moon came and went without Indian attack. Folks didn't ride horses into the saloons anymore, and almost every community had its own church. The old Tilman Chapel that he knew so well was still in use, and it was there that he gave his final sermon. His benediction began with, *"I believe ..."* and he died. At last, the fighting parson's battle was won. Perhaps there is no better statement of faith.

1865—The Midnight Ride of Sophia Butts

Next time you visit an old cemetery, take a look at the number of graves representing men and women. In most cases the women outnumber men by a good majority, especially in the really old cemeteries. The old timers said that Texas was fine for men, horses, and dogs, but hell on women and oxen. Frequently, a man would bury several wives before he either moved on or was also laid to rest.

That wasn't always the case, however. Some women outlived a good many husbands.

Take Sophia Suttonfield, for example. Sophia was born in Indiana in about 1814, and in 1833 she married a fiddle-footed schoolteacher named Jessie Auginbaugh and came with him to Texas. Jessie soon moved on without telling Sophia, and, after getting a divorce for desertion, she married Holland Coffee at Washington-on-the-Brazos in 1837.

Things looked good. They left the Brazos on horseback and made their home at Coffee's Station up on the Red River, where they finally built a nice home and named it Glen Eden. Holland Coffee was cut from good cloth. Back in 1833, he'd come west from Arkansas with forty trappers and established a string of trading posts along the Red River. Active in politics, he served his friends and neighbors well as a member of the Third Congress of

Sophia's Crossing
by Suzy Keller

the Republic of Texas. He was a good husband and a good businessman, but not good enough to keep from passing on when an Indian stabbed him in 1846.

Sophia was left with a plantation, several trading posts, and no husband, again. Being an unmarried woman with property created certain problems in early Texas, so, in 1853, Sophia Suttonfield Auginbaugh Coffee married Major George Butts. Apparently, the marriage proved satisfactory to both parties. Butts gained control of Coffee's plantation and trading posts, and Sophia had a husband. That is, she had a husband until the Civil War came and William Clark Quantrill's raiders killed George in a raid.

That was almost too much. Husbands were hard enough to find, much less keep. Eight counties along the Red River had voted against secession, but Yankee raiders turned the tide. Sophia swore eternal damnation on Quantrill and all Yankee aggression in general. Then, during what became known as the Red River Campaign, regular Union troops advanced in an attempt to invade Texas from the north and east. Sophia wasn't too good at keeping husbands, but, by golly, she wasn't about to lose her home to the Yankees as well.

Friendly Indians reported the approach of Union scouts, who, they said, took a delight in torturing Indians to learn the location of trading posts. Mounting up on one of her late husband's horses, Sophia swam the Red River in the night and made her way to the camp of Confederate Colonel James Bourland to give the alarm. It worked! The Union advance was driven back at the river and on back into Louisiana. Sophia became known as the Paul Revere of the Confederacy.

The closing days of the war were difficult for a widow with property. In 1865 Sophia made her way to Waco to be with friends, and there she met and married Judge James Porter, a former Confederate officer from Missouri. They returned to Glen Eden, but the troubles of "Reconstruction" and the financial problems of farmers in the 1870s led to the Judge's death also. Sophia survived.

Abandoned by one husband, she buried three more before joining them in 1899—remembered best not for her long life, but for her midnight ride.

Advancing the Frontier: 1866-1900

1866—A Long Walk For a Boy, or a Man

The transition from child to adult has little to do with age. It depends more on the willingness (and opportunity) to accept adult responsibility. Because of this we have today a few teenage adults and an unfortunate abundance of 30- and 40-year-old children. The opportunity to grow up often came early on the frontier where folks did not expect a paternal government to solve all of their problems.

The state established Erath County in 1856 from parts of Bosque and Coryell Counties, about 50 miles south of Fort Worth. It was named for old George B. Erath, who, as a graduate of the Vienna Polytechnic Institute, came to Texas in 1833, fought at San Jacinto, and was also the surveyor who ran the first county lines. As soon as the county was formed, it officially opened for settlement, although John M. and William F. Stephen had jumped the gun a bit and established Stephenville in 1854.

Among the first permanent settlers in the new county were Samuel V. and Elizabeth Edwards. Remember that, in 1856, this was *Comanche* country. Settlements were few, and families stood a good chance of losing stock and their lives to every raid. Here, near Stephenville, Samuel V. Edwards, Jr., sometimes called "Pete" to distinguish him from his father, was born in April of 1859. A couple of years later the Civil War came along and the frontier retreated for 100 miles. That's where the acceptance of responsibility began for very young Sam Junior. He tended stock, watched for raiders, and took an active role in the management of a pioneer farm, this during a war that stripped the area of men of fighting age. The Edwards family did not retreat with the frontier. But, Sam Edwards, Sr., did not return from the war.

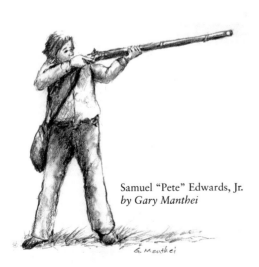

Samuel "Pete" Edwards, Jr.
by Gary Manthei

The war officially ended for most folks in Texas in 1865, when General Gordon Grainger landed in Galveston and proclaimed United States authority. For some, it didn't. Many Confederate veterans, bitter over defeat, the loss of states' rights, and the triumph of "Yankee Aggression," made their way to Mexico rather than live under the destructive policies of the "Reconstruction" government. At the ripe old age of ten, Samuel Edwards Junior, "Pete," left home to join them. His father hadn't owned slaves and cared nothing for those who did. He'd fought and died for the Tenth Amendment to the U.S. Constitution and the right of states to control their own destinies by law. Pete Edwards vowed not to live under the unjust laws that killed his father. He didn't have a horse or a pony, so he walked from Erath County through unsettled Indian country to San Antonio.

His first ten years had taught him to survive. One shot from his old muzzle-loading rifle brought him food. If it brought unwelcome visitors to his camp, he knew how to hide or travel without leaving a trail. Today, by highway, that route is about 240 miles. For a ten-year-old on foot, it could mean a lifetime.

A good long walk can take a lot of bitterness out of anybody. By the time young Pete got to San Antonio, things looked different than they had back near Stephenville. For one thing, he was tired, hungry, and without money. A temporary job "swamping out" a saloon provided a place to stay at night, food, and the opportunity to meet people. When he knew the people and the town, he became a messenger for the buyers and sellers of cattle. Up one street and down the next, and into and out of the hotels and bars, he became sort of a walking commercial, ringing a bell and calling out the names of people for whom he had messages and announcing offers to buy or sell. It really wasn't an easy life—few lives of any worth are—but it made him a well-known figure, and he got to know a lot of the shakers and movers of the growing cattle industry.

Then, in the spring of 1870, he hooked up with a cow outfit headed back south to their home range, which was located near where Millet is in present LaSalle County. They accepted him, so he accepted them, and he decided to stay. He didn't ask them to trust him. That came after he proved that he was a responsible member of the group. By the age of 19 he had spent almost half of his life in the saddle and had been up the cattle trails to Kansas and Nebraska at least six times. In those years he gained a reputation as a fine shot with a pistol, and with a rifle he was a marksman who never missed. More importantly, he also had the reputation for being honest, responsible, and fearless, and for having excellent judgment in dealing with all kinds of people.

It was then that he accepted appointment as a special agent for the newly re-formed State Ranger Service. The Texas Rangers had been abolished and replaced by Governor E.J. Davis with the much-hated Texas State Police of the Reconstruction government. When the Reconstruction administration officially ended, the "Davis" Police were gone, and the Rangers were back in the saddle.

Operating alone, at an age when many of today's young people still depend on three meals a day at home, someone to pay the bills, and free laundry and maid service, Pete Edwards became a peace officer on the frontier. He was responsible for infiltrating the various outlaw bands operating along the cattle trails and then leading them to the point where they could either be surrounded or captured, one-by-one, by the organized Ranger Companies. In two years he became well known—too well known for that kind of work.

In 1881, at age 22, he entered the regular Ranger Service under Captain Joe Sheely. He was young, even then, with more living than most of us see in a lifetime. Maybe he figured it all out on that long walk to San Antonio. Maybe, even at age ten, he understood that only he was responsible for what he made of himself. We don't know what he thought, and never will—but we can see where that long walk led him.

Pete Edwards went on to become the first Special Agent for the Texas State Cattle Raisers' Association (now known as the Texas & Southwestern Cattle Raisers' Association), a deputy sheriff, a sheriff in LaSalle County, and a Mounted Inspector for the U.S. Customs Service. Throughout his lifetime he rode for the law and not against it. He also found time to marry, raise a family, and build a ranch—no small accomplishment in itself.

Responsibility and trust? Samuel V. "Pete" Edwards, Jr., probably would have told you that responsibility comes when you are willing to accept it—no matter how old you are. Trust from family, friends, and that bigger world in which we live is a different matter. Trust must be earned. First comes the willingness to accept responsibility, then comes the practice of responsible acts. Only when responsibility is proven can we expect trust.

1866—The Tree that Charley Planted

The Bible tells us that if you rear a child in the way he should go, he will not depart from it. A proverb tells us that as you bend a twig, so will the tree grow. I guess that they both mean the same thing. The only things that are lacking in the equation are the will and the responsibility necessary to rear the child or bend the twig. From time to time, we can see evidence of that force.

In frontier Texas, education was pretty much a personal matter. Parents taught what they could, and much of what was taught was in the nature of frontier survival skills. From time-to-time, itinerant teachers would move into a community, and, often in exchange for room and board, would teach local children for a year or so. Much "advanced" learning came from unofficial apprenticeships. Future "butchers, bakers and candlestick makers; doctors, lawyers, and [even] Indian chiefs" learned their professions from someone who already knew how.

During the days of the Republic of Texas numerous colleges sprang up, and some of these still exist. However, many parents who were financially able still sent their students "back East" for an education.

Charley Carlton ran away from home in Kent, England, when he was sixteen and decided to go to sea. A lot of boys ran away to sea in the 19th century and found out that it wasn't quite the exciting experience they had anticipated. Work and working conditions were brutal, food was poor and often in short supply, and injuries and sickness were common and often untreated. Charley had sense enough to quit. That's how he ended up as marginally literate and unskilled labor in a Boston shipyard back around 1840.

One day, according to T.U. Taylor, who was once the Dean of the University of Texas, Charley spelled out the word "algebra" in the newspaper and, not knowing what it was, asked his boss. Now, some bosses have patience, and some don't. Charley's did. He suggested that if Charley really wanted to learn about things, he should go to see a fellow named Alexander Campbell who had just opened a place called Bethany College near Wheeling, in what would one day be West Virginia. It was a long rough way from Boston to Wheeling, but Charley made it, and he crammed a lifetime of learning into a few years, graduating in 1849. Then, Charley started teaching. He made his way southwest with the advancing frontier and wound up in Springfield, Missouri.

There he was quite popular, but the turmoil of Missouri border clashes and the coming Civil War pushed him even farther southwest. He spent the war years in Dallas, where he organized what became the Central Christian Church. When the war was over, he started back toward Missouri, but only made it as far as Kentucky Town up in Grayson County. You see, folks up there wanted a school, and that's what Charley wanted to do.

Students came from far and near, and the little school was both crowded and a success. After two years, Charley Carlton moved to Bonham, Texas, where the folks offered him a bigger building and a bunch of books and desks and other "schoolish" things.

That's how Carlton College was born.

Do you know what "college" means? The word comes from the Latin *colligere*, which

Charles Carlton
courtesy of the Fannin County Museum of History

means, "to bind together." In Latin, a *collegium* was a society of people bound together by shared goals and objectives. We get the words "collect" and "colleague" from the same root.

Carlton College was unique in many ways. Today, some folks preach that self-paced learning is a new and dangerous concept. Not so. Socrates in Ancient Greece and Confucius in China taught that way before the birth of Christ. Charley pioneered it in Texas by necessity because he was only one teacher, and there were primary and secondary students and the college students to consider and lead.

There is a great deal of argument today about *how* and *what* a teacher should teach. There are those who say teachers must *"teach from the book"* because *"the book is approved."* This ignores the fact that reading the "book" is the responsibility of the student. It should be the teacher's responsibility to widen the student's horizons by demonstrating that all knowledge is *not* "in the book." Knowledge is found in experimentation and an evaluation of the perspectives of many people who may not be approved by the agency adopting the book. There is a great deal of emphasis today on "standardized" testing (perhaps in an attempt to turn out "standardized" citizens) and teachers must "teach to the test" and cover a specified amount of material each day if they expect their students to do well (and if they expect themselves to be rehired). There are essential elements to cover, and there are mountains of paperwork to distract teachers from what they are really supposed to do—teach.

Charley couldn't do it that way. He became more of a facilitator for the college students than a teacher. Students chose those subjects that they wanted to master and then worked together under the shade of the trees on the campus to reach their goals. When they felt qualified in their lessons, Charley called on them to discuss what was learned, and woe be unto any student who was unprepared. As for Charley, he also taught primary and secondary classes from eight in the morning to six in the evening every day and also taught Sunday school and preached on the weekends. By 1887, there were 240 students, and the tree of learning that Charley planted had already borne fruit.

Back in 1866, when Charley was teaching at Kentucky Town, two brothers who had served together in the Confederate Army came to him for education. They didn't have any money, but they were willing to work and eager to learn. Charley never turned anyone away, and, although they were older than traditional age, Addison and Randolph Clark became excellent students. Bent toward education and the church by Charley's example, the two brothers not only became ministers in the Christian Church, but also, with their father and another brother, opened their own college. It was in Thorp Spring, and they called it Add-Ran Male and Female College. By 1889, they had 395 students, and the ownership of the school was transferred to The Disciples of Christ in Texas and renamed Add-Ran Christian University.

The word "university" comes from the Latin *universalis*, which, in turn, comes from *unus* (one) and *versum* (to turn). Put them together and a university is a place where all things are gathered together and turned into one universal body of knowledge. At least in theory, universities today are a combination of two or more colleges.

By 1893, the enrollment was 445, and, on Christmas day of 1895, the University moved to Waco, where it pioneered the concept of correspondence courses for adults. In 1897, the University played its first collegiate football game, and, in 1898, the students chose the name *The Horned Frog* for their yearbook. In 1902, the University changed its name again, and, when the main building burned in 1910, moved to Fort Worth. By now you've probably guessed that the tree that Charley Carlton planted with love is now called Texas Christian University. Not a bad planting for a boy who ran away to sea.

1868—The Slave Who Became a Senator

When Texas won its independence from Mexico, this did not mean that everyone in Texas was free. In fact, several areas of the Republic of Texas had more African-American slaves than Anglo settlers, and the laws of the republic stated that "free" African-Americans could not live within its boundaries unless special acts of the Congress were passed in their names. Even those so honored had no civil rights.

Being African-American in Texas, whether slave or free, was not an easy situation.

The ultimate result of the Civil War changed things for African-American Texans, but not that much, and not all at once. The proclamation at Galveston by General Gordon Granger on June 19, 1865, freed the slaves

Matthew Gaines and G. T. Ruby addressing the Texas State Legislature
courtesy UTSA's Institute of Texan Cultures at San Antonio

but didn't give them any civil rights. In most cases, the "Freedmen" were worse off than they had been before the war, because they had no owners responsible by law for providing them with food, clothing, and shelter. They had no jobs and were desperately illiterate. It took more than a war to change these conditions, and some changes are still taking place.

Along came the First Reconstruction Act of March 2, 1867, that required, among other things, that Texas create a new constitution and elect new state officers. Among these, the Texas Legislature in 1870 contained two African-American senators and nine African-American representatives. One such senator was George T. Ruby, born free in New York and educated before the Civil War. Ruby had been a newspaper reporter and schoolteacher and had been instrumental in setting up schools for Freedmen in both Louisiana and Texas. The other African-American senator was Matt Gaines.

Matthew Gaines was born into slavery around 1840 over in Louisiana. He never knew who his father was, and his mother died when he was quite young. He grew up in Rapides Parish on the property of Madame Candida Grandi Despallier, who was Spanish-born, and whose son, Charles, died defending the Alamo. Business on the Despallier estate, which included lands in Texas and Louisiana, was conducted in a mixture of Creole French, English, and Spanish. Although he was never allowed to attend school, Matt learned to converse in all three. He also learned to read at night, out in the fields, with books smuggled to him by an Anglo boy who was about his own age who may have been his half brother.

The Despallier estate fell apart in the mid 1850s when Madame Candida died, and the lands were sold to pay off debts. By then, Matt had a family, to the extent that plantation slaves could have families, and they were all sold in different directions. After passing through the hands of several owners, Matt escaped and made his way to Arkansas. When he returned to New Orleans, he was recaptured and sold as "troublesome" to Christopher Columbus Hearne, one of the wealthiest plantation owners along the Brazos River. In 1863, while the Civil War was in progress, Matt escaped from Hearne's plantation in Robertson County and tried to make his way to Mexico. Out at Fort McKavett in Menard County he was captured by a group of local "Home Guards" who called themselves Rangers. He spent the rest of the war doing odd jobs around Fredericksburg, where sentiment against slavery and the war was high.

As for why the Home Guards let Matt go to Fredericksburg instead of sending him back to his owner, as was the custom for regarding recaptured slaves, I have a theory—but that's all that it is. The German settlements that had voted against secession were caught between a rock and a hard place. Agents from the Confederacy raided them to conscript able-bodied for the army, and the Comanche raided them to push back the frontier. Many communities formed their own "ranging companies" to protect themselves from both. My guess is that Matt ran into one of those ranging companies from the German settlements, and that they "arrested" him both to keep him out of harm's way and to provide a one-man labor force for the town from which they came.

Matthew Gaines
by Suzy Keller

Matt Gaines had religion. He preached in Louisiana while still a slave, and when he made his way back to the Brazos after the war, he preached in the little town of Burton. By 1869 he was a political activist, using his pulpit as a political forum much in the same way that Martin Luther King, Jr., did in another century. When the dust settled following that year's election, Matt Gaines found himself sitting in the Texas Senate.

We may not have had a senator quite like him since. Most elected officials attempt to make those who elected them happy with their choice. Matt curried favor from no one. It made no difference to him if a person was African-American, Mexican-American, Anglo, or Native-American. He dumped on them all for not creating a land where everyone could live together in both dignity and harmony. He made a lot of enemies and a lot of friends. He was never the stereotype of the quiet and unobtrusive African-American who tried to stay out of trouble. He stood up to any and every one. According to one biographer, *"He developed a critical, emotional, and apocalyptic style in politics."* Curiously, Matt Gaines received more respect from southern whites than from blacks.

This may not be easy to understand unless you understand the times and the people who lived through them. Most of the former slaves had no education because the slave-era laws forbade it. They'd lived all of their lives as property, not as people who made their own decisions. They just weren't accustomed to the responsibilities and perils, as well as the benefits, of freedom. Matt kept saying that African-Americans didn't deserve their freedom unless they were willing to work for it and not depend on someone to take care of them. He said that true freedom comes from self-reliance and responsibility. No, he certainly was not that popular with much of the black community and was especially unpopular with the Yankee "scalawags" and "carpetbaggers" who bought votes in the black community by handing out favors.

Matt Gaines remarried while in office. His enemies in both parties who wanted to silence him charged him with bigamy because they claimed there was no divorce from his first wife. A jury convicted him, but the Texas Supreme Court overturned the conviction on the grounds that his first marriage as a slave in Louisiana wasn't really legal. In a way, that made it worse. Although he won the next election, the "Scalawag Reconstruction Senate" refused to seat him. They wanted blacks in the Senate, but they wanted only those they could control.

Abandoned by the Reconstruction government, Matthew G. Gaines retired to his pulpit in the rural area between Brenham and Giddings. He made quite a name for himself as a preacher. People called him "the Waterduck" because they said he could "pray down the rain." One time, during a drought, white farmers in the area between Burton and La Grange offered to build him a new church if he could make it rain. He did, and they did, and it became his church.

The Handbook of Texas goes into more detail about what he accomplished in the Senate, but it stops there, saying that he went back to preaching and died in Giddings in 1900.

1869—Have You Ever Heard of Joe McCoy?

Quite a few things we take for granted in Texas start and end somewhere else. In the meantime, Texas gets involved, and so the legend is born. The "Gilded Age" of the latter 19th century created many legends and many fortunes. "Big Business," as represented by "Titans of Industry," made some people very rich indeed. There were very few "middle class" citizens. The Gilded Age also created much unrest among poorly paid laborers in the industrial North and farmers and ranchers in the agricultural South and Southwest who were barely able to survive.

Attempts by laborers and farmers to organize were seen by many as "Socialist" or, in some other way, "un-American." The "Patrons of Husbandry," also known as "The Grange," and several other organizations that became today's farm co-op movement, had their beginnings at this time. At any rate, after the end of the Civil War, the economy was rough in Texas.

Think about Texas after the Civil War. When Johnny came marching home, he found that Texas was poor in everything but carpetbaggers, scalawags, land, and cows. Those cows were walking banks. A $3 cow in Texas was worth $50 in Chicago, and there were lots of cows. Chicago, though, was a long way away.

Cattle drives through Texas were almost as old as the European colonization of North America. The Spanish drove herds north from Mexico even before the first English settlements appeared on the Atlantic coast. After the Texas Revolution, people drove herds as far east as Mobile, as far west as the California gold fields, and as far north as St. Louis. The idea wasn't new.

But, northern farmers noticed something mighty peculiar. When Texas cattle came through their area, all of their local cattle died. They called it "Texas Fever." It didn't take long for folks in Missouri and similar areas to pass laws against Texas cattle and to form vigilante groups to enforce those laws. Texas was covered with cows, and the folks up North were hungry and willing to pay high prices for them. There just seemed to be no way to connect the two.

Despite the law, some folks tried. Take James Dougherty, for instance. He was still nineteen when, in 1866, he tried to drive a herd of 1,000 Texas longhorns to St. Louis along the Sedalia Trail. After crossing the worst rivers and making it safely through the Indian Territory, he and his entire crew were waylaid by local farmers in Missouri, tied to trees with their own ropes, and beaten. The cattle were never seen again.

Then came Joseph G. McCoy, who was born near Springfield, Illinois. He avoided the Civil War by becoming a livestock trader, along with his two older brothers, and supplying food to Union troops. He was rich by

illustration by Gary Manthei

the time the war ended, and so he started looking for a way to expand. He knew that if the dollar-poor, but cow-rich, Texans could be connected with the rich and hungry North, the middleman stood to make a good profit.

According to his biography, Joe came to Texas in 1867 *"with an earnest desire to do something that would alike benefit humanity as well as himself."* With this noble thought in mind, he talked to cattle owners and folks like James Dougherty and then went back to the North with an idea. What was needed, he decided, was a place where both buyer and seller could, *"conveniently meet to transact their business."*

Joe approached the Kansas Pacific Railroad for backing. No, they were not willing to risk a dollar on such a foolish scheme. He then approached the Missouri Pacific with the same result. Finally, the Hannibal & St. Joseph Railroad that ran from Kansas City to Chicago agreed to quote rates and carry cattle—if, that is, he could connect with them on the Union Pacific.

With little help from the railroads, except for an agreement that they would pay him $5 for every carload of cattle, he arranged to ship. With nothing else but an idea, Joe set out to find his *"convenient"* location.

In the spring of 1867, he found what he wanted on the Kansas prairie. He called it, *"a very small, dead place, consisting of about one dozen log huts, low, small, rude affairs, four-fifths of which were covered with dirt for roofing."* He bought most of the town, all 480 acres of it, for the sum of $2,400. In sixty days he transformed the village into a cattle capital, complete with shipping pens, *"a three-story hotel,"* a pair of large Fairbanks scales, a barn, an office, and a sign that read **"ABILENE."**

Riders took the news south. *"There is a place where Texas herds are welcome. Come to Abilene!"* And, come they did. On September 5, 1867, less than a year from the day that Joe McCoy first went to Texas, the first shipment—twenty carloads of cattle—left Abilene for Chicago. By December, the number of cattle shipped had reached 35,000. In a few years the number topped ten million.

As farmers moved onto the plains along with the railroad, their prejudice against Texas cattle moved with them, so the shipping points also moved west, ahead of them, to Ellsworth, to Caldwell, to Wichita, and to Dodge City.

For over twenty years, Texas herds streamed north to the rails. The economy of an entire nation was changed, and our culture was enriched by a thousand stories of tall men from Texas, longhorns, and long, dusty trails.

It all happened just because Joe McCoy had an idea.

1870—A Nest In the West

A long time ago there was a popular song that had as its last line, "We'll build a sweet little nest, somewhere in the West, and let the rest of the world go by." Depending on your point of view, a nest in the West may or may not sound romantic, and your idea of what one would actually look like might not agree with someone else's. Still, most folks agree that a house is only the wrapping on the package. It's the feeling inside that makes it a home or not.

Ella Elgar was born in Lee County, Mississippi, in 1861, and her father was murdered soon after, while he was trying to protect his home from Union "foragers." During what a lot of folks called "The War of Northern Aggression," they were a self-sufficient farming family who lost everything. After the Civil War, she and her sisters and mother moved in with her also-widowed-by-the-war grandmother, and all planned together to leave the destruction in the South and go to the West.

"*Gone to Texas,*" was a common comment in those years. The simplified notice of "GTT" was posted on cabin doors and gutted mansions throughout the South. Court dockets were revised when the initials appeared beside the names of either plaintiffs or the accused, because it was assumed that they'd moved beyond the jurisdiction of the court. Whether they left a sign on the door or not, Ella and her family—three generations of strong-willed women in a single covered wagon—left the South. They left destruction behind and came to Texas—to Johnson County in 1867, a frontier far from *ante-bellum* Mississippi.

By the time she was fifteen, Ella and her family had moved several more times. She wrote, "*Each time I moved, I moved west, finding more Indians, and more sparsely settled territory.*" It was while she was living in Young County on the Texas plains that her new brother-in-law opened their cabin door to a visitor and

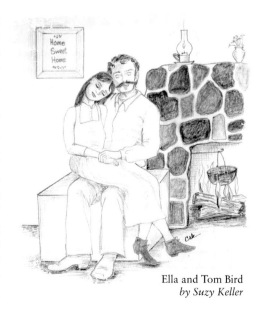

Ella and Tom Bird
by Suzy Keller

she *"...beheld, mounted on the most beautiful big black horse I had ever seen, a man, yes, a man in full western attire, that of a Texas Ranger— gallant and brave in appearance."* Tom Bird was, indeed, a Ranger and a member of the Frontier Battalion of Major John B. Jones, but his enlistment was about to expire.

It was "love at first sight" for both of them. Ella and Tom married in 1876, when she was fifteen. When his enlistment with the Rangers was up, they moved further west to hunt buffalo. Three days after Christmas in 1876, they built their "nest" in the "Croton Breaks" on what would become Bird's Pouroff Canyon Creek, out in the southeast corner of Dickens County. There was nothing of civilization there at the time, and the "Croton Breaks" today remains a rugged and very sparsely populated region.

Ella was a strikingly attractive girl who all of her life had wanted to be a sculptor. There wasn't much opportunity for artistic display in "the Breaks," but she helped to build their new home and described it in her diary:

> *"First we built a frame of small chinaberry poles, split some for rafters, no nails were used, rawhide strings instead. We took dried buffalo hides, tied the legs together and put them around the wall, wool side out, then another tier of hides over these in the same manner to break the joints of those underneath. The roof was made on the same order as the walls, tying down the legs all around the edges. The door was made of a frame of split poles with a buffalo hide stretched over it, legs tied inside. The little rock chimney with fireplace, which was crude, of course, came next. The floor was carpeted with buffalo hides, squared up to fit, wool side up. All was complete and a more clean and comfortable little home you could not find in any of the Eastern cities. We were happy; it was a real little love nest."*

Furniture she made from packing cases, with wooden spools for drawer pulls. Light was a lantern, seldom used because of the scarcity of kerosene.

For three years Ella and Tom lived happily in their "nest in the West" before moving on—proving, perhaps, that it's the quality of the occupants and not the construction that makes a nest a home.

The Bird family moved several more times during the next ten years. They occupied "nests" in Dickens County, where Tom was a line rider for the Pitchfork Ranch, and then on to Cottle County, where Tom rode for the Ross Ranch. Their love and their "nests" produced three children before Tom died suddenly in the vicious winter of 1886.

182

Ella made it on her own for nine years. She reared her family and made ends meet while living in a "dugout," making her living as a seamstress whose gloves, vests, and pants made of buckskin were very popular. Then, in 1895, she married a French-Canadian named Auguste Dumont and began a new "nest" for a new family in the town of Paducah.

Accidents do happen. At age 46, Ella broke her leg. Even in 1907, quality health care was rare in that part of Texas. The accident left her with limited mobility and slowed down the fast pace of her life. But even accidents and handicaps can have a positive side.

While she was a child, before they left Mississippi, Ella (whose first name was really Arrie—but she didn't like it) had begun modeling in clay taken from the family farm. During her life with Tom Bird, and after his death, her artistic talents were confined to making "nests" into homes, rearing a family, and her sewing. Now, with time to spare, she returned to her first love, sculpting. Arrie Ella Elgar Bird Dumont became famous in Texas during the early 20th century for her carvings from the locally available gypsum rock, and finally, in 1928, she wrote her autobiography detailing a succession of "nests" of a type the West will never see again.

Author's note: Ella died and was buried in Paducah in 1943, and, unfortunately, most of her work was either lost, stolen, or disintegrated because of the nature of the "gyprock" she used as her carving medium. Her diary and editorial entries are archived in the Barker Collection in Austin.

1870—Taking Care of "Mama's Children"

As I have told you before, the difference between being a child and an adult has little to do with age but has a lot to do with the willingness and the ability to accept adult responsibility. That is the way it has been in the past, and that is the way it will always be. There are some very young "adults" in our society, but there are even more old "children" who never think of anyone but themselves, refusing to accept any responsibility for anything.

Noah McCuistion was born on May 13, 1857, on a frontier farm in Coryell County. At birth, he had an older brother, John, who was four, and a sister, Mary Jane, who was two. Joshua McCuistion, his father, was a full-bearded, handsome Scot who read the classics and often quoted Robert Burns when he was not busy building his frontier farm. The mother was a feisty Irish lass named Mary Elizabeth O'Neal who was the first graduate of the old Baylor Female College down in Independence, in Washington County. So far, things had worked out well. Then, after another two years, James was born pre-maturely, and the laughing Mary Elizabeth died, leaving Joshua alone to care for three young children and an infant. Of course, there was some help from neighbors. Such situations were far from rare on a frontier where cemeteries were filled with young women who had died in childbirth. Joshua did what he could, but Mary Jane took over the care of Baby Jim and the house. She was four.

Then came the Civil War. Many of those counties along the Red River and in Central Texas voted against secession. Most of the folks there were small independent farmers who didn't like the competition from the big landowners who had slaves to produce their crops. Most folks called them "Free Soilers" but seldom understood that they didn't really oppose slavery—they just didn't want to compete with it economically in their own neighborhood. In any event, not every able-bodied man "rushed to the colors" (enlisted). With his young family to think of, Joshua remained at home.

However, when Confederate troops came through the area drafting men for the army, they picked up Joshua and took him along whether he wanted to go or not. Ten other local men who resisted and said that it wasn't their fight were hanged one night. So, Joshua rode off to war, and "Mama's Children" were left to fend for themselves.

A rule of the universe seems to be "adapt, and survive." "Mama's Children" adapted to the change as was necessary. By this time, Mary Jane was a mature six, and she took over the house. John, at eight, was the oldest, but showed little inclination to do more than sit around and wait to be told what to do. At four, as incredible as it may seem, Noah became the man of the house and did what he could to work the garden and to care for the stock. When their grandfather died, a share of his estate went to Noah, not to the older brother John. At the ripe old age of four, Noah McCuistion invested that money and became a cattle rancher. But, cattle alone, in a land where there were many of them, would not pay the bills. Noah made his first stake when he sold a matched pair of geldings he had raised from foals for $5oo in gold coin.

At best, life on the Texas frontier during the Civil War was harsh and dangerous. Historians agree that the advance of the frontier was pushed back about one hundred miles as the Comanche and other tribes took advantage of the abandonment of most of the military forts. The "Home Guards" who were left to protect the farms and ranches were few in number, often poorly equipped, and, more often, poorly led. Although some were "good men, and true," many were draft dodgers or deserters. From San Antonio to the Red River, homesteads went up in flames. Those who survived Indian attentions were often preyed upon by renegade bands of "Jayhawkers" of mixed background who were frequently more destructive than the Indians. Throughout it all, "Mama's Children" refused to leave the home they were making for themselves. Mary Jane grew into her early teens, and Noah grew in accomplishment, although never much in size. For all of his life, he remained small by frontier standards.

Joshua survived the Civil War and came home to find a strange situation. His oldest son still sat around waiting to be told what to do. Mary Jane was an accomplished homemaker and mother to her youngest brother. Noah tended the farm and to an increasing herd of cattle. It was almost as if a very young couple had taken over the homestead and didn't appreciate interference. No doubt modern social agencies would have a hemorrhage, but Joshua didn't interfere. He remarried and had eight more children,

illustration by Gary Manthei

but built another farm nearby and helped out only when necessary. He was proud that both families prospered, and, when they moved, they moved together—first to Limestone County and then up to Bosque County.

Mary Jane went to school—but not Noah. When she came home each day, Mary Jane taught Noah what she had learned while she prepared their evening meal. Noah farmed and tended the cattle and helped his father build his new farm. John, unwilling to be more than a child, apparently drifted between the two growing families and finally disappeared from the picture.

As time passed, the frontier again moved westward and the family split. Mary Jane got married after brother John moved away. Father Joshua wanted to go to Mexico with his new family and did; and, in 1878, at age 21, Noah McCuistion drove his first herd of cattle to the Panhandle.

Noah's whole crew was made up of young men, boys he knew who grew up in the neighborhood. Will and Lige Wallace went along with Will Hazlewood and "Dusty" Rhoades. Young Jack Haley drove the wagon and did the cooking. They were all young, unattached, full of vinegar, and looking for "The American Dream." They settled in Roberts County and put down roots. But there were other horizons. During the drought and then the killing "Big Die-Up" blizzard of 1886, they added Cleve Coffee to their number and headed for New Mexico and the Datil Mountains. Along the way, Noah borrowed $2,000 for the first year's operations. Things looked good. In the protected basins of the Datil Mountains, they escaped "the big die-up" that cleared the Central Plains of cattle that year; but, in 1888, they lost everything to another severe winter. That, coupled with the New Mexico range wars, made Montana look pretty good, so they tried it there.

Montana was a qualified success. The young men got along well with the Indians, kept clear of trouble, raised a good herd of stock based on cold-tolerant breeds from Europe, and, when the railroad arrived, sold out at a good profit. Noah shipped his best breeding stock back to Texas by rail and came home to Roberts County. By 1897, Noah McCuistion had raised cattle for 36 of his 40 years.

Noah and Mary Jane kept in touch throughout all of this. He once told his sister that they had never been children. They had both been babies, and then they had become adults, who, in taking care of themselves, took care of "Mama's Children." Maybe because of this, Noah loved all children. In Roberts County and the town of Miami, children all called him "Uncle Noah" and flocked around him. He was a small man himself, handsome and with a twinkling eye, but he never laughed out loud. If a kid needed shoes, he got them. If pants had way too many holes for comfort or decency, there was a new pair. There were always nickels and dimes for the candy counter at the store. You might say that "Uncle Noah" adopted a whole generation of children as his own. At the turn of the 20th century, he was not only one of the largest landowners in Roberts and Hemphill counties, he was also the richest in love and respect. He was only doing what came naturally, taking care of "Mama's Children" and raising cattle, like he'd done all of his life.

Noah married Elizabeth Jordan in 1903, when he was 46, and, finally, started his own family. But his other "children" didn't forget him. On Halloween, in 1908, when every outhouse in the town of Miami was tipped over and all of the stock in the railroad pens released to roam the streets, "Uncle Noah's" cattle were found, miraculously loaded in the cars on the siding, ready for the 4 a.m. freight that carried them to market.

1870—"Wild Bill" Longley

Legend has a way of making heroes out of men who are poor choices for the honor. In this way a horse thief, gambler, bunco artist, and crooked cop who was fired for pocketing the fines of prostitutes, became Wyatt Earp, "brave, courageous, and bold," and a habitual drunk who took part in several lynchings and liked to decapitate his victims, became known as Clay Allison, "the gentleman gunfighter." So, it is not too surprising that "Wild Bill" Longley, often called "The Tall Texan," is a hero to some, when, in reality, he wasn't a particularly likable or heroic chap.

William Preston "Wild Bill" Longley
by Suzy Keller

William Preston Longley was born October 16, 1851, along Mill Creek in Austin County, and, with his family, moved to the little town of Evergreen when he was two years old. The frontier was rough and so was growing up, especially when most of the men joined the Confederate Army during the Civil War. Little William had a mind of his own and earned the name of "Wild Bill" at an early age. With most of the men of the community away at war, many boys assumed the responsibilities of running the farms and ranches. Not William. Later, he wrote, *"My first step was disobedience, next whisky-drinking, next carrying pistols, next gambling, and then murder, and I suppose next will be the gallows."*

Wild Bill killed his first man, a black soldier in the Union Army of Occupation, in 1867, when he was 15. They met a few miles from home on the old *El Camino Real*. The soldier was riding a horse and Bill was afoot. There was an argument about right-of-way, and the soldier took a shot at Bill with his rifle. Bill dropped him with a bullet to the head and buried the body in a nearby ditch.

Shortly thereafter, within the same year, Bill and a friend lost heavily on the horse races down in Lexington. They were poor losers. That night they shot up a black street dance, leaving two men dead and several wounded.

Things rocked along pretty calmly for about a year. Then, in December of 1868, Bill took it upon himself to rid the county of three more black men who had *"been causing trouble."* He tracked them to their camp about three miles from Evergreen. In the confusion, two of them managed to escape, but one more stayed in camp with a bullet through his head.

Enough was enough. The local attitude being somewhat chilly, Bill decided to move south and wound up in Karnes County in 1869, working as a cowboy for cattleman John Reagan. The Taylor-Sutton Feud was running hot in that area, and, one day, when Bill rode into Yorktown, he was mistakenly identified as Charles Taylor. Local Union troops had orders to arrest Charles Taylor, so a sergeant and several others made the mistake of trying to arrest Bill. Bill escaped, and the sergeant died for his mistake. Bill was on the run, in the company of a horse thief named Tom Johnson, when they were caught by Union sympathizers and lynched. Johnson died, but Wild Bill was indeed a "tall Texan"—his feet touched the ground. Friends cut him down before he expired, and, for a while, he rode with Cullen Baker's gang until Baker was killed in 1869.

Thinking that another change of climate might do him some good, Bill went along on a trail drive to Kansas to get out of Texas. But poor old Bill (by now an old man of 18) just couldn't seem to get along. Halfway to Kansas and deep in the Indian Nation, Bill had a disagreement with the trail boss over whether he should stand a night watch, and so he shot him, not once, but five times. Apparently, the trail boss was Bill's first white victim. With a score of at least six, Bill drifted on to Kansas. In 1870, in Leavenworth, he killed another soldier in a barroom fight and wound up in jail. That didn't last long either. He bribed the guard and headed for Wyoming, where they didn't know him.

In Wyoming, Bill went to work for the Army as a teamster and formed a business partnership with the post quartermaster to sell stolen army stock at a profit. When his partner confronted him with the fact that Bill was skimming more than his share of the illegal proceeds, Bill killed him and ended up in jail again. This time he was sentenced to 30 years in prison, but he made another escape.

Killing followed killing in regular order. In 1872, it was a young gambler in Parkersville, Kansas. In 1874, he killed a black man who had allegedly insulted a white woman in Comanche County, Texas. In 1875, in Bastrop County, an old boyhood friend killed Bill's cousin, so Bill killed him with a shotgun. Then there was a Bell County hardcase called Bill Scrier, whom Bill filled with 13 bullets. In 1876, near the town of Ben Franklin in Delta County, he added a preacher named Lay to his tally of murder.

With at least 13 killings to his name, and, at the age of 25, Wild Bill retired from outlawry to farming near Keatchie in Louisiana. It was there that two Texas lawmen found him and brought him back to stand trial at Giddings for killing his boyhood chum. Wild Bill complained to the governor. It wasn't fair, he said, to hang him. After all, many of the people he killed were black, and even world-champion desperado John Wesley Hardin had only been sent to the penitentiary at Huntsville.

Five days short of his 27th birthday, Wild Bill Longley was hanged in Giddings. On the first try, his legs still touched the ground. The townspeople and the lawmen wanted to make sure that he didn't escape as he had so many times before, so they shortened the rope and dropped him again. That time, the Tall Texan finally passed to his well-deserved reward.

1871—A Buggy to Kansas

The men and boys who pointed the big herds up the trails from Texas to the Kansas railheads wrote a never-to-be-forgotten chapter in American history. Historians estimate that over 10 million cattle followed those dusty trails between 1867 and 1886. There are no exact figures because folks rarely kept track of such things, but from accounts of the old trail drivers, it usually took about ten men, including the cook and horse wrangler, for every 1,000 cattle. That would mean that one hundred thousand men made the same trip. I don't think I've ever seen that estimate in print. Of course, many men made the same trip many times. Some made as many as 15 trips.

Trail drives could not start in the spring until there was enough new grass to feed the moving herds. Starting as early as April down along the Rio Grande, the herds moved north slowly, chasing the spring. Herds rarely averaged over ten miles each day. To move faster meant that the cattle would lose weight rather than gain it on the trip. Each trip lasted from four to eight or more months, depending on where it began and ended, the weather, stampedes, flooded river crossings, irate farmers and "herd cutters," prairie fires, and, in the fall, snow. Estimates indicate that about 40% of those who herded the cattle were Anglo-Celtic-American, 30% were Hispanic, 25% were African-Americans, and the remaining 5% were a mixture that included Native-Americans and Chinese. The average age of these men was about 20. Today, no one can either prove or disprove

Amanda Burks (in center of rowboat) and others at La Mota Ranch, La Salle County, Texas
courtesy UTSA's Institute of Texan Cultures at San Antonio (Virginia Sturges)

these figures, but they are interesting to think about. Put them all together and the result is a massive amount of human endeavor.

With so much else to remember we sometimes forget that many women followed these same trails and also shared in the cattle drives.

W. F. Burks and his wife Amanda ranched near Banquete in that disputed land below the Nueces River. Back during the 1830s, Mexican businessmen from Matamoros staged a week-long welcoming party for newly-arrived Irish immigrants on the edge of this prairie, and the name *"banquete,"* banquet in Spanish, immortalized the site as an early approach to racial harmony. But, by 1871, things had changed. Mexican "bandits," Unionist "scalawags," Yankee "carpet-baggers," assorted desperados, unreconstructed Confederates, deserters from the armies of both North and South, and the remnants of Emperor Maximilian's Army made every new sunrise seen by law-abiding folks a victory. They called this area between the Nueces and the Rio Grande the "Nueces Strip," and much of it is still pretty wild today. There wasn't much money, but the mesquite thickets were full of old mossy-horned cattle that were even wilder than the men who hunted them.

When the Burks made their decision to take a herd of cattle north, the hazards along the way seemed less formidable to Amanda than staying at home by herself. They trail-branded 1,000 mixed cattle on Penitas Creek, near today's Lake Corpus Christi, in April; and, with ten herders, a cook, and a helper, they hit the trail. Amanda drove a buggy with the herd.

They passed through the sprawling Miller Ranch and crossed the Nueces River near Lagarto. Near Beeville, they had their first stampede. Then they moved north past Helena and Gonzales and on to Lockhart, where, in hope of adding to their own stock, local German farmers stampeded the herd; 30 head were lost and never recovered. They kept Pilot Knob on their left and passed between Austin and Elgin. Spring in Central Texas brought good grass for the slow-moving herd, but it also provided a steady succession of hailstorms with thunder, lightning, and more stampedes.

Passing through Ellis County, Amanda stopped to talk with the first woman she had seen in over a month. The woman said, *"Yes, I'm the first woman that made a track through Dallas County, and I would be back in Tennessee now, only I would have to go through Arkansas to get there. I guess I'll stay right here."* Amanda and her buggy rolled on.

At the Trinity River, there were 15 herds waiting for floodwaters to fall before crossing. Local farmers again stampeded them in hopes of catching strays, and it took weeks to separate the mixed herds. After crossing the Red River into Oklahoma, they lost most of their food and camping supplies, including Amanda's only comb, in a prairie fire set by the Indians to scatter the herd. In all, they endured six more prairie fires without additional loss.

But, in southern Kansas, they lost most of their horses in the year's first blizzard, and the cold was so severe that many of the cattle lost their horns. They also lost their cook after he had a fight with one of the drovers—but the end was in sight. Near Ellsworth, Kansas, they found a buyer. The price wasn't quite as good as they hoped, but it was enough. After paying off the hands and selling the buggy, chuck wagon, and horses, they were able to return home in style—by rail through Missouri, and down to New Orleans, and then by steamboat to Corpus Christi by way of Galveston and Indianola. That round trip took nine months, and Amanda returned home with better health than she had before they left. Friends made a great to-do about her hardships, but her response was, *"What woman, youthful and full of spirit and the love of living, needs sympathy because of availing herself of the opportunity of being with her husband while at his chosen work in the great out-of-door world?"*

1873—A Matter of Semantics

During the last quarter of the 19th century, the American West was much in the minds of European investors. The West offered opportunities in mining, ranching, railroads, and the land development associated with all of these. Most folks don't realize that many of the really big ranches in Texas were owned by European investors. Sometimes, potential investors actually came to look over the situation.

Today, one of the most popular styles of cowboy boots is what is called the "roper." It has a short top, a low heel, and a round toe. A lot of folks think it is traditional; it is, in a way. English gentry, arriving in Texas to look over their investments, found that the Wellington cavalry boot, a mark of distinction back in England, was too hot for normal wear with riding britches. So they had local saddle shops cut them in half, making "Half-Wellingtons," and thus the "roper" style was born. In the late 19th century this style made a fashion statement. Half-Wellington boots said, "I no longer must work for a living and may sit on the porch while I watch others work for me." Any range-riding cowboy who tried to wear a pair would be hooted out of camp. Today we call them "ropers," and the meaning of the name has changed.

A study of words and their meanings is called "semantics." Sometimes, we get confused.

Semantics deals with the meanings of words. That's why many misunderstandings are semantic in origin and begin when people get tangled up in the use of words that sound similar but have different meanings. Now I'm not going to say that there were any arguments, but there were certainly opportunities for misunderstanding when Lady Leah Cahar arrived from Scotland at the end-of-track of the Galveston, Harrisburg, and San Antonio Railroad in 1874. You see, Lady Leah called herself a "sportswoman."

Central Texas in 1874 was not totally unsophisticated. Mixed in with small farmers from the Old South, recent non-English-speaking immigrants from Central Europe, old time ranchers who had fought in the Texas Revolution, and Yankee carpetbaggers, were professionals of all descriptions who had studied at Yale and Harvard, at the Sorbonne, and in Vienna, and who had traveled much of the known world. A little knowledge is a dangerous thing. These gentlemen may never have heard of a Scottish "sportswoman," but a "sporting lady" was a different matter. Sporting ladies were the well-known inhabitants of the "sporting houses" that flourished in all big cities and many rural areas. New Orleans and St. Louis and even Houston and San Antonio were well known for the quality of their sporting houses and their sporting ladies who dispensed their favors for a price. Less discriminating cowboys, fresh off the trail, cavorted with the likes of Big Nose Kate and Buffalo Annie. Yes, sporting ladies were a well-known fact of life, but a "sportswoman"? Well, it sort of sounded like the same thing.

Lady Leah Cahar
by Suzy Keller

Before the Civil War, the railroad pushed its way from Houston to Alleyton on the east bank of the Colorado River. There the war stopped it, and, after the war, there was a lack of capital to get it started again. But, Texans realized that to develop the state, there must be a dependable and reasonably priced system of transportation. That meant railroads. With public land to spare, the state granted over 32 million acres to railroad companies over a 20-year period as an inducement to get them to build. The necessary investment came from all over the world, and special trains brought the investors to "the frontier" to see how their money was being used. That brings us back to our story, and the day in 1874 when Lady Leah Cahar arrived in Caldwell County.

Lady Leah, who called herself a "sportswoman," was from Scotland. She had invested her money and wanted to inspect the results and view the Wild West. In this case, the Wild West had a rather exciting view of Lady Leah. She was preceded from the train by her footman, who was appropriately dressed in knee britches with silver buckles, white silk stockings, black slippers with more silver buckles, a white shirt with ruffles at wrist and throat, a tight short coat, and hair tied "in a club" at the base of his neck. If this apparition were not enough to startle folks at the station, what next emerged set them back on their heels or running for a better look. Lady Leah was a strikingly attractive woman, and she was dressed for dinner at the hotel in a silk gown with a long train, high-piled hair, and a décolleté neckline that bared the shoulders and much more of Lady Leah's bosom than Central Texas was used to seeing. With her footman keeping her skirt from the mud, she progressed to the hotel like a clipper ship through a sea of fishing scows. Two local doctors soon replaced the footman and taught her that, in Texas, the escort carried a lady's train with her hand on his left arm. In all, it must have been an exciting spectacle, diminished only slightly when they found that, in Scotland, a "sportswoman" rode to hounds in fox hunts, angled for trout, danced beautifully, and played rousing games of golf and tennis.

In any event, Lady Leah captured the hearts of the entire area, and on September 10, 1874, at high noon, at a point midway between 5th and 6th Avenues, Lady Leah Cahar, a visiting dignitary, with hammer in hand and a stroke perfected on the tennis court, drove a silver spike in the railroad and proclaimed, *"This is the center of this town I name Luling."*

1874—Billy and the Buffalo Wallow

During the winter of 1874, the lovely Miss Mary Outerbridge, while escaping from the winter of her native Northeast, vacationed in the balmy climes of Bermuda. As were many society belles of the day, she was bored. She had already visited the first American zoo, established that same year in Philadelphia, and was, of course, thrilled by the assorted animals on display. But, watching animals, even strange ones, did not satisfy her need for action and excitement. Then, as an invited guest, she witnessed a competition between several British Army officers in which, suitably attired of course, they pursued a bouncing white ball across the lawn and swatted it over something like a fish net using a strange paddle that looked like the footwear of Arctic explorers. When she returned to her home, Miss Mary's search for excitement in Bermuda ultimately introduced the game of tennis to the United States.

She should have been with Billy Dixon that year. If she had been, who knows what games we might play today?

If you remember anything about Billy Dixon, you probably remember that fantastic shot that he made with his Sharps "Big 50" buffalo rifle on the third day of the fight at Adobe Walls in 1874. They measured it afterward—1,583 yards from the back of Hanrahan's Saloon to the spot on the hill where Billy's bullet knocked the Comanche warrior from his horse. It's quite a story, but that's not what this story is about. This is about what happened to Billy next.

William "Billy" Dixon was born in 1850, and in the spring of 1874, he was making good money as a buffalo hunter up in the Texas Panhandle. On June 27, he and 27 other men and one woman were attacked at the old trading post of Adobe Walls up in the northeast corner of today's Hutchinson County. About 700 Indians from the Comanche, Cheyenne, and Ki-

Dixon's Desperate Fight
by Gary Manthei

owa tribes combined forces for the first time to push the buffalo hunters from the plains. It was an unpleasant few days, and, after his long shot and the Indians left, Billy decided to give up buffalo hunting in favor of a safer and more regular occupation. He applied for, and got, the coveted job as a scout for the U. S. Army under Colonel Nelson A. Miles. Billy thought that meant easy duty and three square meals a day. Not quite.

As a result of the attack at Adobe Walls, the Army abandoned its policy of peaceful negotiation and mounted an all-out effort to clear the Indians from the Panhandle. They called it the Red River War, and it pitted the allied Indian forces of Quanah Parker, Black Horse, Buffalo Hump, and Mow Way of the Comanche; Stone Calf and Little Bear of the Cheyenne; Lone Wolf and Satanta of the Kiowa, and others, against the troops of General W. T. Sherman, General Phil Sheridan, Colonel Nelson Miles, Colonel Ranald Mackenzie, and the rest of the Army. Billy's "safer occupation" put him right in the middle of the action.

Dawn of September 12, 1874—less than three months after his long shot—found Billy, another scout named Amos Chapman, and four enlisted men, including Sgt. Woodall and Pvts. Roth, Harrington, and Smith, in the middle of what is now Hemphill County, looking for a wagon train loaded with supplies. They didn't know that the supply train was, even at that moment, under attack about ten miles away.

Suddenly, they were surrounded by about 125 Indians and saw no place to hide. Within a few minutes every man of the detail was wounded, and they found themselves near a buffalo wallow, a small depression in the otherwise flat plains.

The buffalo, or more accurately, the bison, were not immune to infestations of ticks. In order to rid themselves of the little rascals, and scratch at the same time, they liked to roll in the dirt. Once such a "wallow" was established, it usually grew larger as subsequent sufferers rolled away their unwanted visitors.

This wallow was about ten feet wide and only a foot or so deep, but it was all the cover the scouts could find. All but Smith and Chapman made it to the hole. As one man fired to keep the Indians at a distance, the others dug deeper with their knives and hands. The air was strangely still and oppressive. It was hot and dry, and they baked in the depression without water. Soon, ammunition ran low, and the loss of blood and the heat made every man weak.

Then came the "blue norther," with lightning and rain that turned to sleet and snow and filled their refuge with muddy—and bloody—water. Billy and Pvt. Roth dragged Smith into the hole with them, and then made windbreaks of tumbleweeds to provide some shelter from the wind. In the morning, no Indians were in sight, so Billy took off on foot to find help.

A few miles away he ran into four companies of the Eighth Cavalry and thought his troubles were over. Major William A. Price, with his 255 men from Fort Union, New Mexico, looked at the wounded men in the mud hole, decided they needed more help than he had to offer, and left them there without even a horse. Price later explained that he was in need of rations for his men and couldn't be detained. It was midnight before Billy could find another troop and lead them to his comrades. With the exception of Smith, who was buried in the wallow, all the others survived.

On Colonel Miles' recommendation, all six men who fought in the buffalo wallow received the Medal of Honor authorized by Congress for *"skill, courage, and determined fortitude"* in the face of the enemy. It is the only time in history when all participants in a particular battle were so honored.

A few years later, Congress changed its mind. According to the bureaucrats, Billy Dixon and Amos Chapman were only "employees" of the Army and not real soldiers. They were not entitled to such a decoration. Congress wanted the medals back. We don't know exactly what Billy thought about that, but he kept his medal, and it hangs today in the Panhandle Plains Historical Museum in Canyon.

1875—Sarah Did Dallas

Written history is almost always selective. The ethnic group, gender, religion, or any other social category that writes the book usually gets credit for the good things, while others are rarely mentioned. Or, if they are, they receive negative comment. Editors who try to even-out the reporting usually catch the discontent from all sides. Unbiased reporting is hard to come by. A lot depends on the reader's willingness to accept new ideas. For instance, I always thought that the person who built Dallas was John Neely Bryan. That's what most of the books and Chamber of Commerce handouts say. And, after all, there's that cabin of his in the park downtown.

John Neely Bryan did, indeed, begin what is today the city of Dallas. He was born in Fayetteville, Tennessee, in 1810, and, after a varied life as a farmer, Indian trader, and lawyer, came to Texas in 1839. After exploring the western lands of the Caddo in 1840, he claimed a head right in what was known as the Peters Colony, and built a cabin on the Trinity River near today's Dallas Courthouse Square in 1841. Apparently, he had plans for a community from the beginning, and the name "Dallas" was there before

Sarah Cockrell
by Suzy Keller

any other settlers, although no one knows for sure just which of the dozen or so claimants of the name was honored. All he is reported to have said is, *"I'll name it for my old friend Dallas."*

Bryan married Margaret Beeman, the daughter of a new settler, in 1843, and, by 1844, the booming metropolis had two cabins and a population of ten, or twelve, if you went far enough out in the country. Bryan's cabin became the first post office, and, when Dallas County was formed in 1846, the first courthouse. For a while, Bryan gave a city lot as a wedding present to every newly married couple, and the town began to grow. In 1849, James Latimer started a newspaper called the *Dallas Herald*, and, by 1851, there was a total urban population of 163 people, including 37 slaves. But, you see, such big city life was boring to a pioneer like Bryan, so he went to the gold fields in California with the 49ers. In 1852 he sold his town, all of it, lock, stock, and barrel, to Alexander Cockrell who already owned an adjacent 640 acres.

Now, Alexander Cockrell was a builder, but he could neither read nor write, and it was his wife, Sarah, who organized things, kept the books, wrote the records, attracted new colonists, and, generally, "did for" the town. While Alex made the bricks, Sarah built the first hotel, a three-story affair, and began to entertain everyone moving west. Alex built the first wooden bridge over the Trinity River, but it washed away, and Sarah operated a ferry when the water was high. Then, in 1858, Alexander Cockrell was killed in a fight over a bad debt, and Sarah, a widow with four children, became the proprietor of Dallas in name, as well as in deed. She could have sold out and gone back to the East. She could have done nothing but complain about how bad her luck was and how the government should take care of widows and orphans. Instead, she went to work.

When most of the town burned in 1860, folks rebuilt it with bricks from Sarah Cockrell's Brick Yard. Throughout the Civil War, it was Sarah who kept Dallas growing, and, in the boom years to follow, she leased land but didn't sell it. She formed her own corporation and built an iron toll bridge over the Trinity River to replace her ferry. In 1872, there was a resident population of 1,200, but the transient population was larger. There were banks and buyers of buffalo hides from the Panhandle. The Houston and Texas Central Railroad arrived that year, and it was old John Neely Bryan, back from California and the war and full of speeches, who greeted it; but his stake in the operation was small. That same year, Sarah bought a one-third interest in the first flourmill in the area. The Texas and Pacific Railroad arrived in 1873, and 725 buildings popped up on land mostly owned by, you guessed it, Sarah. Income from the hotel alone would have kept Sarah in the forefront of developers. But, with the bridge, the brick factory, the flourmill (which by 1877 was grossing $3 million a year), and her other varied ventures, Sarah Cockrell was easily the richest person in the county, if not in North Texas.

The only picture I've seen of Sarah shows a small woman wearing a plain dark dress; she has a rather sad, but not severe, expression on her face. Maybe, for someone who had carved a city from the wilderness, she longed for a simpler way of life. By 1900, the population of Dallas was over 40,000. The first Dallas City Directory listed Sarah's occupation as "*Capitalist.*" When she died, she owned fully one-fourth of the downtown business district and hundreds of acres of development in the suburbs. Her will was so complex that it was printed in book form. Not bad for a little lady who once poled a ferry across the river.

I don't care who writes the story. They should give Sarah the credit for "doing" Dallas.

1875—The "Bride" of Company D

In 1875, the states of Bosnia and Herzegovina were involved in a bloody civil war within the Turkish Empire. In London, entrepreneurs opened the first roller-skating rink, and, in the United States, an ex-riverboat pilot named Samuel Clemens wrote The Adventures of Huckleberry Finn. *Meanwhile, in Texas, "Redeemer Democrats" had ousted the "Reconstruction" Texas State Police and reinstated the Texas Rangers as a force for both internal and external protection.*

When Luvenia Conway married Captain Daniel Webster Roberts of Company D, Texas Rangers, they had to hold the train. You see, it was 1875, and there was only one train a day headed west through Columbus down in Colorado County. The preacher, the Reverend Dr. Archer, came in on the train, there was a ceremony on the platform, and, as the Columbus Times reported, *"The gallant groom and his accomplished bride departed on the train immediately after the ceremony."*

It might not have happened that way if it had not been for the value the State of Texas placed on Roberts' service, the understanding wit of a commanding officer, and the courage of a girl who had no experience with the "wild frontier."

Luvenia Roberts and the
Company D Rangers
by Suzy Keller

Luvenia was living in Columbus when Ranger Dan Roberts came to town. It seems that there was just a mite of a question about the ownership of some cattle that had made their way into West Texas. When that problem was solved, the Ranger stayed around a while because he'd decided that Luvenia was more interesting than chasing the bad guys. In any event, when he went back to his company out in Menard, it was with the intention of resigning and coming "back East" to live.

His commanding officer saw things in a different light. Major John B. Jones of the Texas Ranger Frontier Battalion realized that when the heart was involved, the brain often ceased to function. He wasn't about to lose one of his best men just because Cupid's arrow had found its mark. Instead of accepting the resignation, the major promoted Roberts to the command of his company and told him to bring his bride with him. Of course, they both forgot to consult with the bride-to-be.

The honeymoon was short. After picking up a Ranger escort in Austin they moved west—right into the middle of the Mason County War. We don't hear too much about the Mason County War today. It was not only a very brutal affair that left memories which are still too near the surface, but also it was an ethnic war of extermination as severe as what was going on in Bosnia at the time. In general, the "war" pitted Anglo-American ranchers from the "Deep South" against German farmers fresh from Europe. There were barn-burnings, stock-killings, and lynchings, as well as assorted individual murders and organized mayhem.

At first, Ranger Roberts thought it safest for Luvenia to stay with friends in the town of Mason, while the new captain and his company went about the business of calming things down. At the first lodging she tried, two men waving guns rode up to her window right after there was a shooting in the street. That didn't seem too safe, so she moved to a home that was set well back from the street and was surrounded by a fence. There, twenty more gun-wavers with torches came through the garden, looking for a man that they wanted to hang.

That did it! Luvenia put her foot down. She wasn't going to live in a dangerous place like that any longer. She packed up, bag and baggage, and moved—into a tent at the Ranger camp. That beat a stuffy old town any day.

She wrote, *"The camp was located in a fine pecan grove on the river about two miles below Menard. I wish I could describe the country as it was at that time. Beautiful nature had not been marred by the hand of man. It was thrilling."*

Luvenia became the "bride of the company." The Rangers took turns taking her riding, hunting, fishing, or to visit military wives at Fort McKavett. She was embarrassed to be with Company D and not be armed, so they bought her a new Remington rifle, with which she became as proficient as any man in the camp. The Rangers kept her supplied with a variety of pets. There were squirrels, prairie dogs, a hound dog, a canary—and a bear. The bear cub was okay when he was little, but became a real grouch as he got older.

Drinking and card playing were not allowed in camp, but there were horse races and evenings of music when the Rangers would bring out their instruments to play and sing. The croquet set got a good workout every Sunday. In all, being the "bride" of Company D wasn't all that bad. Although the Austin Daily Statesman reported that she suffered the hardships of a frontier life, Luvenia lived happily in that tent for six years.

The Austin Daily Statesman reported, *"Mrs. Roberts is a lady of culture and refinement, and for six years she was in camp with Captain Roberts and his company on the extreme frontier, suffering the hardships of a frontier life and braving the dangers of Indian warfare. Her womanly graces and indomitable courage were the admiration of the entire force of Rangers, and Company D, commanded by her husband, idolized her."*

1875—The Kid With the Butcher Knife

The vast majority of parents have the best interests of their children at heart. Unfortunately, what parents consider to be in the best interest doesn't always agree with what the children want to do. It's almost like an endemic disease. Once children reach about ten years of age, it becomes obvious to them that their parents are about as obsolete as the old "Dick and Jane" readers. Some recover quickly, and, by about age 16, are almost human. Others never seem to recover.

Parents don't always know *what is best for a particular child. Coming from a different generation, they have different perspectives. Sometimes the contrary opinions of the child work to his or her advantage.*

Charles L. "Charlie" Nevill was born near Tuscaloosa in Hale County, Alabama, in 1855. While he was still holding on to the tablecloth to toddle around the table, his family moved to Texas, and by 1858, they were located in Fayette County. Then came the Civil War, and Charlie's dad, Z.L. Nevill, went off to fight with Terry's Texas Rangers, where he watched both his brother and brother-in-law die in battle. When he returned home, he found that his wife, Anne, had died in 1864. After that, it was just father and son to carry on. Understandably, Z.L. Nevill had no use for war, and so worked the rest of his life to build a farm to leave to Charlie.

Charlie, however, had other ideas. You see, Charlie didn't remember the war the way his father did, and the idea of following the hind end of a mule around a field for the rest of his life didn't fit with his world view, which, in the 1870s, was filled with cattle drives, railroads, Indian wars, and the growth of a nation. Charlie wanted some action.

So, he decided to join the Texas Rangers. Now, in those days, to join the Rangers you had to provide your own horse, your own weapons, and your own clothes. Charlie had clothes. Of course, they weren't "Ranger" clothes and were better suited to sod busting than to chasing the bad guys, but they covered his body in the necessary places. However, he had no horse, no gun, no boots—and no permission from his father. Daddy Nevill had seen the effects of war and didn't want his son involved with violence in any way. To Dad, the equation read, *"No horse plus no gun equals no Ranger."* He didn't count on Charlie being just as stubborn as he was.

At eighteen, Charlie drew a line in the sand for himself, crossed it, ran away from father, home, and mule, and presented himself for service with Company D, Texas Rangers, wearing only ragged overalls, bare-footed, and carrying a butcher knife from Daddy Nevill's smoke house. "Progressive" authorities today would lock him up because, obviously, he had violent tendencies. For his own good (and to protect society) they would put him away in a place where he would *really* learn not only violence but also contempt for authority.

Well, the Texas Rangers of the 1870s were not particularly concerned with spit and polish and education. They looked more for spirit and integrity than anything else. Call it what you will—*esprit, chutzpah, cajones,* or just plain guts. For a gangly, bare-footed farm kid, dressed in overalls and carrying nothing but a butcher knife, to show up to enlist on the frontier took more guts than facing down an Indian attack. They let him stay. Within a month, Charlie had a horse (on credit) and a pis-

Charlie Nevill
by Gary Manthei

203

tol (also on credit) and had changed his overalls for more appropriate (but still ragged) jeans. He even got himself a worn-out pair of boots. It was just the beginning. In five years, he was Captain of Company E, charged with the protection of the state treasury in Austin.

As rails moved west and more and more of the Trans-Pecos region became occupied by ranches, so did conflicts increase along the border. Presidio County is still a wild and relatively untamed area today, with a population of only about 6,000 people. In the 1880s it saw everything from the last Indian attacks to bandit raids and general all-around hard times. Captain Charlie and his company were transferred there, and, after his regular tour of duty with the Rangers was over, Charlie stayed on as the county sheriff for six years. During that time, Charlie turned thirty and married Sallie Crosson.

In 1889, Charlie and Sallie moved to San Antonio. That was where Sallie's home was, and it seemed to be a good place to rear the eight children that the couple produced. Charlie, the kid with the butcher knife, first became the Tax Collector for Bexar County, and then, for four years, was the chief deputy for Sheriff Tobin, the man who "wrote the book" for running frontier towns peacefully. In 1904, he was elected as Clerk of the Court, simultaneously, for districts 37, 45, and 57, and he served in that capacity until he died unexpectedly in 1906. He was only 51.

When you look at it one way, maybe Charlie's dad was right. Z.L. Nevill outlived his son. As a planter in Brazos County, he had eight grandchildren, but no son to leave with his estate. But, what about what Charlie wanted? According to one friend, *"Beyond all wealth, honor, or even health is the attachment we form with noble souls, because to become one with the good, generous, and true, is to become in a measure good, generous and true ourselves."* It was not a bad epitaph for a bare-footed kid who ran away from home with a butcher knife.

1876—Meet "Bet-A-Million" Gates

There are more "overachievers" in the world than we would like to admit. Most of them didn't start that way. Most of them rolled through at least a part of their lives like a ball in an old pin-ball machine—falling in some holes, ringing some bells, but eternally being swatted back to try it again. In his poem "The Men That Don't Fit In," Robert Service described some of these as:

> "They say: 'Could I find my proper groove,
> What a deep mark I would make!'
> So they chop and change, and each fresh move
> Is only a fresh mistake."

And yet, some do find that "proper groove," and our heritage and economy are the better for it.

There may have been some bigger and more colorful businessmen in history, but you've got to hunt for them. Although John W. Gates was born in 1855 in Northern Illinois, you might say that, from the beginning, he and Texas were made for each other, and we wouldn't be quite the same without him.

John W. Gates
by Suzy Keller

In the days when a young man was often apprenticed to learn a trade at ten or twelve years of age, John just didn't fit in, and it wasn't until he was nineteen that he finally landed a job with a fellow who was a friend of the husband of a woman who was distantly related to his mother. It's not that John wouldn't work, you understand—it's just that his ways were, well, unique. Most employers just didn't cotton to him. However hard it was for him to land that first real job, once he did, he never looked back.

You see, the fellow who hired him was unique also. They called him "Colonel Ike" Ellwood, and he had a strange new product to

205

sell, something called "barbed wire." And that is how John Gates came to be on the Military Plaza in San Antonio near the end of the year in 1876.

San Antonio in the 1870s was everything that the modern moviemakers would have us believe, and more. The city was old, older than Texas, and had been the crossroads of empire, a battleground, the seat of government, a bastion of the Church, and, then, the capital of a cattle empire. It was in the hotels and saloons and on the shaded plazas of Old San Antonio that the new "Lords of the Cattle Hoards" planned their campaigns to send millions of Texas cattle over the trails to railheads in Kansas. And, it was there that "Colonel Ike" sent John Gates to peddle a brand new invention.

Barbed wire was new. Even though a fellow named Grinninger, who lived in Austin, used a fence with barbs after the Civil War, barbed wire, as we know it today, wasn't patented until 1873 up in DeKalb County, Illinois. So, not only was barbed wire new in 1876, it was a "Yankee" thing, and no one thought it would work. Why, everybody knew that a Texas longhorn steer, if he had a mind to, could go through anything constructed by men.

So, John had an idea. He got permission from the city officials to build a corral on the Military Plaza between San Fernando Cathedral and the *Comandancia*, that we now call the Old Spanish Governor's Palace. The old San Antonio city hall is on that site now, but back then, it was an open block of land surrounded by trees. It was a good location. His work attracted a lot of attention and comment. The posts were too far apart. There were no planks in evidence to build the fence. *"What's that fool Yankee think he's doing, anyhow?"*

According to Chris Emmett, who wrote the biography of "Shanghai" Pierce, Gates then strung his wire and said:

> *"This is the finest fence in the world. Light as air. Stronger than whisky, cheaper than dirt, all steel, and miles long. The cattle ain't been born that can get through it. Bring on your steers, gentlemen!"*

Accounts vary. Some folks later reported that they put 25 longhorn steers in the pen and hazed them from horseback. Others said there were 60, and some said 135. Some say men hazed them with torches at night. Bets were made. Whether or not Gates actually bet a million dollars, the name caught and held. So did the fence. By nightfall "Bet-A-Million" Gates had sold hundreds of miles of barbed wire at the going rate of 18 cents a pound.

Barbed wire came to Texas, and "Bet-A-Million" Gates made a personal fortune, a name for himself, and a place in Texas history as the one who made the systematic management of cattle possible. If the story stopped there, we'd have more than enough for a legend—but it didn't.

John "Bet-A-Million" Gates became one of the shakers and movers of the "Gilded Age" industrial revolution. He followed his barbed wire success with years of "unique" salesmanship and business. To make barbed wire, he needed wire and barbs. He started buying wire mills, and then iron-ore deposits and coalmines, to make the steel for the wire. Then came shares of stock in the railroads to carry his products to markets. Today, the economists call that both vertical and horizontal integration. Back then it was simply called good business.

He wasn't always successful, but, at the start of the 20th century, he was again in the right place at the right time. His American Steel and Wire Company went with Andrew Carnegie into the combine that became the world's first billion-dollar corporation, United States Steel, and, being semi-retired, he had a few million dollars to invest. He had an interest in the Kansas City Southern Railroad, and, because he liked the fishing and duck hunting along the Texas Gulf Coast, started the process of building the city of Port Arthur at that line's southern terminus. Then, on January 10, 1901, Spindletop blew the lid off of the future of oil.

Spindletop is another story, but in the months that followed the discovery of what was then the largest oil field in the world, oil was available, and cheap, but you had to get it to market. Due to his location on both rail and water shipping routes and his available cash, "Bet-A-Million" Gates did it again, and provided operating capital and much-needed shipping facilities to the small Texas Fuel Company in exchange for a seat on its board of directors. They changed the company name, and TEXACO was born.

Cattle and oil are a big part of the Texas legacy. Where might we have been without "Bet-A-Million" Gates?

1877—Renty and the Texas Black Watch

Some time ago, I saw an advertisement for a performance of England's (or rather, Scotland's) famed Black Watch Regiment pipe and drum corps. They tour the United States occasionally, and, if you've never seen and heard them, you should. Not only are the pomp and circumstance of the performance and the music good, but also, for several hundred years, that outfit has been known for containing some of the world's best fighting men. They have quite a reputation.

Well, you might say that Texas also once had a Black Watch, and, although they didn't wear kilts and march to the stirring sounds of pipe and drum, they, too, were well known as fighting men. I'm not talking about the famed "Buffalo Soldiers" of the black 9th and 10th U.S. Cavalry regiments and the 24th and 25th U.S. Infantry regiments who, for more than thirty years, guarded the Texas frontier. I'm talking about the little band of Seminole Negro Scouts that led the way in battles throughout the American Southwest from the Mexican border to Palo Duro Canyon and beyond. That brings us to the story of Corporal Renty Grayson of the Texas Black Watch.

Renty was called a Seminole Negro. The term "Negro" is not popular today, but I use it here with respect because it was applied to a very special group of people. Many of the Seminole Indians, usually identified with the Southern Florida Everglades, originally lived in the area now known as Southern Alabama, Georgia, and North Florida. They were a branch of the *Muskhogean* tribe and one of the five "civilized" tribes of the Southeast. There were many tribes in the area, and most folks, including the government, lumped them all together and called them *Creeks*. When the Spanish left Florida in 1763, the remnants of the once-numerous

Corporal Renty Grayson of the Seminole Scouts
by Sam Woodfin

208

Timucua Indians went with them and left a virtual geographic vacuum. Seminoles and Creeks from Alabama soon filled this void. Their name in the Muskhogean dialect held the connotation of "emigrant" or "frontiersman" or "people who live at a distance." Among these Seminoles were escaped slaves from the southern plantations. They made their lives with the Seminoles, adopted their language and culture, and, by 1800, had become a separate but recognized part of the tribe.

When the U.S. Government had dealings with the Creeks, those dealings did not include the Seminoles, because they lived in Spanish territory. In 1821 Spanish West Florida officially became part of the United States, but, by that time, the *Seminoles* were recognized as a different group.

Then folks found gold on the Cherokee lands up around Dahlonega, Georgia, and this was followed by the Indian Removal Act of 1830, in which President Andrew Jackson required the removal of all Indian tribes in the East to points west of the Mississippi River. Although the Supreme Court said that the act was unconstitutional and illegal, it was enforced by the military, and those Seminoles who didn't flee to the Everglades were rounded up like cattle and herded to the West. Collectively, Indian groups from the Southeast refer to their removal as "The Trail of Tears." Some settled in Arkansas, Louisiana, and Oklahoma, and others moved into Texas. Here, they found more trouble.

You see, although they had considered themselves Seminoles for many generations, the Seminole Negroes were still black. Under the Texas law sponsored by Mirabeau B. Lamar, no free black person could live in the Republic without a special act passed in his or her name by the Congress, no matter what they called themselves. If you were black and you weren't protected by such an act, you were subject to enslavement.

Because of this persecution, in 1855 most of the Seminole Negroes gathered together and headed for Mexico, where chattel slavery was illegal. According to Lamar's standing orders regarding the status of unregistered free blacks, three companies of Texas Rangers, led by James Hughes Callahan, pursued them. The capture of such a large assortment of supposed "runaway slaves" and their subsequent sale would make a lot of money for those involved, so Callahan crossed the Rio Grande into Mexico on their trail. When they met resistance from Mexican authorities, Callahan's rangers contented themselves with looting and burning the town of *Piedras Negras* before returning to Texas.

The Seminole Negroes remained in Mexico and became well known as tough warriors. For generations they had been fighting for their existence. Just in order to survive, they had along the way learned several Indian dialects, along with English and Spanish. They were fierce fighters and could track a cockroach across a rocky desert. When everybody is your enemy, you learn to be tough or you die.

After the Civil War, about 150 of these Seminole Negroes drifted back across the Rio Grande down near Eagle Pass. There, they came to the attention of a young Army Lieutenant named John Lapham Bullis. Bullis was from New York, had served during the Civil War, and had earned the rank of captain in the 118th United States Infantry, Colored. Having served with black troops before, Bullis saw in the Seminole Negroes a unique resource and discussed them with his Colonel, Zenas Randall Bliss. On July 4, 1871, the entire Seminole Indian adult male population enlisted in the U.S. Army as mounted scouts. They were stationed at Fort Clark, and someone along the way started calling them the "Texas Black Watch."

Renty Grayson was there. He took the oath and put on the uniform, and, with the others, took his place at the head of the columns of black and white troops that fought bandits, the Apache, the Kiowa, and the Comanche. He never talked much about what he and the other scouts of his race did. For that, you'll have to read the after-action reports from skirmishes all over the West. Usually the white officers who wrote the reports simply called them the "Seminole Scouts," and you'll find that name in military records on up to the First World War.

On September 22, 1874, Renty Grayson was the scout for Troop A of the U.S. 4th Cavalry, serving up in the Panhandle. It was Renty who led Troop A to the Palo Duro Canyon battle that finally broke the power of the combined tribes of the southern Great Plains. But, somehow, his name wasn't on the published after-action muster roll. Some folks seem to get lost in the bureaucratic shuffle even today, and just because some over-worked company clerk didn't include his name, Renty Grayson, like the old soldier of the song, just faded away. As far as the Army was concerned, he ceased to exist.

But those men of A Troop of the 4th Cavalry, even though they were white, knew who had led them and knew he had survived. They didn't forget, and, for them, Renty did not fade away. Not only those who fought at the Palo Duro, but also succeeding generations of troopers remembered him. Remembering Renty's contribution became something of a tradition for the 4th Cavalry.

It is extremely hard for anyone in a position of power to admit to a mistake. It is much harder for a government. According to the Army, he was there when they started, and he was not there when they stopped, and that was the end of it.

The American frontier was officially closed in 1890. The government said that it no longer existed. Then came the Spanish American War, and participation in the Chinese "Boxer" Rebellion, and the Philippine Insurrection. There were skirmishes in Honduras and Guatemala, and "Black Jack" Pershing followed Seminole Scouts on his "punitive expedition" into Mexico after Pancho Villa. In Europe we fought "the war to end all wars," and Johnny came marching home again—again. A lot of time had passed, many battles were fought, and a lot of brave men had died. But, still, some remembered.

Finally, because those that he led on that bleak morning in 1874 refused to give up, the Army "found" Renty Grayson again. In November of 1923, almost 50 years after that Palo Duro morning, Renty got his back pay and a pension.

1877—Knowledge, Drumheads and "Garden Sass"

Folks leave last wills and testaments for a variety of reasons. Mostly it is to make sure that the sticky-fingered government has as little impact in the distribution of their worldly goods as possible and to relieve the survivors of other unnecessary complications. Sometimes it is to limit the avaricious nature of some of those whose business survival depends on legal obfuscation or on burying people. But a primary function has always been to divide what is left and determine who gets what. Wills are usually interesting. Sometimes they are bizarre. More frequently than we suspect, folks and the courts pay little attention to them.

James Edward Singleton came from a *"highly respected Christian family."* He was about 22 years old, quite literate, and he had a good sense of humor. He was also drunk on the night in 1876 when he killed a man in Beeville.

In one of his novels, western writer Louis L'Amour said that James Singleton was a notorious outlaw. Now folks, that's just not so. He was a pleasant young fellow who just had too much to

illustration by Gary Manthei

drink and killed another pleasant young fellow during an argument. The courts today would probably ignore the fact that someone had died and simply tell him not to do it again. Things were different back then when folks tended to believe in the biblical injunction, *"an eye for an eye, tooth for a tooth ..."*

Local feeling ran high. In order to protect his prisoner from mob violence, Sheriff D. A. T. Walton at first kept Singleton locked in the corncrib on his farm and later, when things got even hotter, had him chained to a tree in a sheltered and well-hidden spot on his ranch. In due time the trial was held up in Galveston, and the verdict was guilty. The penalty was common on a frontier that didn't pander to drawn-out appeals processes. If you were found guilty by a jury of your peers, you were punished then, not twenty years later. Singleton was sentenced to hang until *"dead, dead, dead."* Several days before the sentence was carried out, Singleton wrote to his mother that he *"did not commit the crime with malice aforethought in [his] heart nor was [he] actuated by any hope of gain—it was caused from a quarrel over a trifle."*

No one else at the jail knew how to tie a hangman's noose, so, with a laugh, he tied it himself. Then he sat down to compose one of the strangest wills in our history. Here it is. I've filled in a few missing words that were eaten by critters in the court files:

> *"In the name of the Omnipotent, Omnipresent, Omniscient of science and common sense, Amen. I, J. E. Singleton (cosmopolitan), now sojourning in Galveston Jail, State of Texas, and, being of sound mind, Do by these presents, will, devise, and bequeath, (for the diffusion of anatomical knowledge among mankind)—my mortal remains to J.J. Swan, on the following conditions.*
>
> *"First, that my skeletal body—after execution—be prepared in the most scientific and skillful manner known in anatomical art, and placed in his office, in the Courthouse in Beeville or other temple of Justice.*
>
> *"Second, it is my express desire—if Dave Walton has no objections—that two drumheads, be made of my skin. On one of which shall be written in indelible characters Pope's universal prayer, and on the other the following verdict,*
>
> *"'We, the Jury, find the defendant, Jas. E. Singleton, guilty of murder in the first degree, as charged in the indictment, and assess the penalty of death.'*

"The said drumheads to be presented to my distinguished friend and fellow citizen, Frank Boggus—drummer for Tom Holly's volunteers—on the following conditions that he, the aforesaid Frank Boggus, shall beat, or cause to be beaten on said drumheads, a popular tune in front of the courthouse on the 8th day of June annually.

"The viscera, and other parts of my body, useless for anatomical purposes, I wish composted for a fertilizer, and presented to Mr. Barclay, proprietor of the Grand Palace Hotel, in Beeville, to be used by him for the purpose of nourishing the growth of cabbage, turnips, pertaters, and other garden sass, that the worthy people of Bee County, or at least the masculine portion thereof, may have something to relieve the monotony of hash and dried apples, during their brief sojourn at the aforesaid Hotel while assembled in Beeville, for the purpose of dishing out Justice to Violators of the Law."

Unfortunately for those in need of anatomical knowledge, those in need of *"garden sass,"* and those who liked to hear Frank Boggus beat on his drums, no one was found who was willing to carry out all of the details of the will. James Edward Singleton, a pleasant young man with a sense of humor, was buried after the trap was sprung on April 27, 1877.

1877—"What Shall We Do With Our Daughters?"

Throughout the animal kingdom, most parents, at least for a little while, care for their young. None, however, lavish the attention on their offspring as do representatives of Homo sapiens—us. The care and training of children has always been a problem. Not only do humans accept this responsibility for a major portion of their lives, they also often drive themselves to near dementia worrying about how to do it. Without this responsibility and worry, legions of writers from the annals of medicine to the supermarket tabloids would be out of business. It seems that we are always looking for new ideas when the old ones really work just as well.

Those of you who have "California Dreamin'" on your minds may be interested to know that 300 acres in the San Joaquin Valley, stocked with 115 cattle and sporting a six-room house with a well and a picket fence, sold for $6,000 in 1878. Or, that 500 acres located four miles from San Jose went for $65 per acre. These interesting, but currently useless, statis-

213

James Theodore Dudley Wilson
courtesy Jeff Carroll

Mrs. Cornelia Wilson
courtesy Jeff Carroll

tics come from the back of a clipping from the Santa Clara Argus of that date. We'll get to the front of that clipping in a minute.

You will remember reading earlier in the book about the desirable rules of life and conduct laid down by a mother to a son going away from a basically rural home in Houston to Yale College in 1847. Things haven't changed that much. A son would do well to follow those rules today. But, what about daughters? Surely they can, and, perhaps should, follow the same rules of common prudence and decency; but what should they know before leaving the family nest?

James Theodore Dudley Wilson, who fought as a boy in the Texas Revolution and led wagon trains of cotton into Mexico during the Civil War to bypass the Union naval blockade, had three rambunctious sons. He also had two daughters, Cora Trula Belle and Cornelia Estelle Beranese, who gave him cause for worry. They were just as headstrong as the boys. The five of them kept things humming in Houston, where they were occasionally referred to as *"The Wild Wilsons."*

That's probably why J. T. D., while on a business trip to California after serving his terms as mayor of Houston, went to the trouble of clipping an item from the Santa Clara Argus and enclosing it in a letter to his wife. Most of what was said in 1878 makes pretty good sense today, if you modernize some of the terminology.

Here's the front of that clipping.

"What Shall We Do With Our Daughters?

Teach them self-reliance.
Teach them to make bread.
Teach them to make skirts.
Teach them to total store bills.
Teach them not to wear false hair.
Teach them not to wear paint or powder.
Teach them to wear thick warm socks.
Teach them to wash and iron clothes.
Bring them up in the way that they should go.
Teach them how to make their own dresses.
Teach them that a dollar is only a hundred cents.
Teach them to cook a good meal of victuals.
Teach them every day, dry, hard, practical common sense.
Teach them how to darn stockings and sew on buttons.
Give them a good substantial school education.
Teach them to say "NO" and mean it; or "YES" and
stick to it.
Teach them to regard the morals and not the money.
Teach them to wear calico dresses, and do it like a queen.
Teach them all the mysteries of the kitchen, the dining
room, the parlor, and the bedroom.
Teach them that a good rosy romp is worth fifty
consumptive pills.
Teach them to have nothing to do with intemperate and
dissolute young men.
Teach them that the more one lives within his income,
the more he will save.
Teach them the further one lives beyond his income, the
nearer he is to the poor house.
Teach them the accomplishments—music, painting,
drawing, if you have the time and money to do it with.
Teach them to cultivate a garden and drive a road team
or farm wagon.
Teach them that God made them in his own image, and
no amount of tight lacing will improve the model.
Teach them that a good steady mechanic without a cent
is worth a dozen oil-patent loafers in broadcloth.
Rely upon it that upon your teaching depends in a great

> *measure the weal or the woe of their after life.*
> *Teach them the essentials of life—truth, honesty,*
> *uprighteousness—and then, at a suitable age, let*
> *them marry."*

It must have worked. J. T. D.'s daughters turned out well, and one of them kept and treasured the clipping. Maybe we should all try it.

Author's Note (Sequel):
You know, it's kind of funny. When I first shared this clipping with a modern audience, I got a lot of complaints from some women who said I was trying to promote an inferior place for women in modern society. I was surprised. Granted, I am male and I was once kicked in the shin by a babysitter when I opened the car door for her, but, having helped in the successful rearing of two daughters (both of whom now occupy management positions once restricted to men only), I feel that I am not totally insensitive when it comes to gender relations. The complaints bothered me. Was it insensitive to suggest, even in 1878 prose, that women should be taught to be independent in both thought and deed?

Then came the second wave of response. It would take several more pages to catalog the comments, but the general consensus was that many

"The Wild Wilsons" (L-R) Hubert S. H., Cora Trula Belle, Harvey T. D.,
Cornelia Estelle Beranise, Robert E. C.
courtesy Jeff Carroll

modern women wished that their parents had cared enough about them to teach some of these basic survival skills. The modern woman who can't cook; can't sew; can't drive; can't balance a check book; can't take pride in her appearance in either a party frock, business suit, or jeans; pops pills instead of exercises; and can't evaluate the character of the men in her life—is in for a heap of hurt because it guarantees her dependence on someone else, not her independence.

Well, I still get letters of both kinds. I suspect that what we should or should not know in life is a matter of perspective.

1880—A Tale of Two Henrys

In Shakespeare's Romeo and Juliet, *the young lady in question asks, "What's in a name ...?" Often, names get us in trouble. We may call someone by an inappropriate name and lose a friendship for life, or go to jail. The names of close friends can also be a problem. We either forget them or can't forget them, and either way, we have problems. Sometimes there is confusion when two or more people share the same name. Sometimes it is a basis for a strong friendship.*

Henry F. Hoyt came to old Tascosa up on the Canadian River in the Western Panhandle in the fall of 1877. Now, folks, Tascosa was a rowdy sort of place, and in 1877, like the Marine Corps recruiters say, it needed a few good men. Henry figured he would fit right in. Besides, old John Chisum himself told him that he was really needed up there. It seems that the friction between buffalo hunters and Indians; and the occasional local misunderstandings between gamblers, cowboys, and the few permanent residents, continued to fill large holes up on Boot Hill. You see, Henry Hoyt was an ambitious young medical doctor, and he figured that Tascosa should offer a lot of business.

Henry F. Hoyt was born up near St. Paul,

Hoyt & McCarty
by Gary Manthei

Minnesota, in 1854. After attending a wide variety of medical schools he got the itch to see the frontier, and that was what landed him in Tascosa.

He was just in time. Dr. Henry hit town about the same time as a smallpox epidemic. Among others, he saved the life of Piedad, the beautiful daughter of Casimíro Romero, the Castilian sheep rancher who had first settled the area. The fact that he used a poultice made of gunpowder and water to save lives, rather than using it the conventional way to take them, made him an instant hero.

The trouble was that employment as a doctor wasn't regular. Smallpox epidemics didn't happen every day; there weren't enough women around to have many babies; and those citizens intent on shooting up the town usually only came in from the range about once a month—and even then, they had more interest in the dances at "Hog Town" across the river than in destruction and general mayhem. But, Dr. Henry was determined to stay in the area, so it wasn't long before he had a part-time job as the mail carrier between Tascosa and Fort Bascom. Whether hurrying to deliver a baby or the mail, he needed a good horse—more about that horse later.

About that time, another Henry came to town. He was born in New York, but he went to New Mexico with his mother at an early age. As he grew, he involved himself in various aspects of the cattle and horse-ranching industry. For some reason, he didn't call himself Henry, but seemed to prefer William, or Billy. When he showed up in Tascosa, this second Henry (Billy) was riding a beautiful sorrel chestnut racehorse named Dandy Dick. He was in company with a group of other young men who were driving a herd of horses and looking for buyers. All in all, the horses looked good. The young men deported themselves in a seemly fashion, and, while waiting for buyers, they made friends in old Tascosa.

Dr. Henry met Henry (Billy) during a card game, and they became good friends. They were not too far apart in age, and both had a desire to get ahead in life. Besides, they also had a name to share. Dr. Henry once gave Henry (Billy) a lady's gold watch that he had won in a poker game, this so his new friend could give it as a gift to one of the girls in Hog Town. As I said, they were good friends, and when, a short time later, Dr. Henry decided to move his practice of medicine to Las Vegas, New Mexico, Henry (Billy) gave him his horse, Dandy Dick, as a going-away present.

By now, you may have figured out that the second Henry was Henry McCarty, who also called himself Henry Antrim, William Bonney, and Billy the Kid. Dandy Dick had once belonged to William Brady, the sheriff of Lincoln County, New Mexico, and had come into Billy's possession after he and the other "seemly" young men had killed Brady in a shoot-out in April of that year. Dandy Dick was, indeed, a good and swift horse, and he served Dr. Henry well for many years. The bill of sale transferring ownership is now in the Panhandle Plains Museum up in Canyon.

You already know what happened to that second Henry. On the night of July 14, 1881, he was ambushed and killed by his old friend Pat Garrett when he stepped out to slice a steak from a side of beef hanging in Pete Maxwell's meat house in Fort Sumner, New Mexico. He certainly made a name for himself, and you'll find him mentioned somewhere in most history books. Assemble the evidence yourself and judge the right or wrong of his life. It is a matter of perspective. The "good guys" are not always good and the "bad guys" are not always bad.

Young Dr. Henry also made a name for himself. He rode Dandy Dick to Las Vegas, New Mexico, and there became one of the best-known medical practitioners on the western frontier. Dr. Henry F. Hoyt parted company with Dandy Dick when he was called to serve his country, to wear the uniform, stars, and saber of the Surgeon General for the United States Army in the Philippines during the Spanish-American War. After the war, he returned to Texas and continued to practice medicine in El Paso and, later, in California. His book, *A Frontier Doctor*, is a classic on life in the Panhandle during the high tide of the cattle empire.

Tascosa isn't what it used to be. The total population of Oldham County hovers around 2,500. Vega is now the county seat. Hog Town is gone, as are the saloons where the two Henrys played poker and where a woman named "Frenchy" dealt *monte* and married a fellow named "Mick." A well-populated Boot Hill is still there, just off of U.S. Highway 385, where it crosses the Canadian River. Today, however, the most important thing around that area is Cal Farley's Boys' Ranch. Cal took over the old town and turned it into a place of refuge for boys who, but for the opportunity and the education, might take the wrong trails. I think both Henrys would approve.

1880—Shanghai Pierce, King of the Coasters

The Texas Department of Transportation, in its infinite wisdom, makes it slightly confusing to locate this spot if you haven't been there. But, if you want to find relative peace and quiet in a well-kept setting and think about people who made a big impact on Texas, it's a good place to spend a few minutes or to share a picnic with one of the real legend-makers.

Abel Head "Shanghai" Pierce
courtesy Wharton County Historical Museum

Abel Head Pierce was born in Rhode Island in 1834 (the same year that Antonio López de Santa Anna declared that Mexico was not ready for democratic rule), and, at age 14, he was sent to Petersburg, Virginia, to serve as an apprentice in his uncle's general store. In 1854, when Abel turned 20, he decided that the life of a clerk in a musty store didn't appeal to him, and he stowed-away on a schooner bound for Texas. When he poked his head up for air a few days out of port, the crew caught him and put him to work handling cargo. He was big and strong, and, some folks say, the captain joked about the fact that his presence saved him from having to "shanghai" (kidnap and force into service) additional crewmembers. In any event, the name stuck, and many folks who later did business with Shanghai Pierce never knew that it wasn't his real name.

Shanghai first landed at the busy port of Indianola and then moved up the bay to Port Lavaca. There he jumped ship and put his size to work splitting fence rails and learning the job of cowboy on the old Richard Grimes ranch. In time, he followed tradition and began to burn his own brand, AP, on some of the wild cattle he found in the brush, and, in 1860, his brother, Jonathan Edwards Pierce, joined him. Then came what some folks call the "War for Southern Independence."

August C. Buchel, a locally prominent businessman who had not only served as a military instructor to the Turkish Army under Ali Pasha, but

220

also had been aide-de-camp for General Zachary Taylor during the Mexican War, raised a volunteer company of Confederate cavalry. Shanghai and his brother went along to fight their way through the Red River Campaign and the battles of Pleasant Hill and Mansfield, Louisiana. When General E. Kirby Smith surrendered the Trans-Mississippi Department in 1864, the brothers came home to find that the "AP" wild cows had followed the biblical injunction to *"be fruitful and multiply,"* and the brush was full of available cattle. That wasn't all that they found. The two brothers married the two daughters of William Demetris Lacey, and, together, the two new families formed the Rancho Grande Cattle Company along the Trespalacious River in Wharton County. Then the legends began.

George W. Saunders, who was, for years, the President of the Old Time Trail Drivers' Association, said that Shanghai's record in the cattle industry was never surpassed and never equaled. Shanghai traveled all over South Texas, followed by a trusted servant and a pack mule loaded with gold and silver coins. At each ranch he would buy cattle and pay cash until he had enough to make a herd. He would then hire a crew and start the herd on its long walk up the trails to the railheads in Kansas.

Cattle purchased in the late summer were wintered on the salt grass flats of Matagorda Island and, in the spring, started up the trail by first swimming Matagorda Bay. Shanghai called them his "sea lions," and folks called Shanghai *"The King of the Coasters."*

"To see him was to hear him," wrote cattleman Ralph Records. *"He had a booming voice to match his body and personality."* Many visitors told of him standing on the balcony of his home and shouting orders to his crew at the stock pens, which were almost a mile away. Every trail boss and vaquero had his own special Shanghai story to tell. He was on the old Military Plaza in San Antonio when "Bet-A-Million" Gates first demonstrated barbed wire, and he swore that he would never treat his cattle that way. But, by the mid-1880s, he had fenced most of Matagorda County and made the

Pierce at a later age
courtesy Wharton County Historical Museum

221

organized management of breeding possible. When Texas cattle were excluded from Missouri and most of Kansas because of "Texas Fever," he may have been the first to proclaim that it wasn't the cattle but the ticks that did the damage. He searched the world for cattle that were resistant to ticks, and, after Shanghai's death, his brother became the first major importer and breeder of Brahman cattle on the Southern range. Shanghai fought bandits and blizzards, Indians and politicians, neighbors and strangers, and it took the Galveston Storm of 1900 (in which he lost over $1,250,000), a bank failure, the failure of the Gulf Island Railroad, and a cerebral hemorrhage to finally put him down, fighting to the last.

That's why, when you want to relax in a well-kept quiet spot, you should visit the old Hawley Cemetery. It's in the same grove of mossy live oaks that it's always been in, just off of Highway 31, about a mile north of its new junction with Texas 71 in lower Matagorda County. The graves of Shanghai and his brother and their extended families are there, along with both older and more recent graves. It's about three miles east of the town he named Blessing, and there you'll find King of the Coasters at peace.

1880—Some Good Advice

Now and then it pays to take advice. Not all of the time, mind you, because quite often free advice is worth just what you pay for it. But, every so often you get "the word," and it is best to act accordingly. The case of the Ballard brothers shows you just how important advice can sometimes be.

If you draw a line from Galveston to San Antonio and then extend it south to Corpus Christi, you include a large chunk of real estate well-known for colorful characters, fierce feuds, and the proponents of individualism. Austin's, DeWitt's and De Leon's original colonies were there, and so were most of the battles of the Texas Revolution. Among the Texian and Tejano residents there were Indian fighters and Texas Rangers, cattle barons, good solid farmers, and tradesmen. In such a diverse population there were bound to be a few whose personal attitudes toward the private property of others were somewhat creative.

Bill and Charlie Ballard were perfect examples. In the 1880s they were pretty well known down in Colorado, Lavaca, and Jackson counties. If you dig through court records and the newspapers of the time, you will have no trouble collecting a sizable list of their activities, including disturbing the peace, petty theft, willfully burning the fence of another, burglary, theft of branded cattle, shooting another man's dog, aggravated assault, theft of unbranded stock, and more. In fact, you could get a pretty good education in the law just by reviewing their cases.

A visiting correspondent for Scribner's Magazine once wrote that Texas stockmen, *"despite the many dangers and vexations which beset them, are a healthy, happy set. Their manners have a tinge of Spanish gravity and courtesy."* Even so, the most mannerly of men can lose patience. As John Dryden wrote, *"Beware the anger of a patient man."*

So it was that in October, 1891, while rounding up their cattle on the open range east of the Navidad River, some stockmen encountered brother Bill Ballard in questionable circumstances with certain stock not

illustration by Gary Manthei

his own, a hot fire, and several "running" irons. Running irons, if you are unfamiliar with the term, were usually straight pieces of wagon tail-gate tie rods which were often used in open country to picket a horse, but which could also, when red hot, be used to "run" one man's brand on the hide of a horse or cow so that it would look like someone else's. Once the new burn of the run healed, it was hard to tell from the outside whose brand was first. You could tell from the inside, but, to do that, you had to kill and skin the cow.

Enough was enough! Bill had escaped the courts on too many occasions. A running gun battle ensued, and Criminal Docket No. 3252 of the District Court of Lavaca County reported that one participant stated, *"That last shot of mine wound up his little ball of yarn."*

Meanwhile, brother Charley was in jail in Jackson County, awaiting trial for selling mortgaged property. While there, he received some advice in the form of a grave and courteous letter:

223

"*Mr. Charley Ballard.*
Dear Sir,

We, thee Stockmen in general, understand that you plan to return to this country again with thee view of making it your Home in The future. Now, Mr. Ballard We call own you to stop and think for yourself, do you think that best? Shurely not. Man that has conducted Himself as you have hear in all time past, we ask you again think, ought we allow it and will we is something you should consider well. Remember your Brother, had you not better leave at once? We have know confidence in you and have know causes whatever to have and to be very plain with you we never will have. We don't want you hear, take warning lest you are found as your Brother Bill was. You have nothing to hold you in this country and while you are left to your own thoughts for a while consider the life you have led. We have put up with the like long enough, you can't stay hear is just the fact in the case. If you stay we the Stockmen of the three joining countys will have to leave. You can leave with less trouble than we and we say to you, go.

Lava, Jac and Colorado Countys"

A copy of the letter was printed in the Hallettsville Herald on January 28, 1892. While it was far from being grammatically correct, it had a certain appeal to Charlie's self-interest. Today, when the courts spend more time protecting the criminals than they do protecting the rights of the victims, the writers of such a missive would be arrested, while Charley would be free to continue his career. Back then, "the people" made the law, and, under the circumstances, that letter sounded like pretty good advice. Apparently Charley also thought the advice was good. He never reappeared on a court docket in the area.

1880—Temple at the Bar

Two stories deserve re-telling, not because they are necessarily true, but because they fit, whether true or not. The first concerns a shooting match between two teenagers up in old Tascosa. Bat Masterson, the buffalo hunter, army scout, and noted lawman, acted as a civic-minded citizen to conduct the match between two newcomers to the Panhandle—one from New Mexico, and one from Brazoria County down on the Gulf. His objective, so the story goes, was to peacefully sidetrack any confrontation between the two youngsters, who had each already built quite a reputation. After an inconclusive round of shooting the necks from bottles behind a saloon, Bat threw a plug of Navy chewing tobacco in the air. The kid from the mouth of the Brazos drew one of his two Colts and shot the metal star trademark out of the flying plug, whereupon the kid from New Mexico conceded that no one could do better. The match ended in friendship.

The second story begins in a courtroom where a local cowboy with an unsavory reputation was on trial for killing a man. The defendant claimed that the shooting was in self-defense, but public opinion was to the contrary, and his attorney knew that he'd never get a fair trial. All day long, the defense attorney acted strangely. His rattlesnake skin string tie didn't go with his long Prince Albert coat which, when he turned quickly, flowed out like a girl's party dress to reveal the fact that he wore two Colts at his waist. He began his summation from the back of the courtroom, his words low and jerky as he slipped from one supporting pillar to another. The closer he got to the jury, the louder and more erratic became his voice and behavior. He leapt over the rail, approached the jury box, and, nose-to-nose with the poor souls there assembled, he thundered, "So, to save his life, the defendant shot the malefactor." At the height of this last eye-rolling outburst, he drew both guns and stampeded the courtroom by firing into the ceiling. Although he was fined by the judge, he won a new trial and a change of venue on the grounds that the jury had "mingled" with the crowd before giving their verdict.

Temple tames the jury
by Gary Manthei

The first story probably isn't true because the dates don't match.

Henry McCartney (also known as William H. Bonney, Henry Antrim, and Billy the Kid) was in his grave and probably last visited old Tascosa two years before Temple Lea Houston, the 18-year-old new District Attorney of the 35th Judicial District, arrived. The second story is probably true and involves the same Temple Houston.

Temple Lea (named for his grandfather on his mother's side) Houston was the last child of the eight born to Sam Houston and his wife, the beautiful Margaret Lea. Although Sam was 26 years older than his young wife, he proved that "the older you get, the less difference age makes," and Temple probably carried more of his father's fire than any of his siblings. He was the first child born in today's Texas Governor's Mansion in 1860. He was tall, handsome, and a seasoned trail driver and a night clerk on a Mississippi riverboat by age 14. At age 15 he became a page in the U.S. Senate in Washington. There, in his spare time, he read law. He passed the Texas bar exam to become the youngest practicing lawyer in Texas and, at 18, was elected District Attorney of Brazoria County. Not content to let others have all of the fun, he had a habit of riding with the sheriff to make arrests. His words in court matched his baritone voice and his growing reputation.

When J. N. "Honest Jim" Browning resigned as District Attorney of the 35th Judicial District, the "Jumbo District" that covered all 26 counties of the Panhandle, Temple was appointed to fill his place, and the real legend began. He rode the circuit that included the courts at Tascosa, Clarendon, Fort Elliott, and Mobeetie. Depending on the circumstances, he prosecuted or defended everyone from high to low. Later, after he'd married and reached the age of 24, he became senator for the 56th District of Texas and served in the Nineteenth and Twentieth Legislatures. On May 16, 1888, Temple Lea Houston gave the dedication speech at our new Capitol in Austin.

After he practiced law as a private citizen in the Panhandle and became the primary attorney for the Santa Fe Railroad, Temple moved his family to Oklahoma to practice law in the Oklahoma Territory. There, in Woodward in 1890, he made what many folks consider his most famous speech in defense of Minnie Stacey, accused of prostitution.

> *"Let us judge her gently. You know the story of the prodigal son, yet the story of the prodigal daughter is incomplete. The Master, while on this earth, spoke in wrath and rebuke against kings and rulers. He never reproached a woman such as we see here today. One he forgave. Another he acquitted. Who will cast the first stone and say*

'I am holier than thou?' No, Gentlemen of the jury, do as
your Master did twice. Tell her to go and sin no more."

And let her go, they did.

1880—Tom Munson's Grapes

*No one knows who invented wine. It's been around for at least 4,000
years and is, traditionally, made by the fermentation of grape juice. Actually, you can make wine out of almost anything that will ferment, and I
once tried some turnip wine that wasn't all bad. Despite the fact that most
Texans are quite proud of their state and are convinced that Texas has a
major world impact on such things as oil, cattle, cotton, football, and
pretty girls, they might be surprised to learn that we also rate high in our
world impact on grapes. Grapes?*

The Texas Agricultural Extension Service recently reported that Texas
now ranks fifth or sixth nationally in wine production and that over twenty-five Texas wineries cultivate over 5,500 acres of grapes. I'm not surprised. After all, Texas grapes and a Texan once saved the wine production
of France and, through that, fine wine production throughout the world.

The story actually begins back on September 26, 1843, when Thomas Volney Munson was born in Astoria, Illinois. After attending a business college and teaching school for a few years, he earned a degree from
Kentucky State Agricultural College (now the University of Kentucky) in
1873 with a thesis entitled *Trees and Forests of Texas*. His interest in
Texas came naturally. Back in 1872, his
younger brother, William B. Munson,
had helped establish the town of Denison up in Grayson County on the site of
an old stop of the Butterfield Overland
Stage Line that also became a stop on the
Missouri, Kansas, and Texas Railroad.

In 1876, Thomas and his wife Ellen
joined brother William in Denison and
opened a nursery. Back in Kentucky,
one of Munson's professors had interested him in grapes and viniculture. Soon,
Tom Munson became the world's leading authority on native Texas grapes and

illustration by Nathan Smith

227

was recognized for his classification and understanding of all grapes in general. Thirty years later he wrote that he *"traveled through 40 of the states and territories of the Union, never neglecting one opportunity to hunt and study the wild plants, especially grapes and other fruits."* On these trips he traveled not less than 50,000 miles by railway and many hundreds more on horseback and on foot. He studied thousands of vines of nearly every species of American grape where they grew in their own natural habitats.

Disaster struck in the early 1880s. In France, the wine capital of the world, the tiny insect *phylloxera* attacked the vineyards. The little critter bored its way into the roots; the roots enlarged, strangled themselves, and died. Whole vineyards were wiped out. Pierre Viala, a leading authority on viniculture who had corresponded with Tom Munson (and after whom Munson's daughter was named), thought of his friend in Texas. Munson knew that the insect could not be destroyed, so his solution was to graft the desirable strains of grapes onto rootstock resistant to the insect.

From Bell County in Central Texas, a shipment of rootstock from the native Texas Mustang Grape reached French authorities. Their experiment worked. In 1888, Pierre Viala, by then the French Minister of Agriculture, came personally to Denison to confer on Munson the title *Chevalier du Merit Agricole* and induct Tom Munson into the French *Legion du Honor*. Only once before had an American received France's highest civilian award. That went to Thomas A. Edison. This time, French wine was saved and the newly resistant French vines were exported all over the world—even back to America.

In 1885, Munson's classification system was presented at the New Orleans Cotton Centennial Exposition and officially adopted by the American Horticultural Society. At the 1893 Columbian Exposition in Chicago, his display of grape species was the most complete ever assembled.

By 1909, Tom Munson's book, *Foundations of American Grape Culture*, became the author-

illustration by Gary Manthei

ity for viniculture throughout the United States. Before Thomas Munson's death from pneumonia in 1913, he saw over 300 new grape varieties created by his hybridizing experiments.

Prohibition once wiped out the Texas wine industry, but, with Tom Munson's work as history, we are now back in business on a grand scale.

1881—"Frenchy"

Not everyone who came to Texas came in search of land. There were those who, having, as they said, "run out their string" in other locations, came for a new beginning. The myth of the American frontier was that there would always be the opportunity to start over. Some were drifters who never put down roots. Others came and decided to stay.

Frenchy
by Suzy Keller

The barroom girls and honky-tonk queens of the old West weren't particularly noted for their looks, fastidious manners, or moral decorum. In the adobe *cantinas* along the border, in the dugouts of the Staked Plains, and even in the plush velvet bordellos of the few growing cities, a certain amount of compliance was all that was necessary to practice their profession. Also, they were not well known for their dependability. They were generally as footloose as the men they followed, and moved from town to town on a regular, if unpredictable, basis. They forgot and were forgotten with the changing seasons. That is why those few who don't fit this model stand out.

"Frenchy" was beautiful in the ripe style of the 1880s. She was well educated. She could sing and dance. She was obviously cultured. Frenchy had no past. Although she used the name Elizabeth McGraw on legal papers, she admitted that it was false. In her old age she stated that, *"No one will ever find out who I am."* It was a secret that would make a great story, but she carried it to her grave. What we do know is story enough.

Apparently she was born in 1852, near Baton Rouge, Louisiana, and appeared, without a name, in Dodge City during the 1870s. There, a Texas cowboy, fresh off the trail, said, *"I want to dance with that 'Frenchy,'"* and the name stuck. The year 1880 found her in old Mobeetie, the free-wheeling county seat of Wheeler County, catering to buffalo hunters, cowboys, and troops from nearby Fort Elliott. It was there that Mickey McCormick found her.

Mickey was a gambler by preference and a buffalo hunter and livery-stable operator by necessity when the cards weren't with him. He was young and handsome, had a small mustache, and he always seemed to win when Frenchy stood beside him. To him, she was "My Luck." When he left Mobeetie and went west to old Tascosa, Frenchy went with him. There, she learned to deal *monte* and helped Mickey run the gambling room behind a saloon.

Tascosa was as raw a town as ever existed. Once the center of a New Mexican Hispanic culture based on sheep, it had changed. Hide-hunters, soldiers, drifters, outlaws, lawmen, cowboys, ranchers—all of the drifting tide of the West—came there, and Frenchy welcomed them and played cards with them all. But that was as far as it went. She was *"Mickey's Woman,"* and when Oldham County was organized in 1881 with Tascosa as the county seat, Scotty Wilson, the bartender and first Justice of the Peace, married her and Mickey.

Mickey built her a two-room adobe cottage just west of Atascosa Creek, about three blocks off of Main Street, which, in turn, became the road, or trail, to Dodge City. There she settled down to prove to the world, and perhaps to herself as well, that she was different. In later years she said, *"Mick and I discussed the fact that we had lived somewhat on the seamy side, and then he took my hands in his, and we pledged to stick to each other and to the town of Tascosa."*

And, stick they did. When the town folded and the county seat moved to Vega, Mickey and Frenchy stayed put. With his hunting and her garden they did well.

Finally, in 1912, Mickey's string ran out, and he died in the town that he had helped to build but was no more. Frenchy buried him in sight of the house with a marker that simply said *"M. McCormick, February 17, 1848 - October 7, 1912."*

Frenchy in her dance hall costume
by Suzy Keller

230

The town was dead, and Mickey was dead, but she had promised to stick with them both. She could have gone almost anywhere because she was already a legend, but she stayed, the last resident.

In 1939 she became unable to care for herself and allowed her many friends to move her to Channing, only after exacting a sacred promise to return her to be by *"My Mick"* when she died.

On January 12, 1941, Frenchy rejoined her Mick at last. The dance hall girl whose true name no one will ever know and Mickey the gambler now lay side-by-side near the home they shared above the river in Old Tascosa.

1881—How the Gospel Came to Mobeetie

The years between 1875 and 1880 were far more than complicated for many parts of the world. In 1875, Bosnia and Herzegovina began an uprising against Turkish rule, and the "Cuba Libre" movement started in Cuba. In 1876 (while we celebrated the centennial of the signing of the U.S. Declaration of Independence) Korea became independent from China; Serbia and Montenegro joined in the war on Turkey; and the Turkish troops retaliated by massacring the Bulgarians. In 1877, Russia got into the act by declaring war against Turkey and celebrated by invading Rumania. Meanwhile, Queen Victoria of England proclaimed herself "Empress of India," and there was civil war in Japan. In 1878, Greece went to war against Turkey; an attempt by socialists to assassinate Emperor William I of Germany failed; and Italy began a campaign against Austria. Then, in 1879, the first Zulu War began in Africa; the British Army occupied the Khyber Pass between Pakistan and Afghanistan; and Moslem extremists massacred the British legation in Kabul. As something of an afterthought, Germany decided to take the Alsace-Lorraine away from France. The year 1880 was almost peaceful by comparison—France captured Tahiti; the Boers in the Transvaal declared themselves independent from Britain and started the Boer War; and Chile went to war against both Bolivia and Peru.

Not everything that happened in that timeframe was disastrous. Mark Twain wrote Tom Sawyer, *and Joel Chandler Harris wrote* Nights With Uncle Remus. *The world's first roller-skating rink opened in London, and the first lawn-tennis championship was played at Wimbledon. The game of "BINGO" was invented, and, in 1881, the Gospel came to Mobeetie.*

Old Mobeetie is about the oldest town in the Texas Panhandle. As time goes, that doesn't make it especially old. In comparison with Santa

Fe, it is a juvenile upstart, and it is young when considered in company with San Antonio and even Austin. But, for Panhandle towns, it is old. Up in northwestern Wheeler County, Mobeetie began life as a trading post for Fort Elliott back in 1875. First they called it "Hidetown," when a collection of buffalo hunters clustered around the fort for protection, and their mountainous stacks of raw buffalo hides perfumed the air. Then it became "Sweetwater," named for Sweetwater Creek. But when it got a post office in 1879, they found out that there was another town by that name, and so the local Indian word for Sweetwater, *mobeetie*, triumphed.

Mobeetie and Fort Elliott had just about everything, including a reputation that matched the aroma of the buffalo hides. There was a 50-foot flagpole made from two cedar trees hauled by J. J. Long from the Antelope Hills 30 miles away. It had a booming business district of 13 saloons and regular freight and mail service to Dodge City and St. Louis. Bat Masterson killed his first white man there in a fight over a card game. The fact that the fight also killed Mollie Brennon, Bat's current lady friend, was deemed

illustration by Gary Manthei

immaterial at the time. She just should not have gotten in the way. There were assorted cowboys from the big spreads that were pushing their way onto the plains, and there were the famed black "Buffalo Soldiers" from the fort. There was a "sort of a school" with occasional classes. There was a courthouse where Judge Emanuel Dubbs dispensed frontier justice, and flamboyant Temple Houston, last son of the old general, swirled the long tails of his frock coat to reveal his pearl-handled revolvers to judge and jury alike. These minions of the law were supported in 1886 by a brand-new stone jail that cost $17,300, plus an additional $120 for a new state-recommended, state-of-the-art, guaranteed one-drop, hangman's device. Yes sir folks, Mobeetie had just about everything—except a church.

Newton Willis once remembered how the Gospel came to Mobeetie. He said that in 1881 there was no church or Sunday school until his grandfather started to preach in his home. He wasn't a preacher, but he was a devout Presbyterian and felt that someone needed to do something. He started a Sunday school in his home and, considering the general tone of things in Mobeetie, was doing pretty well.

Then some cowboys, in town for a frolic, reported seeing a couple of men hiding out in a creek bottom south of town. Now, folks that hid out in creek bottoms were not new to the Mobeetie area. More often than not, they were somewhat chicanerous in nature, and their apprehension provided both a festive occasion for folks to gather at the courthouse and fresh occupants for the new jail. You never knew—there just might be the opportunity to test that new hanging contraption. So, a delegation of leading citizens from the local bars paid them a social call to inquire into their health and occupation. Now as it turned out, they were two preachers who were on their way to somewhere in Colorado and, considering Mobeetie's reputation, had decided to give the town a wide berth. Since there were no laws against preachers in Mobeetie (that is, if they conducted themselves in a decorous manner), it just wouldn't do for them to slip away unnoticed.

Newton's grandfather and another civic delegation made up of somewhat different folks, paid another social call to the camp in the gully and asked the preachers to preach. They passed the hat and collected a right sizable donation in advance, just to show their good will, and the service proceeded. Despite the absence of hymnals, the cowboys and local citizens alike harmonized on a song everyone seemed to know: *"Talk about your good things; Talk about your glory. When you get to Heaven, You'll all be hunky dory."* There was a bunch of praying, and one preacher preached. Then they sang the song again and prayed some more, and the other preacher preached so as to get his share of the contents of the hat. Then they prayed some more and sang some more and all had a good time. Even

233

the bartenders agreed it was a good show, 'cause all that praying and singing made folks right thirsty.

Things went so well, in fact, that the town officially called upon the Reverend C. W. Alexander, a Presbyterian minister from Sherman, to come to Mobeetie. He held services in the school for two years, until he died of pneumonia. His widow and five children filed on a 640-acre section of land (probably the first woman in the Panhandle to file a claim in her own name) and hauled buffalo bones for $3 a ton to make a living. But, that's another story.

Next came the circuit-riding Methodist Reverend Joe Bloodworth, whose non-denominational revivals saw to the founding of the First Baptist Church. By accident and design the Gospel finally came to old Mobeetie. The harsher element sought more fertile ground for their occupations, and, despite a few rough edges, Mobeetie joined the ranks of upstanding Victorian communities.

1883—Ed Nichols and the Barefoot Caper

Back in 1943, Ruby Nichols Cutbirth transcribed a delightful little book called Ed Nichols Rode A Horse. *I say she transcribed it because her father, the Ed Nichols of the title, dictated it to her when he was well along in years and, in his words, "blind as a sun-struck owl." There ought to be more books like this because they convey the flavor of Texas history without the indigestion of overly "professional" writing. Here's my version of one of Ed's stories.*

Ed's daddy, it seems, came to Texas from up in New York back in 1843, and like most folks, moved around a bit before he finally settled in Bosque County in 1859. Ed was born there in 1863, and in that neck of the woods he grew up. Despite the fact that the family was well educated and served as pillars of the community, Ed grew up rather wild and became well-known in local pool halls, emporiums of pleasure, and assorted gambling establishments. Sometimes he won and sometimes he lost. When he lost, he'd sell a yearling steer and get back in the game.

That's about the way it was one night at the poker table over in Morgan. Ed felt lucky, and the cards fell right. All together, he stacked up a couple of hundred dollars at a time when cowboys generally got paid $30 a month and what they could eat. Feeling pretty good about it, he heard of a game over in Cleburne that had been going on for several days and showed no signs of getting smaller. For whatever reason, Ed rode over to take

illustration by Gary Manthei

a hand. Now back when I played for matchsticks, I'd occasionally see things like this happen. The cards just kept falling right, and Ed left the game with a roll of $50 bills in one pocket, $20 bills in another, and so on. Things were looking better and better.

From the tops of the hills in Bosque County today you can see the lights of Waco. It really wasn't that far, only 40 or 50 miles, and Ed figured that the really big money was just sitting down there waiting for him. In a wet blue norther, Ed Nichols forked his horse and headed south.

Somewhere around Hillsboro on this dark and stormy night, Ed took a wrong turn. Lost, cold, and wet, he ended up at a little, shabby, two by twice cabin in the woods. When he hailed the house, they invited him in. People did that in those days. The latchstring was usually out for anyone in need, especially lost travelers. Now, those were poor folks. There was one stool on the place, and they let Ed have that. There was a fire, and they had the stub of one candle, but they made room for him. About the only thing those folks had plenty of was kids, and all of them were girls. As Ed remembered, there must have been at least eleven of them, including several sets of twins. But the thing he noticed most in that screaming wet norther was that there wasn't a pair of shoes in the house.

There was a tradition in Texas at one time that you always took in and cared for a stranger. That night Ed slept on the only bed in the place and, apparently, used the only blanket. The next morning he ate what may have been the last piece of bacon and drank the last tin cup of coffee. That's kind of the way it was. Folks did for folks and didn't expect anything in return. If you couldn't make it on your own and still take care of the less fortunate, then you didn't belong on the frontier.

Before he rode out for Waco the next morning, however, Ed reached in his pocket and started passing out $20 bills to every hand in the family. It would be nice to say he was rewarded for his good deed at the Waco tables, but that just wasn't the case. He was right, though, there was big money there. The big money players had it, and they cleaned him out. But, you

235

see, it wasn't all lost. Back in the woods, a stranger and his covey of bare-foot young 'uns were able to pay off the note on their rawhide farm, and, we hope, buy some shoes.

1886—Mr. Pettibone and the Onion

Perhaps the two most important things happening in Texas during the period from 1865 to 1900 were the trailing of 10 million cattle to Kansas railheads, which ended about 1886, and the linkages between small rail-road lines and the big ones to create a web over most of the state. Before the Civil War, Texas was basically a self-sufficient economy. Small farm-ers grew that which they used themselves or traded to their neighbors. There was no "market economy" because there was no satisfactory way to haul produce to market. Travel on the rivers was unreliable at best, and there were only about 310 miles of railroad. Other roads had no surfacing and were impassable much of the year.

The railroads made it possible for even small farmers to ship their produce to far-away buyers. New towns sprang up by the hundreds along the tracks. Some towns literally moved to the tracks. Some towns found ways to bring a railroad spur line to them. Towns without rails died.

If you've ever been over in San Saba County, you'll remember seeing a lot of sheep and goats and pecans along with cattle and a wide variety of home-garden produce. But, it may not be evident that the area was once one of the leading shippers of farm produce in the state. Talk to the old-timers. They'll be glad to tell you about how Mr. Pettibone's onion built a railroad.

Even before Texas independence, the Spanish and Mexicans recog-nized the valley of the San Saba as a good place to live. Not far away they established a mission and a small *presidio*, or fort, to protect both the mis-sion and a silver mine somewhere in the vicinity. The Comanche destroyed the fort and mission but left the land. The town of San Saba was founded before the Civil War, and the valley was full of small self-sufficient farms. During the 1870s and '80s, cattle from the valley moved north to the Kan-sas railheads and west to stock ranges in New Mexico and Colorado. The county was full of schools and churches. As far as the folks there were concerned, they had everything for a good life except a railroad. Finally, in 1886, the Santa Fe Railroad passed about twenty-five miles away.

Most of the farmers started planting extra plots of assorted produce so that they'd have something to haul to the railroad for sale. Herds of San

Saba Valley cattle filled the shipping pens. Everybody was doing pretty well, but 25 miles with a wagonload of produce was still a long haul. They wanted a railroad of their own.

Mr. F. G. Pettibone was the vice-president and general manager of the Santa Fe Railroad. The odds are that he was a pretty nice guy, but he wasn't in the business of handing out expensive favors to farmers. When he was approached about building a line into the valley, he balked. Railroads cost money. What did the valley have that would pay back the investment? Without some guarantee of payment and profit, a new railroad line, even one only 25 miles long, made about as much sense as hip pockets on a hog. That's where Professor L. C. Hill entered the picture. Professor Hill was a horticulturist, hired by the railroad to solve such problems. Cattle weren't enough. There had to be cash crops.

How about onions? Mr. Pettibone liked onions. Not only were they good to eat, they were also a good cash crop that you couldn't put in a herd and drive to another part of the state. *"Next year, cut loose on onions,"* said Professor Hill. *"Let's see what you can do."*

Now, I mean, everybody planted onions. There were fields of them and town lots full of them. Backyards were full of onions planted right up to the doors of the privies, and there were 40-acre patches the whole length of the valley sandwiched in between the pecan trees. In addition, some folks also tried cabbages, potatoes, and melons. In August they started

illustration by Gary Manthei

digging, and every day there were wagon trains of onions headed north for the railroad siding at Lometa. When they were told to try onions, those folks gave it their best shot. The first year's crop filled 40 boxcars with the onions, plus a bunch more of the potatoes, tomatoes, cabbages, and pecans gathered in the woods. In a time when money was really scarce for the farmers, they cleared over $18,000.

True to his word, Mr. Pettibone started plans to build a spur line into the valley. Most folks don't remember that there was a big depression during the 1890s, and that toward the end of that decade we went to war with Spain. Then, in 1907, there was another financial panic, and, what with one thing and another, it took a long time to lay that track.

Lay it they did, though. On August 8, 1911, Mr. Pettibone himself arrived on the first passenger train. All together, there were probably 10,000 men, women, and children on hand to open the railroad built by Mr. Pettibone's onions.

While this story is interesting, it is far from unique. Tomatoes brought the railroad to Yoakum. Spinach brought the rails to Crystal City. Oranges, lemons, and grapefruit brought them to Harlingen, and figs brought them to Port Lavaca. Strawberries brought the rails to Poteet. Timber spread rails throughout East Texas, and peanuts brought them to Pleasanton. The list is almost endless. By 1900, Texas had more miles of track than any other state in the Union, and each mile brought hundreds of home-seekers to try to make a living on the land. The economy changed from an introspective, local one to one that looked beyond state borders by necessity. For the next fifty years, railroads reigned supreme.

1883—The Dreams of "80 John"

We all have dreams. Some of us sit around and wait for them to come true and blame others when they don't. Some, with limited expectations, say that you can't expect more. Some see no limits to their dreams and work toward them. In Rogers' and Hammerstein's version of South Pacific, *a song tells us, "You've got to have a dream. If you don't have a dream, how you gonna make a dream come true?"*

Daniel Webster (80 John) Wallace wearing a cattleman's association badge
courtesy UTSA's Institute of Texan Cultures at San Antonio (D. W. Wallace Estate)

When "80 John" Wallace bought two sections of land southeast of Loraine in Mitchell County and, in 1885, moved his herd of cattle to that new grass, he was only doing what thousands of other young men did. He had always wanted to be not just a cowboy but also an independent rancher. It was a dream shared by many, but there was a difference. Sometimes we fall into the trap of believing that people who look different have different dreams. "80 John" is a good case in point.

You see, Daniel Webster Wallace was born a slave in 1860 down in Victoria County. Mary Wallace, his mother, was the property of another Mary—Mary O'Daniel. Both Mary Wallace and Mary O'Daniel had sons about the same age, and they were reared side-by-side. Maybe that's why young Daniel Webster Wallace shared the dreams of his white companion.

By the time he was old enough to work, the Civil War was over and Webster Wallace was free. He was only a boy in years but seemed to have a way with horses, cattle, and men. He hired on with a trail crew and, for $15, helped push a herd up to Coleman County. Then came years of life on the open range in the company of such frontier notables as C. C. Slaughter, "Ike" Ellwood (of barbed-wire fame), Sam Gholson (the Indian fighter),

239

and cattle baron John Nunn. According to one source, that's where he got his nickname "80 John." He was still only a boy, but when asked to help round up some cattle, he reportedly said, *"I'll bring in 80, Mr. John."* No one believed him, but he did what he said he'd do.

At age 17 he stood 6 feet, 3 inches tall, weighed about 200 lbs., and had the strength to match. No one could stand up to his pace at branding time when he could throw, cut, and brand calves single-handedly. In a short time he became Clay Mann's foreman and trusted companion. When, at age 25, he branched out on his own, it was with the help of money saved for him by Mann and cattle he had bought and pastured with Mann's herd.

In 1885 Mitchell County could still be called the frontier, and to get ahead meant a willingness to face frontier dangers and the ability to stick with a job. It also meant a lonely life for ranchers. "80 John" had the grit to stick with a job, but he also had a dream of being educated and having a family. So, with a ranch and cattle left in the care of friends, he started to school in the equivalent of the first grade. It took him two years to finish 12 years of education.

There, spending waking hours in learning, he not only learned reading and writing and arithmetic, but he also met Miss Laura Deloach Owens. She was graduating and wanted to be a teacher. Then all of the dreams came together. The ranch, the cattle, the education, and the family came true. They married on April 8, 1888, and, together, they pioneered the Texas frontier, building their own holdings and working for others when times were hard.

They drilled wells and bought more land. They experimented with cotton and grain and reared a family. As the first African-American member of the Texas and Southwestern Cattle Raisers Association, "80 John" Wallace attended statewide meetings for 30 years. His holdings grew to support not only a growing herd but also ten tenant farmers. In the depths of the Great Depression, while others went broke and fled the country for the cities, "80 John" owned twelve and a half sections (8,000 acres), 600 registered Hereford cattle, and had no debts.

The dreams came true, helped along by hard work, responsibility, and love. That's what it takes. Things weren't easy, but then they seldom are. "80 John" said that you had to fight the storm, not let it blow you away. Maybe that's why, when he was dying in 1939, he requested that they sing *"On Jordan's Stormy Banks I Stand."* Today, if you go to the town of Loraine, you will find a historical marker telling his story, but I suspect the monument that he would most appreciate is the school named for him in Colorado City.

1889—The House of 10,000 Washings

They say that cleanliness is next to godliness—could be. In any event, both were fairly rare on the Texas frontier. Personal bathing was still considered a dangerous affectation of the well-to-do elite, and harsh, homemade soap left a bit to be desired. Anyway, in a society where everybody smells bad, nobody smells bad. Clothing was different. If you didn't wash fabric occasionally, it rotted.

When the Southern Pacific Railroad punched its way from California through the desert and arrived in El Paso on May 19, 1881, it added more than a quick commercial link with the West Coast. It brought the Chinese. The new tracks, built predominantly with Chinese labor, produced the first "Chinatown" in the state.

The Chinese formed their own community. In the area generally stretching today from Mills Street, south to Fourth Street, and between Stanton and El Paso Streets, they built shops, restaurants, laundries, and other professional pursuits. The addition of the laundries and vegetable gardens provided a more balanced diet and clean clothes to the frontier community not particularly noted for either.

You see, it isn't that folks in El Paso were habitually dirty; it's just that their efforts toward cleanliness weren't always successful. Water was a problem. Every day Mexican and Anglo women met on the banks of the Rio Grande and pummeled their washing in flowing silt that was "too thick to drink and too thin to plow." The resulting shirts, pants, and dresses may have smelled better but had a certain abrasive quality that wore as much on the spirit as on the skin.

Following age-old tradition, however, the Chinese carried their water to settling barrels where the silt slowly drifted to the bottom—to be added later to enrich the gardens—and the resulting clean water was boiled—how else could you get clean clothes and add starch? By

illustration by Gary Manthei

241

1889, the Chinese held a virtual monopoly in the El Paso laundry business. There were 18 laundries, and all were Chinese. This brought cries of unfair competition from the public and the press, but you really can't argue with clean sheets. When a competitor advertised that his product was *"Cleaner than River Sand,"* Wong Wun made advertising history by opening The House of 10,000 Washings at 401 North Stanton. For 40 years, the business prospered. If he had anticipated the examples of various future fast food dispensaries, Wong Wun could probably have changed the name to The House of 10,000,000 Washings, but the old name was good enough. Sheets were cleaned for one dollar, and ladies' starched drawers went for fifty cents.

Since Anglo and Mexican names were too confusing, Wong Wun used his own system of identification. Each article of clothing carried the web-like Chinese characters identifying the owners as *"Fat man with long fingernails," "Sneezing man who scratches head," "Unhappy lady who coughs,"* and other distinctive traits. Don't laugh; it worked. Just think about the folks you know and imagine one symbol that would identify them forever.

Along with clean clothes there was, however, a problem with the disposal of the wash water. Boiling soapy and starchy water has its own aroma. Much water went into the streets or into gardens or into the pigpens that provided pork, duck, and chicken to the increasing number of Chinese restaurants. One newspaper quipped that *"The House of 10,000 Stinks"* would be a more appropriate name. In any event, a city ordinance soon banned the pigpens, and, in the fullness of time, sewage systems kept water out of the streets.

Although The House of 10,000 Washings has gone on to a well deserved resting-place, the Chinese community of El Paso is still a vibrant and vital part of Texas.

1890—Cotton Conjuring

Folklore covers many things we do with an umbrella of "but we've always done it that way." Some things get so deeply seated in our cultures that no one questions them. Broken mirrors, spilled salt, black cats, and left-handed handshakes—all of these have a place in the unquestioned patterns of our lives. We should not be surprised to learn that every human endeavor from newspaper printing to farming has its own set of rules for good living.

To understand the depth of this, you must first understand the word. "Folk" simply refers to "the people." "Lore" is knowledge. Therefore, folklore is the collected knowledge of the people. Too many times we think of folklore as just a collection of superstitions. They are a part of it, of course, but even superstitions sometimes turn out to hold a grain of truth.

For over 100 years, cotton was the number one cash crop in Texas. In many respects, cotton, and the control of the land that produced it, brought the Anglo-Americans who fought for independence. During the Civil War,

illustration by Gary Manthei

243

cotton was the only commodity that Texas had to offer the world market. Successive generations poured their sweat and blood into the land to produce the fibers needed by the mills of Massachusetts and Manchester. It is no wonder that a rich heritage of folklore circles around cotton plants like flies around road kill. There is no question but that cotton was the "king" of Texas agriculture. As with any "king," you must treat cotton with special respect because it has the power to change your life.

Now I hope that you are ready to pay attention. The whole remainder of your life may depend upon whether you understand what I'm going to say and act on it. Of course, it may also depend on whether or not they still grow cotton in your neighborhood.

For good luck in life and love, plant cotton at night while the weather is damp. Divide a cotton boll into seven pieces and put them at different places in the family Bible. If you are a woman, wear a green dress when you pick cotton on Friday. Be sure to pick the first boll of cotton to open in a field, pick out the seeds, and put the seeds under the back door step while the cotton lint goes over the front door, outside. Place a piece of cotton from the first picking in your sugar bowl. Always use a woolen sack to pick your cotton. And, if you go fishing on a windy day, be sure to float twenty dried cottonseeds on the water—the fish will surely bite.

Be careful!! Cotton can bring bad luck, too! Never let a black cat sleep on or near cotton sacks or picked cotton. Don't allow your children, or anyone else, to mix the cotton they've picked in each other's sacks—if you do, a relative is sure to die. Never allow a bride to use a cotton tablecloth on her wedding day—if she does, her children will be crippled. Don't start picking on one row and shift to another before you reach the end—if you do, a snake will be waiting for you at the end of the row. Never start your cotton picking on a Friday, and never pick cotton after noon on Friday the thirteenth. Cottonseeds handled by children under two years old won't grow. And, you should never plant cotton with your left hand because the bolls won't open.

I hope that you are absorbing all of this …

Don't forget that cotton plays an important part in your love life, too. If a young woman steals the first boll of cotton to open from an unmarried farmer's field, she will surely marry him. I guess that's because he won't have that cotton to put over his front door. As long as that particular boll of cotton remains white, the couple will be happy together. If an unmarried girl picks a twin boll of cotton, two men will ask to marry her. If the first cotton to open in a couple's field is a twin boll, they will have twins to help pick cotton in the future. If an unmarried man dreams that his cotton is all baled and shipped, he will marry before the year is out. If a farmer sits on top of his bale of cotton with his legs crossed while he is hauling it to the railroad in his wagon, he will have a big family. If a girl is in a cotton field at night and the wind blows loose cotton toward her, she'll soon marry. And, don't forget that good luck comes to any couple that makes love while planting or picking cotton—unless they slept on a cotton mattress on their wedding night.

Are you sure that you are getting all of this? Like I said, this is important stuff.

Here are some general things to remember. A wad of cotton held on your tooth will cure a toothache, and a wad held under your upper lip will stop nosebleed. If your first load of cotton makes exactly one 500-pound bale, you'll be rich. If you see a rabbit in your row while you're picking, turn around three times to fool the devil. Never start a cook-stove fire with cotton. Don't pick up cotton that falls from your wagon on the way to the gin. It's all right though, if you pick up someone else's cotton. Never leave a tortoise upside down in a cotton field. Never sleep under a tree in a cotton field if that tree has a bird's nest in it. If you mix pepper with cotton and wear it in a sack around your neck, your lost love will return to you. It is bad luck to see someone else picking cotton in your field at midnight— I'm not sure if that means bad luck for you, or bad luck for him. Early spring snow means a good crop, so long as you don't plant in April. And, above all, don't carry your baby to the cotton field unless you want it to grow up to be a cotton farmer.

1890—Kate, the Sidesaddle Bronc Buster

Now, I've been to some pretty fair shade-tree rodeos, and I've seen a bunch of "cowgirls" stick to the backs of barrel racers and cutting horses like cockleburs. But, I've never seen a girl broncobuster. Don't get me wrong. I know there must be plenty of them, but I just haven'st seen one. There was, though, one that I really would have liked to watch. Her name was Kate Anderson, and she would probably have been a real showstopper.

Kate's "Papa" came to Texas from South Carolina after the Civil War and the death of his young wife. Up in Freestone County he married the widow of another Confederate soldier, and it was later that Kate was born, in 1879 to be exact. They lost a herd of good Durham cattle—and with them, most of their money—to rustlers, and when the herd of goats they bought with what money was lcft died from breaking out of their pen and eating too much of a neighbor's cotton seed, they were left in pretty sad

245

financial shape. That's when they left "civilization" and moved into the Big Bend country.

When you visit the Big Bend National Park today it's still a long trip. In 1890, when Kate was 12, there wasn't a fence south of Marathon, and it was a good 90 miles from town to their camp. And, camp it was. You see, Papa Anderson, Kate, and her brother all had a contract to kill cougars that had been killing stock. That's right, Kate, at age 13, killed cougars for a living and, though I hadn't mentioned it before, wore skirts and rode sidesaddle because no "lady" would ride "astride."

Just in case you're thinking the men folks just let her go along for the ride, you're wrong. Kate had a .38-55 Winchester that was given to her by a family friend after she'd used it to kill one deer and nine javalinas in one day. She also carried a .38 Smith and Wesson pistol, just in case. She was quite an athletic young lady. One time she lowered herself on a rope over the edge of Nine-Point Mesa to kill a cougar on a ledge. After he fell off the ledge it took a two-mile ride to reach the carcass. Another time, tangled up with dogs and cougars in a good old rolling fight, she made her

Kate Takes Aim
by Suzy Keller

kill by jamming the rifle barrel down the cat's throat. He measured eleven feet from tip of nose to tip of tail.

But, this isn't about "Cougar Kate"—that's another story. It's about her bronc busting. You see, she'd learned to ride, she said, when she had to climb the horse's leg and swing herself up by holding onto the saddle strings. She was a big girl and was shoeing horses by the time she was ten. Down at the camp by Government Springs, she started her own horse herd and did all of her own breaking, training, and shoeing for market. Whatever her methods, they worked. Kate's horses always fetched a premium price when the Army needed remounts, and they had a standing contract for as many as she could spare.

She'd start a horse slow and easy, tying one hind foot to the head to hold the horse until she got him saddled. After a few days of getting him used to the saddle, she'd run a rope from the stirrups to the bridle bit and let the horse get used to the pressure in his mouth. Then it was time for the first ride. If you've ever seen a sidesaddle, it's about the most uncomfortable-looking thing you can imagine. There are a lot of things to get tangled up in if you're trying to get on or off in a hurry. Add to that the fact that Kate always wore full skirts with little lead weights in the hem that had a tendency to flap around the horse's flanks. Sometimes that first ride lasted for 20 miles through the brush. Kate said she didn't get pitched off many times, but when she did, she learned how to fall and sometimes left part of the skirt hung on the saddle.

In fact, that's about the condition she was in when she first met her future husband. Kate, her Papa, and her brother had ridden down to Cedar Springs one day to clean out the spring. Along the way about half of that flopping skirt had hung up on assorted branches, and, after spending the day knee-deep in the spring with a shovel, she must have been quite a sight. Along about the middle of the afternoon a couple of fellows who'd been "brush popping" for cattle showed up, and, if anything, they were more ragged than Kate. They were more than somewhat surprised to find a comely young lady in tattered attire standing in the spring where they hoped to get a drink. It didn't look like a rosy beginning, but Kate invited one of them on her next cougar hunt, and that seemed to turn the trick. On January 25, 1905, Kate Anderson and Frank Rogers married. With Kate's horses and Frank's cows, they homesteaded a place of their own and later moved to Kerrville and Uvalde.

You might not think that was much of a life for a young lady, but Kate would have disagreed. She wrote, *"The life we led was wholesome, and we lived a great deal closer to the Creator. I know that the years my eyes looked on the beauty I saw everywhere, were years added to my life."*

1890—Nick Clayton, Master Builder

Venice, Rome, Paris, London, New York ... and others; mention any one of them and your mind usually projects an architectural image. Every city has its own flavor, and, for each flavor, there must be a flavoring agent. No city in Texas was more "Victorian" than Galveston in the late 1800s. One man was the responsible flavoring agent.

Nicholas J. Clayton
(public domain)

The first thing he did when he stepped off of the train in Galveston in December of 1872 was to buy two clocks and a ceramic Madonna and Child from a pawn shop on Market Street. Then he walked to St. Mary's Cathedral, met the Bishop, and Galveston was never the same again.

Think about it. Besides the beach and assorted fun-in-the-sun, what is it that makes Galveston distinctive? If you've been there, traveled the streets, and looked around a bit, you haven't missed the architecture of the homes and buildings. Along the streets you can see some of the finest examples of Victorian architecture in the United States. People literally come from all over the world to tour the "Bishop's Palace." What really gave Galveston this flavor was primarily the work of Nicholas J. Clayton.

Nick Clayton's father died of the plague and "the great hunger" in Cork, Ireland, about 1842. If they had stayed in Ireland, Nick and his widowed mother might have joined the million or more other Irish who died as the result of the Potato Famine and English indifference. But, they came to the United States soon after to live with her brother, who made shoe buckles up in Cincinnati. I don't know where Nick went to school. Cincinnati was on the frontier then, and schooling for poor Irish kids was hard to come by. Whoever gave him the drive to succeed and then taught him did a good job. His military records state that he worked in the building trades as a plasterer in Cincinnati, Memphis, New Orleans, Louisville, and St. Louis before serving as a yeoman in the U.S. Navy during the Civil War years of 1862-1865. After the war, in Cincinnati, he became a marble carver and an architectural draftsman. He relocated to Houston in 1871, and, when he came to Galveston at age 32, he came as supervising architect and superintendent of construction on the old Tremont Hotel and the First Presbyterian Church. He came, and he stayed.

Nick's first love was designing churches. No matter what denomination they were, they all deserved special attention. Sacred Heart Church and Academy, St. Mary's, Eaton Memorial Chapel, Grace Church, Trinity Episcopal, Temple B'Nai Israel, and others—he designed, built, or remodeled them all. Then came schools. There were at least eleven of them in Galveston. Homes? You should go and see some that are left. The home he built for Colonel Walter Gresham is now called "The Bishop's Palace" and ranks second only to the beach as a tourist attraction. Commercial buildings from banks to bars to office blocks sprang up under his hand on every street. Look also at the original John Sealy Hospital and Masonic Temple and the old Galveston News Building—the first fireproof, steel-beamed structure built in Texas.

He was what we call today a "workaholic." Between big jobs he built porches, chimneys, and even outhouses. He didn't confine himself to Galveston. You'll find his buildings in Victoria, Columbus, Austin, Ennis, and Palestine. Some of his best are gone, lost to fire, hurricane, or modern development, but there are still enough to enrich our culture.

Nick Clayton didn't get rich in the process. He made only $500 on the home, bank, and opera house he built for cattle baron Bob Stafford out in Columbus. His records show payment of lesser amounts for even larger

The Bishop's Palace in Galveston, Texas
(public domain)

249

projects. One of his sons said he was a good architect but a poor business-man. He never financially recovered from a blow involving the new Galveston County Courthouse. His plans and specifications were approved. He posted a personal bond of $80,000 and went to Florida on business. What happened then is, to some, a mystery. Apparently, a coalition of envious builders and county officials altered the plans slightly, started work in his absence, and forced the forfeiture of his bond. Sometimes folks in government act like that. Although the case stayed in court for ten years, he lost and became bankrupt. The 1900 storm completely washed away 40 building lots that he had purchased for development near Fort Crockett, south of what is now 61st Street.

When Nicholas Clayton died, he was buried in a plot donated by a long-time friend, Judge Joseph Franklin. There is a simple stone to mark his death there in Calvary Cemetery—a cemetery that he himself designed. But, you won't have to look far to find monuments to his life. In Galveston, they're everywhere you look.

1890—The Cattle Queen of Coleman County

Not too long ago there was a popular TV program that involved an extensive ranch, owned and operated by a woman. Although we don't hear much about them, women often ran big ranches in Texas, and they still do.

In 1790, Doña Maria Hinojosa de Balli inherited her husband's extensive grants in South Texas. From her headquarters at La Feria she controlled about one third of the entire Rio Grande Valley, including Padre Island, which was named after one of her sons, a priest.

In 1814, while Mexico was fighting for independence from Spain, Doña Maria del Carmen Calvillo inherited from her father El Rancho de las Cabras, located in what is today's Wilson County. She scandalized her neighbors by dressing as a man, riding her white stallion astride, and supervising the work of twenty families. Near where Floresville stands today, her people constructed a sugar mill and irrigation systems. They created a mixed herd of cattle, goats, sheep, and horses.

The Battle of San Jacinto was fought on the ranch of Margaret "Peggy" McCormick, from whom "Peggy's Lake" (where the greatest slaughter of the battle took place) got its name. "Cowgirls" were not, and are not, confined to rodeos and the "singing cowboy" western movies.

William Henry Day was a very active sort of fellow. By the time he was 44 he had a degree in engineering from Cumberland University, he had

Mabel Doss Day wearing her wedding dress in a studio portrait
courtesy UTSA's Institute of Texan Cultures at San Antonio (Lilliam Maverick Padgitt)

served throughout the Civil War in the 1st Regiment of Texas Mounted Riflemen, built and run sawmills in East Texas, dusted cattle herds up the trail to Kansas 19 times, and started fencing over 80,000 acres in Coleman County where the Concho River meets the Colorado. That's when he decided to get married.

Coleman County straddled the western prong of the trails from the Rio Grande to Kansas. There were times during the 1870s and early 1880s when, from the top of Santa Anna Mountain, you could see the dust clouds of as many as a dozen herds at one time. There was plenty of grass and, along the Colorado River, water. That's where Bill bought his land from the state for 45 cents an acre with $500 down payment. And that's where Bill brought his bride, to a small rock house near the Rich Coffee Post Office. (Richard Coffee had a store/post office. It had nothing to do with what he drank.)

Tommye Mabel Doss came from Denison, where she taught music. The name "Tommye" wasn't ladylike enough for a Victorian-Age music teacher, but "Mabel" was okay. Miss Mabel (to her students) and Miss Doss (to her suitors) became Mrs. Mabel Doss Day on January 26, 1879, in the First Presbyterian Church at Sherman. For a while things were fine. Mabel wrote, *"We have a good stone house with four rooms and a front porch, a smoke house full of hams and breakfast bacon, flour, meal, dried apples, beans, maple syrup by the barrel, splendid pickles, canned corn, tomatoes, grapes, blackberries, strawberries, sugar, coffee, and catsup."* Her nearest neighbor was seven miles away, and she entertained by playing the guitar and singing. A daughter, Willie Mabel Day, was born in 1880.

Then came tragedy. Bill was killed in a stampede almost at his front door. His death left Mabel with an infant daughter, the largest ranch in the area, and a debt of $117,000. Many a person would have folded the tents and left the country. Not Mabel. Although women were not welcomed in the business world, she incorporated and re-financed for $200,000. The entire operation became the Day Cattle Ranch and Company—and she kept the controlling interest. With the extra capital she finished fencing the entire ranch, making it, for a time, the largest fenced ranch in Texas.

Then came the fence wars of 1883. The tradition of open range allowed many men to run large herds of cattle without owning any land. Fences aroused a great deal of bitterness. During the peak of the wars, Mabel lost over 100 miles of fence. Most folks knew who the fence cutters were but felt like one citizen did when asked to report: *I love to live too well to do that.* In 1884, Governor Ireland and the legislature made fence-cutting illegal, and the Texas Rangers got into the business of tracking down the cutters. It didn't all stop at once. Soon, Mabel was left with a lot of posts, a lot of cut wire, 9,000 cattle, and another tremendous debt.

This time she borrowed, at times paying as much as 18 percent in interest. Somehow, she survived when others failed all around her.

In 1889, Mabel, widowed but successful, and known throughout Texas, Colorado, Kansas, and the Oklahoma Territory as the Cattle Queen of Coleman County, remarried. Joe Lea was a rancher and the developer of Roswell, New Mexico. He was a widower with two children of his own. In combining families they also combined an interest in developing the land.

At the turn of the century, the railroad brought thousands of settlers to West Texas. In the role of developer, Mabel cut the Day holdings into farm-size blocks and established two towns: Lea Day and Voss. She built hotels and sold lots. Over 500 families moved to the area. Where there had been open prairie, there were fields and towns and businesses and people, with schools and churches. Mabel saw it all. The music teacher and frontier bride, who became the Cattle Queen of Coleman County, also became a developer that opened the West. When she died in 1906, the era of open range died with her.

There's not a whole lot left of Lea Day and Voss today. There is a new lake on the Colorado River where Lea Day used to be, but the old cemetery is on top of a hill at the end of a dirt road that still passes through Day Ranch lands. They've moved the occupants of several other flooded cemeteries to the site. A mile or so away the Lea Day church sits on a hill above the lake. It looks relatively new. There is a campground and, I suspect, some pretty good fishing. Beyond that, most of the land for miles around is about like it was when Mabel had her adventure. Check it out.

1890—The Night the Whole Train Danced

When Texas entered the Union in 1846, its public lands remained intact, the property of the state and people of Texas. We are the only state where this is true. Except for purchased or donated land, there is not, and never has been, any federally owned land in the state. This is important for several reasons. In the first place, the royalties from oil fields on lands once owned by the state form the foundation for the funds for state educational facilities. For another, the vast and unpeopled lands of West Texas were available for development during the last half of the 19th century. To encourage this development, the state was able to give away to railroad companies, as incentives to build, more land than is now in the State of Alabama. Added to this, one must count the millions of acres donated to the railroads by private individuals who wanted to open their own land for development. By 1900, Texas had more miles of railroad than any other state in the Union. The growth of the railroad system is the story of the transition from ranching to commercial agriculture in much of Texas. Since it disrupted traditional systems, it was not always welcome.

The special excursion train on the rail siding sat dark and empty, fires drawn and pressure down in the engine. The cool November night in the South Texas brush country was a night devoted to quiet good cheer at the little trackside Renner Hotel. Talk was of planning and encouragement and rest. Tomorrow was to be a big day; the morning would bring an opportunity for home-seekers from the North to view, and perhaps choose, sites for farms along the right-of-way of the San Antonio and Aransas Pass Railroad spur line that stretched southward to the tiny town of Alice which, from 1888 to 1893, had been the largest cattle shipping point in the world.

Few migrations of people in history equal that generated by railroad construction in the United States following the Civil War. In Texas,

A Wild Ride
by Gary Manthei

the 310 miles of rails that existed in 1865 expanded to 9,839 miles by 1900, and the state had granted to railroad companies over 32 million acres of land as an incentive to build. To this, you must add additional millions of acres of land donated to the railroads by landowners who wanted the rails to come in their directions. More people meant more business for the railroads, and towns sprang up like mushrooms along the tracks. Special excursion trains brought floods of home-seekers from the Northeast and Midwest who were eager to escape cold winters. Many of the newly developed towns flourished and still prosper today. Many more died because of poor soil, poor water, and poor planning. In some parts of the state, residents who knew the limitations of their land called the small-farm home-seekers "home-suckers."

That night, in the Renner Hotel, a party was in progress. Local bankers and merchants were entertaining a trainload of new home-seekers with the best that they could offer—thick steaks, potatoes, and gravy. The dining room was full. Extra tables were set in the halls and hotel lobby, and two extra girls were hired to help serve the meal. Across the street, in one of the town's saloons, good cheer was also flowing freely. A block away, in the railroad freight office, young Walter Overton sat at his desk in the spill of light from his kerosene lamp and wrestled to balance his books with a pile of loose bills, silver dollars, and some small change.

As dinner was served in the hotel and Walter sorted and stacked his money for counting, there were two shots in the saloon. You never knew what shots in the night might mean. The odds are that they weren't heard up at the hotel, but Walt Overton heard them and quickly blew out his light and swept his carefully made stacks of cash into a strong box. Across the street, a tall cadaverous body staggered out of the saloon to draw a rifle from his saddle scabbard. Too late! The saloon's double doors slammed shut and the bar was dropped in place. No more fun there.

The potatoes and gravy were on the tables and the steaks on the way when horse and rider came across the front porch and through the screen doors. Unsteady on his feet, the rider was firm in the saddle. Tables, chairs, potatoes, gravy, steaks, home-seekers, and pitchers of punch and water scattered. *"Dance!"* he commanded, but they didn't understand. I mean, these were mostly middle-aged and stolid Midwestern farmers and their wives.

"Dance!" Shots punctuated the command, and, this time, they got the idea. The whole train load of home-seekers, and the bankers, and the merchants, and the cooks and serving girls danced. They jigged in the potatoes and gravy. They pirouetted in the punch and fresh bread. They lost their shoes. Petticoats slid down to join the mess, while the rider set the pace with alternate shots from his pistol and rifle. The little hotel shook, and,

one-by-one, exhausted dancers sank to the mess on the floor—only to find renewed strength and interest as the horse moved in their direction.

For some people it lasted a lifetime, but it probably only took fifteen or twenty minutes for Sheriff Hinnant and his son Archie to arrive on the scene. They had the riding dance enthusiast boxed neatly, front door and back, and he went peacefully. Besides, he'd used up most of his ammunition. Crying, but too scared to curse, the home-seekers barricaded themselves in the train while disheveled volunteers stoked the fire. By morning the train was gone to whence it came.

The rider? Well, his name was Jake, and he was a good old boy who had been up the trail and guarded herds for local ranchers for a long time. He probably mourned the passing of his way of life. Friends flocked to his assistance, and the collected money more than paid the hotel for damages and lost revenue. Except for the bankers, most town folks not only understood Jake's actions but also secretly supported them. Jake went back to his little cabin where he lived on a small pension granted by the family of his old employer, Richard King, founder of the King Ranch. In a way, he was a hero to local ranchers who didn't want to see the land cut into small farms. Their only regret was that more of them had not been there to see the night one old cowboy made a whole train dance.

1895—A Flower for "Bones"

Governments and private citizens give many awards. There are Medals of Honor and Victoria Crosses. There are Nobel Prizes in a variety of categories. Local Chambers of Commerce give keys to the city, and the American Red Cross gives little drop-shaped pins for blood donations. All of these are important, as are others. Few, however, demonstrate the sincerity of one white flower.

Back in 1886, one of the larger ranches along the Pecos River was the JRE, and when the grassy plains of the Panhandle opened up to grazing, they moved their cattle to the area around Clarendon in Donley County. Along with the cattle came the cowboys, and among them was Matthew Hooks, better known as "Bones."

Bones came originally from Robertson County, where his parents had been slaves in the cotton fields along the Brazos. Although most of the uplands in that area are now in cattle production, it was cotton from horizon to horizon after the Civil War, and Bones had no desire to follow the stooped life in the fields. So, at age seven, he left home and took a job

Matthew "Bones" Hooks
*courtesy UTSA's Institute of Texan Cultures
at San Antonio*

driving a meat wagon for an itinerant butcher. As young as he was, he was good with the horses, and, by age nine, he had graduated from the meat wagon to a ranch where he took care of the *remuda* (a small horse herd). By twelve, he was considered the best rider and trainer in the area, and he moved from ranch to ranch, always working his way west toward open country.

The 1870s saw a million or more cattle move up the trails to Kansas. By 1880, Bones was involved, not only as a herder of horses, but also as a top hand drawing top-hand wages. Few folks realize, and the movies don't show us, that perhaps as many as 35% of the cowboys who made the cattle drives were either former slaves or the sons of slaves.

The winter of 1886 brought a turning point for the cattle industry and for Bones. Three years of drought followed by a major blizzard wiped out the plains cattle from the Canadian border to the Panhandle. Folks called it *"the Big Die-Up,"* and, when northern ranges were restocked, it was with more cold-hardy breeds from northern Europe. For the most part, it brought an end to the big cattle drives and the free-ranging way of life. When Bones came to Clarendon, he was looking for a place to settle down.

Clarendon, unlike a lot of Panhandle towns at that time, was often called *"Saints' Roost"* because of the religious atmosphere of the community. That suited Bones, and, although African-Americans were scarce in the area, his skill with horses allowed him to fit in with the range crowd. He became a trainer of horses for all of the big ranchers, including Charlie Goodnight's "JA." The rancher he admired most was Tom Clayton. By 1890, Bones and Clayton entered into a partnership. Tom Clayton bought the horses, Bones trained them, and they shared the profits. It was a good arrangement, because they each had what the other did not, and they trusted each other. Then, a few years later, Tom Clayton died, and Bones carried a bunch of white wildflowers to the funeral.

That started a tradition. Every time one of the pioneer ranchmen died, if he had been a good and honest man, Bones brought a white flower for the casket. Pretty soon, folks began to respect the African-American cowboy for more than his ability with horses. A white flower from Bones was public recognition of a good life and a job well done. The family treasured such flowers. In a way, it is a little strange that this simple, unadorned recognition of a job well done from an un-schooled African-American cowboy should be so important. But, folks in the Panhandle attached great value to its significance, and the word spread. So did the scope of Bones' tradition. By 1900, you didn't have to die to receive recognition from Bones for a job well done. Several presidents received white flowers from Bones and felt honored. Other white flowers went to world leaders. A white flower from Bones became the Panhandle equivalent of the Nobel Peace Prize.

Bones never smoked or drank, and, as more and more African-Americans filtered into the area with their families, he built for them the first African-American church in the Panhandle. Then, in 1909, at age 42, Matthew "Bones" Hooks left the range and became a porter on the Santa Fe Railroad. No one seems to know why he traded the four-legged for the iron horse, but his respect and the tradition of the white flower followed him. When he retired in 1930, he made Amarillo his home and settled down to become one of the community's strongest civic leaders. In Amarillo, Bones became the first African-American to sit on the Potter County Grand Jury. His membership was solicited by most civic organizations, and he became a member of several old settlers' associations. It was Bones who founded the North Heights addition to Amarillo, and it was Bones who founded the "Dogie Club" for underprivileged African-American boys.

When Bones died in 1951, every mourner brought a single white flower.

A New Century, New Frontiers: 1900–Present

1900—A.D. Mebane, "King Of Cotton"

We owe a lot to the Amerinds. This is one of the new politically correct and generic names that some folks use for all of those native peoples found by European explorers in North and South America. For a long time we called them Indians. That was because Columbus figured he had sailed right past Japan and China and found India. Then, for a while, we called them "Red" Indians, to make sure that we weren't talking about folks from India. Then they were "Native-Americans," but the dictionary defines a native as one who is born in a certain place and that makes most of us "Native-Americans." A few years ago the accepted word was "Indigenes," for people who were indigenous to a given area.

It is all very confusing, but the fact remains that roughly three-fifths of the world's agricultural pro-*duction during the 20th century originated with Amerind (or whatever else we should call them) farmers. Maize (corn), Irish potatoes, sweet potatoes, tobacco, beans, squash, pumpkins, peanuts, tomatoes, and chocolate originated here, as well as the inedible rubber and the wearable long-staple cotton. Other, more dubious, plants are hemp (Marijuana) and coca (from which they extract cocaine). To balance that is the bark from the cinchona tree from which we get Quinine. There are many others, and each one of them created empires around their culture.*

In the South, and in Texas, cotton was king.

Alexander Duff Mebane
courtesy Lockhart Post Register, Lockhart, Texas

Cotton farming was never easy. In the old days, it required a lot of hard work. First there was the clearing of the land. Then came the plowing and the planting and the hoeing of the crop, followed by the picking. Although, on good land, cotton often grew tall, there were few bolls of the fluffy white stuff on the plant and very stiff and sharp points on the opened burrs protected these. In addition, there was a lot more seed than there was cotton. Even in a good year it often took at least 1800 to 2000 pounds of cotton from the plants to produce one standard 500-pound bale after the seeds were removed. That was with a good crop. Most often, the bolls didn't open at the same time, and by the time all of it was ready to pick, you had lost a lot of the earlier-opening bolls to bad weather. Some years you lost the whole crop. Eli Whitney's invention of the cotton gin made it easier to pick the seeds from the cotton but did nothing for the production of the cotton itself.

One man changed a lot of that. Alexander Duff Mebane was born in North Carolina on April 8, 1855. Like most of us who live in the Southwest, the Mebane family was made up of movers. They came from Ireland before the American Revolution and, by the time A. D. was born, had spread family branches all over the East Coast. The Civil War took its toll, and A. D.'s parents left the devastated South and came to Texas in 1872. By 1873 they had settled in Caldwell County near Lockhart and started farming cotton.

In 1882, the Mebanes lost most of their crop to wind and a rainstorm. While he was surveying the destruction of a full year's work, A. D. noticed that some few plants had survived with their bolls fully opened but pointing down so that the cotton was protected from the elements by the opened burr, which formed an umbrella. A. D. was 27 at the time, and he decided that, just maybe, seed from those plants would produce more storm-resistant cotton. Now, A. D. Mebane was no scientist and had probably never heard of such a thing as genetics. However, he was a careful observer. He collected that seed and kept it separate along with notes about how that individual plant grew. The next year those seeds were planted separately, more seeds were collected, and more notes kept. He didn't realize it, but he was following a "scientific method" and, in the process of trying to save his own crop, ultimately saved most of the cotton farmers in the South. Each year brought an improvement in A. D.'s crop. Not only was his cotton more resistant to storms, it also produced more bolls per plant; the bolls themselves had more cotton lint in relation to the number of seeds, opened at the same time, and had softer spines on their burrs. Often his fields produced twice as much cotton per acre as did his neighbors'.

His fame spread. In 1900 the U.S. Department of Agriculture sent representatives to investigate. They found that through selective planting of his cotton crop, A. D. had produced a new breed of cotton that would reproduce naturally. They named *it "Mebane Triumph."*

By 1913, the Lockhart Post reported, *"Directly or indirectly, every business enterprise of any importance in Caldwell County is supported by Mebane Triumph cotton."* State inspection and certification of seed followed, and the seeds were not only sold throughout the South but also shipped to Egypt, India, and Australia. With "40 acres and a mule" and Mebane Triumph a farmer could double his crop. The whole world benefited. In 1917 a grateful county and state threw a Bar-B-Q to top them all as a salute to A. D. Mebane. Ten thousand pounds of fresh beef ended up in a 300-foot long pit, and there were trimmings galore, all free, in honor of the man who had insured the reign of King Cotton.

1900—Doctor Sofie

A popular television drama of the 1990s recounted the trials and tribulations of a female doctor of medicine on the western frontier. I'm in no position to judge either the accuracy or quality of the program, but I think they could have written it about someone else, someone who actually existed.

There was, indeed, a great deal of prejudice against female practitioners of medicine. It wasn't restricted to the frontier. Colonial America expected that men might occasionally buy a corpse or dig up the dead to study anatomy, but a woman who sought this kind of information was considered a witch and was treated accordingly. During the Victorian 19th century, women were considered to be too fragile in emotion and strength to even discuss the dead, much less treat the sick and injured. Despite the fact that Clara Barton and thousands of other women saved lives in hospitals and on Civil War battlefields, the practice of medicine was "just not right" for a "true woman." Even as late as 1933, the Board of Regents of the University of Texas proclaimed that women who insisted on studying medicine *"... cease largely to be women. They simply cannot follow the profession of medicine and be a wife and mother."* I guess the regents had never heard of Dr. Sofie.

Sofie Dalia was born in Austria in 1846, the daughter of a prominent physician. At age 14 she married Dr. August Herzog, and, together, they began creating a family that totaled 15 children, eight of whom died in infancy. Dr. August Herzog brought his family to New York City in 1886 when he accepted a position as surgeon at the United States Naval Hospital. There, in New York, Sofie began the study of medicine. Being a

woman, she was forced out of the school and returned with her younger children to Vienna, where she completed her medical training and received her degree from the prestigious University of Graz. Apparently, she had no difficulty mixing medicine with motherhood. Back in the United States, she "hung out her shingle" in Hoboken, New Jersey, and had a successful practice for nine years.

Meanwhile, Sofie's youngest daughter, Elfriede Marie, completed her education and began teaching school down in Philadelphia. There she met a young visitor by the name of Randolph Prell from Brazo-

Dr. Sofie Dalia Herzog
courtesy Brazoria County Historical Museum

ria, Texas, and it was, apparently, love at first sight. They married in 1894, and he took his new bride home to the banks of the Brazos River, where he owned a mercantile store. The next year, Sofie's husband died.

Sofie, at age 50, had reared her family and watched them scatter to new locations. With her husband gone there was only her practice to hold her. I'm not going to suggest that there was any kind of "mid-life crisis" involved, but the fact is that many people at that age look for a change and a new beginning. Sofie left the grimy winters of Hoboken and came to Texas.

There was no welcome mat, and few towns would accept a woman as a doctor. Here in Texas, the first woman licensed as a physician was Dr. Margaret Holland. She graduated from the Chicago Woman's Medical College in 1871 and set up a practice in Houston, where most of her patients were other women who refused to be examined by a man. Dr. Josephine Kingsley graduated from the University of Michigan in 1873 and set up her practice in San Antonio with the same clientele. No women were allowed to graduate from a medical school in Texas until 1897. Dr. Sofie came to Texas in 1895.

Dr. Sofie, in her new life, settled in Brazoria near her daughter and, again, "hung out her shingle." Folks just didn't know what to think, but she made friends quickly, not so much among the elite of society, but among the sharecroppers and cowboys and laboring class. To them she simply became

"Dr. Sofie," and her fame spread as one who could handle any emergency and did not require instant payment.

When it was chartered in 1903, she became the head surgeon for the St. Louis, Brownsville, and Mexico Railway Company. The company, later known as the Gulf Coast Line, was building through South Texas and headed for the center of revolution-torn Mexico. Dr. Sofie had more than enough business. Since everyone simply called her "Dr. Sofie," managers "Back East" apparently assumed that Sofie was a surname. When they found out she was a woman, they asked her to resign. She refused. She said that they could fire her if she failed to give good service, but she wouldn't quit.

Folks along the railroad got used to the woman doctor who rode astride in a split riding skirt and wore a hat like a man. Not only did she ride horses, but she also hitched rides on locomotives or resorted to pumping a handcar along the track en route to the scene of an accident or altercation. Fights and major injuries were commonplace in railroad camps, and, to encourage those who wondered about her abilities, she wore a necklace made of bullets extracted successfully from former patients. There were 24 assorted slugs, ranging in size from buck shot to .45 caliber and on up to thumb-sized chunks of lead from a shotgun, all held together with gold links. No doubt it was heavy, but it proved her point and impressed her clients. She was capable and not too fragile to handle any case a man could handle. Workers may not have known her name, but everyone knew of the "Lady Doctor with the Necklace."

In addition to her railroad practice, Dr. Sofie maintained her practice in Brazoria, built a drugstore and a hotel, and bought a considerable amount of real estate in the rich Brazos Valley farmland. At age 67 she remarried and moved out of town to her new husband's plantation. She decided that, at her age, riding a horse wasn't the pleasure it once was, and so she bought one of Henry Ford's new runabouts. Retire? No way! She maintained her practice for another ten years. Finally, a stroke at age 79 ended her career. She died in a Houston hospital in 1925.

Dr. Sofie Herzog proved that women had a place on the frontier and in medicine. Like her necklace of bullets, her life was an example that could not be questioned or ignored. At her request, when she died, she was buried wearing that necklace, but you can still see part of her office in the Brazoria Community Museum.

1900—The Fence that Leaked

In the United States it started in Lowell, Massachusetts, around 1822. For the first time, manufacturing mills needed more workers than were readily available in the immediate area. Housing for workers was provided, and those workers were rigidly controlled in their activities so that they would be available when the mill owners wanted them. Company housing and company towns became a fact of life for our growing industries. They offered both advantages and disadvantages, depending on who managed them and how the owners regarded the workers—as people, or as expendable raw material.

Throughout history, folks have built fences or walls of one kind or another to either keep things in or keep them out. The Great Wall of China worked for a while, and so did the walls of Troy. The Berlin Wall didn't last as long as most garden fences, but, for a while, it also worked. In most cases, when the fence is designed to control people, some really determined folks will find a way to get through.

The turn of the century was the mid-point of boom time for the logging industry in East Texas. The timber, transportation, money to invest, and markets all came together with available manpower. According to the 1910 Texas Almanac, there were 625 sawmills in the state, and about 100

illustration by Gary Manthei

of these were what we would call "big." Big mills were like the coalmines. They devoured whole generations of manpower along with the trees. They offered low pay, long hours, an uncertain future, and the frequent opportunity for serious accident without compensation. As "benefits" to the workers, they also offered company housing and the company store where things cost only about twice as much as they did elsewhere.

Now, on the surface that doesn't seem so bad. Texas, in 1900, offered very few cash-paying jobs to rural families, especially those who lived in the East Texas Piney Woods where just keeping a kitchen garden free from Sweet Gum sprouts was a full-time job. Folks just naturally gravitated toward big sawmill operations. At the mill they were often offered the opportunity to live in company housing. There the men would be available to work the eleven-hour shifts, and the women would have someone to talk to. The company store provided the necessary food and supplies. Both the house rent and the store operated on credit, payable at the end of the month. The difference between what was owed to the store and what was paid to the worker at the end of the month depended on the mill owners or the willingness of the employee to eat only once a day. If the worker actually had something coming to him, it was usually paid in tokens that were redeemable only at the company store. Do you remember Tennessee Ernie's hit song back in the '50s? *"Saint Peter, don't you call me cause I can't go; I owe my soul to the company store."*

In 1899, R. M. Keith, an agent for the Central Coal and Coke Company of Kansas City, began buying timberland in Houston County. A special branch of the company called the Louisiana and Texas Lumber Company was organized in 1901, and a mill began operation in 1902. That mill grew. The "4-C mill," as it was called, was a triple band-saw operation with one extra-long carriage for bridge timbers and a gang saw that could cut fifty-two boards at one time. There were planing mills, dry kilns, shops, storage sheds, and even a short railroad connecting directly with the Cotton Belt Line. You may not understand the workings of a sawmill, but what it boils down to is that the 4-C could, and did, produce 300,000 board feet of lumber every day. That's enough to build at least twenty 5-room frame houses each day.

The 4-C also had company housing and a company store. Stockholders in Kansas really didn't care too much about the employees. After living in the company housing and buying at the company store for just one month, you were hooked, couldn't get out of debt on what you were paid, and couldn't leave because you owed your own soul and those of your wife and kids.

That's when some enterprising folks built the community of Ratcliff on a piece of privately owned land near the mill. Folks could live there and buy there without going into debt with the company. Somehow, that just didn't suit the 4-C. I mean, they had a good thing going until honest competition showed up. So, like that Berlin Wall, the folks of 4-C management built a fence. I'd hate to calculate the amount of lumber that went into it, but it was a solid sixteen feet high and completely separated 4-C from the town of Ratcliff. If you worked for 4-C, you were supposed to stay on their side of the fence.

Texans have never liked being told what they can and cannot do, and I think that old song, *"Don't Fence Me In,"* was written with Texans in mind. That fence leaked like a sieve. If they couldn't go over it or around it, they could go through it. Dynamite was readily available at the stores in Ratcliff. Pretty soon, 4-C had to hire even more men to keep rebuilding that fence and patrolling it at night. The total "net" output of the mill faltered. More lumber went into building and repairing the fence than to the markets.

The 4-C didn't own enough land to keep supporting a mill that size, and, let's face it, the people didn't really support 4-C. By 1918, the company had about run out of timber and had lost so much money that it had to close. For quite a few years, the old 4-C lands looked like the wrath to come, but then, during the Big Depression of the 1930s, the Forest Service of the Department of Agriculture bought the ruined land, added it to the Davy Crockett National Forest, and replanted the cutover devastation. Then, the Civilian Conservation Corps boys moved in and cleaned up the old mill site, removing what was left of the fence. They built shelters and picnic tables and turned the place with its millpond into a recreation area called Ratcliff Lake. Today, people camp under trees that look like they've been there forever and swim, fish, and boat in what was once the log pond for the mill. I guess you could call that recreation lake a monument to the fence that leaked.

1900—The Hobby and the Hurricane

We live in a throwaway society. This should come as no surprise to those who seek convenience, whether it is in diapers, beverage containers, or automobiles. Unfortunately, in our haste to dispose of the unneeded and unwanted—those things that have outlived their usefulness—we often throw out people, too. There is a tremendous waste of love, understanding, and both factual knowledge and experience every time we decide that, just because folks are old, they no longer have anything to offer society.

His hobby met him at the gate when he finally managed to reach his little frame house on the afternoon of Saturday, September 8, 1900.

W. H. Plummer was getting on in years. Already retired from a life spent at sea off the Northeast Coast, he was called "Captain" or simply "Cap" by his friends. Unable to find regular work because folks said he was too old, he was a part-time employee of the Galveston Police—cleaning the station and making sure the doors were locked. His hobby reminded him of his youth; it was a small-scale and carefully handcrafted boat built on the lines of the sturdy crafts used by Maine lobstermen. Floating free from her chocks in the already waist-high water, she seemed eager to be off. Around him, in the rising wind and water, a city was dying in what would soon be called "The Great Galveston Storm."

Whenever we are faced with a natural or man-made disaster, we see those who prey on the misfortunes of others. Fortunately, we also see those who have led unspectacular lives suddenly rise above the call of ordinary duty in their service and acceptance of responsibility. This was something Cap knew and something he could do! He and the sea were old adversaries, and his hobby was waiting to prove her strength.

Cap Plummer didn't wait. He put on his boots and his old slicker, took his two grown sons and four stout hand-carved oars, kicked down what was left of his picket fence, and started out to save as much of his adopted city as he could.

Cap Plummer's "Hobby"
by Gary Manthei

Huracan, the *Quiche* Indian god of thunder, lightning, and evil winds, had ravaged Galveston before. The pirate/privateer Jean LaFitte had once sailed his ships completely across the island during such a storm. The storm of October 3, 1867, did more damage than the Civil War and Yankee occupation combined, but this was different. In 1900, Galveston was a Victorian Queen of Commerce and Culture and was built accordingly. "The Strand" was the Wall Street of the American Southwest. Mansions dedicated to both style and opulence nestled in private gardens or flaunted their excesses next to the streets. The port was as busy as that of Liverpool or Shanghai. People, however, tend to forget the awesome power of wind and water. A city engineer, E. M. Hartrick had said, *"The people of Galveston will go on living in fancied security as they always have."* Now, in the false security of Victorian mansions, they were dying.

Cap's hobby was only 14 feet long. With the crew of three at the oars, that left room for only a handful of people. At first, Cap tried to carry survivors from their destroyed homes to higher ground, but there was no higher ground. The waves were already crossing the island. Neighbors first. In the area between 1st and 7th Streets they often had to split up families, but they kept coming back.

Cap saw his little home demolished, with all those around it, early in the afternoon. He plucked men, women, and children from the floating wreckage and ferried them in the long haul to the red brick security of St. Mary's Infirmary. Then there was the longer haul back against the wind and waves for more survivors. Each trip was more difficult. On each trip, as their strength failed, he found fewer survivors in the wreckage. As buildings large and small were reduced to floating wreckage, the little boat and its crew continued to pick their way through water that rose higher than the second story of Old St. Mary's. Finally, they could do no more. Capsized and broken, the hobby was tied to a window casing, and Cap and his sons joined those they had saved.

We'll never know how many people died in The Great Galveston Storm, but a median estimate of 7,200 makes it by far our biggest natural disaster in terms of lives lost. There were, of course, many survivors, and among them were over 200 at St. Mary's who would not have made it if it had not been for Cap Plummer and his hobby … and something else—his acceptance of responsibility and his value to the community.

1901—Sunday on the Sea Wall Special

On September 8, 1900, a hurricane roared out of the Gulf of Mexico and danced across Galveston Island, destroying much of the city and taking from 6,000 to 10,000 lives. In addition to leveling public and private buildings and the wharves, the wind and storm surge also carried away the wagon bridge and several railroad bridges that spanned Galveston Bay and connected the island with the mainland. Although that wagon bridge was never rebuilt, it took only a few days to put a two-mile-long railroad trestle back in operation. Until completion of the new causeway in 1911 that carried both vehicular traffic and the rails of the Galveston-Houston Electric Interurban line, that one railroad trestle served all six of the steam railroad systems that connected Galveston to the rest of the world. And, that's where this story begins.

You see, folks in Houston and Galveston were pretty resilient. Before the year was out, Galveston began to rebuild and to protect itself from future inundation with a concrete seawall that, just coincidentally, also provided a way for tourists to get a fine view of the Gulf. By the summer of 1901, Galveston Beach was again a tourist attraction—especially on Sundays, when the folks from Houston could hop on the train, have an exciting ride, and spend the day in the sun and surf before returning at night.

All six railroad systems offered "Sea-Wall Specials" to carry the visitors and, of course, those who got there first got the pick of the best spots on the beach. Now, just about the only thing that would make a Sunday on the beach more exciting was to add a sporting element to getting there. Each of those Sea-Wall Specials, except one, left their respective stations in and around Houston at the same time, loaded with young and old and prams and picnic hampers, and then raced for that one remaining railroad trestle. Today the Occupational Safety and Health Administration and the National Transportation Safety Board, and Lord knows how many other bureaucratic outfits, including Homeland Security, would scream and run for the nearest court order. Back then, folks thought it was great fun, and the results of the Sunday Sea-Wall Special race appeared in the papers on Monday morning.

A while back, I said that all but one left at the same time. Well, they tried to be fair about it. The Galveston, Houston, and Henderson Railroad's right-of-way was the oldest and shortest, and so that train had a handicap; that is, it had to leave Houston later. Much of the time, however, that handicap made no difference. The GH&H had a few other things going for it and usually won by reaching the trestle first.

269

Galveston, Houston and Henderson
RAILROAD!

ONLY RAIL LINE

FROM GALVESTON TO HOUSTON

THREE DAILY PASSENGER TRAINS

Close and Reliable

CONNECTIONS WITH ALL ROADS and STEAMERS

AT GALVESTON With MORGAN'S LINE U. S. MAIL STEAMERS, for New Orleans and all Southeastern Points.

AT HOUSTON With G. H. & S. A. R. W., for San Antonio, Richmond and Columbus, and all Points in Western Texas.

AT HOUSTON With TEXAS CENTRAL and I. & G. N. R. R., for all Places reached via their Lines.

 THROUGH TICKETS

To all Points in Texas and the United States, for sale at Galveston, Houston and Henderson Railroad Depot, Avenue A, between Tremont and Twenty-fourth streets, Galveston, Texas.

J. H. MILLER, Ticket Agent.

O. G. MURRAY,
General Freight and Passenger Agent.

H. M. HOXIE,
Vice President and Manager

Advertisement for the Galveston, Houston and Henderson Railroad
courtesy UTSA's Institute of Texan Cultures at San Antonio

A lot of that "edge" belonged to the pride of their fleet, Engine Number 82, a 4-4-0 Baldwin locomotive that was, in 1902, the first railroad engine in the world that was factory-built to burn oil. That meant it needed no fireman to shovel coal or sling wood into the firebox. It meant more even and controllable steam pressures, and it gave both the engineer and the fireman more time to look out for stray cows and other odds-n-ends that might slow down the run. That wasn't all. The 15-to-18 open-platform wooden coaches behind Engine Number 82 usually had a low-geared switch engine at the rear that gave them a jump-start before dropping off and returning to the station. Added to this, the GH&H had a straight 50-mile level run with no stops—that allowed speeds from 70 to 80 miles per hour.

Now folks, if you want to spice up your Sunday outing, you and the family just grab a bench in an open wooden coach behind a screaming, black, smoke-belching monster, and race five more trains at 80 miles an hour toward a single bridge.

Like I said, the GH&H usually won. It may have been the engine; it may have been the jump-start; it may have been the straight track or the experience of the engineer. Or, it may have been that nobody wanted to get in the way.

1902—J. Edgar Pew and the Missing Barber

There are quite a few people in the world who believe that everything happens for some pre-planned reason. There are probably an equal number who believe that all of life is a continuing game of chance, that accident has more to do with history than do the plans anyone makes. Certainly, there is supporting evidence for each perspective. I guess, however, that in the absence of any scientifically monitored system of checking daily events, we'll never know while we're on this earth. Do things happen "just by chance" or are the "accidents" pre-planned to happen that way? Consider the case of J. Edgar Pew.

The odds are pretty good that you don't recognize the name of J. Edgar Pew. I confess that I never heard of him before he popped-up in some research. No matter how well you think you know a story, there is always something left for you to learn. I guess that's the way it's supposed to be. That's why we should never stop learning.

The case in point is Spindletop and the first Texas oil boom. We all know that the Lucas Gusher on Spindletop Hill ushered in the "age of oil" back in 1901. Texas and oil and wheeler-dealers became synonymous.

There was so much happening that thousands of good stories got lost in the shuffle. That's why I want to tell you about J. Edgar Pew and the missing barber.

Back in 1859, two fellows named Bowditsch and Drake hired "Billy" Smith to dig a well at Titusville, Pennsylvania. On August 28th of that year, and at a depth of 69½ feet, Billy struck oil. It was the first well in the United States to produce oil in commercial quantities, and, using a narrow water-well bucket, they managed to dip out about 400 gallons a day. There really wasn't much demand for the product, but it gave folks something to think about.

A few years earlier, in 1855, Dr. Samuel M. Kier, down in Pittsburgh, Pennsylvania, distilled and refined oil skimmed from a creek and sold "Kier's Rock Oil" as a laxative for fifty cents for a half pint. He proved that you could do something with the stuff besides grease wheels, but no one knew just how far the distilling process could go. Then, in 1857, a fellow named A. C. Ferris took the lighter fractions of distilled oil, called it "Carbon Oil," and patented a lamp to burn it. Today we call that stuff kerosene. Everyone wanted light. The Ferris lamp provided much more light than candles at a price (seventy cents a gallon) much cheaper than the lamps that burned the oil from sperm whales. So far, however, the process still involved oil skimmed from ponds and creeks. That was when Billy started dipping it out at 400 barrels a day.

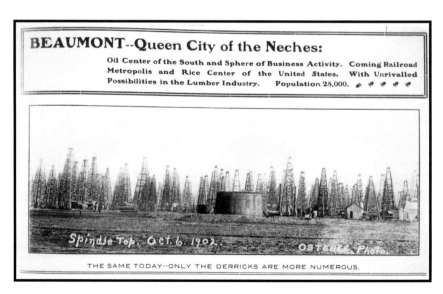

Panorama of the Spindletop Oilfield circa 1902
courtesy UTSA's Institute of Texan Cultures at San Antonio

In 1860 William Barnsdall and William Abbott built the country's first commercial oil refinery up in Oil Creek Valley, Pennsylvania, and the crude oil from the Drake well and others that sprouted in the area arrived at the plant in wooden tank wagons. It wasn't until 1865 that Samuel Van Sickle built the first successful crude oil pipeline from Miller's Farm to Pithole, Pennsylvania, a distance of four miles. Soon, lots of folks in Pennsylvania were involved in the oil business at a time when we were looking for new sources of power. Pretty soon, Standard Oil of Pennsylvania had consolidated most of the small producers and created an almost perfect monopoly.

Joseph Newton Pew was the son of a Pennsylvania farmer and, at the turn of the 20th century, a small but successful gas producer and salesman who had not been gobbled up by Standard Oil. It was Pew's company that supplied the gas to make Pittsburgh the first city to use natural gas for heating, lighting, and cooking. Like I said, he was small but successful. However, with Standard Oil holding a virtual monopoly on the oil business, especially in the North, Joseph Newton's little heating and lighting Sun Oil Company didn't stand much of a chance of getting bigger.

Then came Spindletop and the breakup of the Standard Oil monopoly. There was a chance for the small companies to grow, that is, if someone was in the right place at the right time.

J. Edgar Pew was Joseph Newton Pew's nephew. When he was sixteen he went to work in the Pew refinery as a plumber's helper. By the time he was thirty he was traveling scout and front man for the company. That was why, when the Lucas Gusher blew in, J. Edgar came to Beaumont. He saw that the reports had not been exaggerated. There was great opportunity.

There seemed to be more oil under Spindletop and nearby Sour Lake than anyone had dreamed. Most of it, however, belonged to other people on lands sewed-up by big leases. The small leases, down to one-twelfth of an acre, changed hands rapidly, and millions of dollars were made and lost each day. There wasn't much room in production for a small, conservative, and independently owned company. There might, however, be a need for storage and sales while one waited for a chance at bigger game.

Back in Pennsylvania the company bought the old Lindenthorpe Pleasure Park on the Delaware River and started building a modern refinery. Down in Texas, J. Edgar bought a 40-acre tract of high land along the Neches River where ships and barges could dock and built a storage facility capable of holding over a million barrels of oil.

Then the bottom fell out. Oil was in such great supply that the price dropped to three cents a barrel. There simply was no market for the stuff—we had not started our great love affair with internal combustion engines on four wheels, and few railroad locomotives and steamships had been converted to the new fuel. At that low rate, J. Edgar filled his tanks with enough oil to last for years. But, there was always the question, *"Couldn't he do better?"* What about the dream of sewing-up production as well?

The Lone Star and Crescent Oil Company had good leases, producing wells, pipelines, and additional storage facilities. The company had a good future. In fact, Lone Star and Crescent had just signed a contract to provide England with ten million barrels of oil at that production price of three cents a barrel. Then, suddenly, the wells stopped gushing. There were so many holes on Spindletop Hill that the pressure faded away, and the price of oil jumped to thirty cents a barrel, or ten times what it had been. Unable to meet their contract with England at the higher production price, the Lone Star and Crescent folded their whole operation. The assets were auctioned on the courthouse steps in Beaumont. On Decoration Day, 1902, J. Edgar Pew, acting for the Sun Oil Company, bought a property worth over one million dollars for one hundred thousand. His was the only bid offered.

But, there was a catch. The sheriff required one-fourth of the money that day to seal the bargain. No problem. J. Edgar went to the bank where Sun Oil had its accounts. It was closed. Folks in Pennsylvania didn't know that on Confederate Decoration Day the banks and many other folks down South closed their doors in honor of those who died in The War of Northern Aggression. No money, no deal. The next day would be too late.

Wandering the crowded street and wondering what to do, J. Edgar stopped at his usual barbershop for a trim. The door was open and there was a lot of activity, but no barber. It seemed that the barber had just made $8,000 on an oil lease sale and had sold the barbershop to some other folks who wanted to open a new bank. J. Edgar rushed up to the well-dressed gentleman who was directing the removal of barber chairs and mirrors and said that, if they were opening a new bank, he wanted to be their first customer.

To a banker, business is business, holiday or no. Sun Oil had a good reputation, and, anyway, he was already at his new office, incomplete as it was. A cashier's check was issued, the sheriff got his money, and the papers were signed the next day. By "accident" Sun Oil became one of the largest oil companies in the nation, and the brand new Gulf National Bank had its first and one of its best customers.

1903—Life on the Shoestring

Sour Lake! Now there's a name not calculated to win friends and influence people. It's not like Sweetwater (where there wasn't any water at all). No sir, the folks that named that place told it like it was. Actually, it was originally Sour Springs Lake, and the town was settled back in 1835 while Texas was still a part of Mexico. The Indians had been there a long time before the first Anglo settlers came snooping around and found out, like the Indians had, that the awful tasting water from the springs would cure a lot of what ails you, especially when you mixed it with that shiny stuff that floated on the water from where it seeped out of the ground. By 1850 there was a health resort on the lake, and even Sam Houston went there to "take the waters."

Well on Sour Lake
by Gary Manthei

Well, folks didn't pay much attention to that funny-smelling, funny-tasting water, except to drink it and sit in it on occasion, until the Spindle-top Oil Field blew in down by Beaumont back in 1901. So that's what that funny stuff was—oil! In 1902, the discovery well at Sour Lake blew in with a roar from a depth of only 646 feet, and, by 1903, there were 150 wells producing 50,000 barrels a day.

During the first week of October, 1903, Charlie Jeffries blew into town. Later he wrote, *"Boll weevils had ruined the cotton in my part of the country, and, like thousands of others, I went to the oil field to tide me over a hard time. By pawning my fiddle and my six-shooter and borrowing fifty cents from a friend, I got there without a cent."*

What he found was like a bad dream of that special corner of Hell reserved for child beaters and crooked politicians. There were no laws regulating where or how you drilled. You could buy land in one thirty-second of an acre lots. That's a square about 37 feet on a side, just enough to anchor the corners of a wooden derrick. Slush from the drilling spilled out on the ground, making it a bottomless sea of mud, and gas seepage rolled in yellow clouds along the ground to kill men and animals and then explode when it found an open flame. The throbbing heart of this inferno was called the "Shoestring."

You see, the surveyors weren't always right. Sometimes their measurements were a bit off, especially when they started at two ends and worked toward the middle. Sometimes conflicting claims overlapped. Sometimes they didn't quite meet. I know of one case where, when surveyors for the General Land Office were making the first survey of unoccupied land, they ran into Indian trouble. When they came back the next year, they came from the other direction and measured to where they thought they stopped, drew their map, and went on their way, leaving an unclaimed strip of land almost a mile wide and almost ten miles long that, technically, belonged to no one—not even the government. The Shoestring was like that, a narrow strip of land between recognized ownerships that sprouted derricks like a forest. There was no land uncovered. The workers made their way from rig to rig on pipes and planks. A photograph shows ten derricks in less than one hundred yards. There were no roads and no vehicles on the Shoestring, nothing but mud, gas, spilled oil, and men who worked hard and played harder.

Charlie remembered the Derrick Saloon (built on the working deck of an abandoned derrick) and the Big Thicket Saloon. Then there was the House of Lords, where successful drillers drank when they "broke out" (were promoted) to "work on the big wheel" (assume a position of administrative power) and become "high rafter bats" (those who roost in the barn above all others and shower those below). Also, there was Dad's Saloon, where you could die quicker from a knife than from a gas explosion. If you wanted to sleep, you rented a cot by the hour (blanket extra). Companionship, of very dubious quality, was available. If you wanted to eat, well, you ate what was offered in the saloons or went hungry. There was no place to take a bath, and the privies emptied into the slop below the rigs.

They poked so many holes in the Sour Lake Field that by the end of 1903 the bottom fell out of both the market and the gas pressure. The price of oil dropped to three cents a barrel, and half of the wells stopped flowing. The boomers like Charlie, who built the Shoestring, drifted away to new fields and new towns with names like Petrolia, Electra, Ranger, Tyler, and Burkburnett. No matter what the name, they had the same mud, the same smell, and the same recreational opportunities.

They still have oil around Sour Lake, and the town's population holds at around 2,000. Lots of folks go over that way to hunt and fish, and the Big Thicket National Preserve contains some of the wildest country in the South. But, I bet it's not as wild as life once was on the Shoestring.

1907—The Six-Cylinder Stage

I forget who made the observation that a new idea is one of the most painful afflictions of humanity, but it's true. Most of us reject new ideas because they will disrupt traditional patterns and make us think. Others reject new ideas because they have a vested interest in keeping things the way they are. In any event, we are cursed with the inertia of rest and run from ideas as if they carried the plague.

> *"Dear Sir, ... Our opinions are only given on mechanical affairs of known factors. We do not act on theories of what might happen."*

Well, so much for the government. In that year of 1899 the telegraph had long-since spanned the continent and the oceans. Railroads and oil pipelines linked North, South, East, and West. Streets and factories were bright with electric lights, and, in Germany, Count Ferdinand von Zeppelin was building a monstrous machine that would fly through the air. In the United States the government was continuing to act in true bureaucratic form.

"Dear Sir, Replying to your letter of the 14th, beg to say you must have been kicked in the head by a mule when a small boy ...."

So, it was back to the drawing board for W. B. Chenoweth. Chenoweth was a visionary, but he was also a practical man. As the chief draftsman for the Illinois and Great Northern Railroad, with his office over in Palestine in East Texas, he knew the value of mass transit. He also knew that railroads could not connect every little town and that they couldn't function economically with only a dozen passengers. He decided that the world needed a modern replacement for the stagecoach so he designed a bus. From his drawing board came a motor stage, the world's first six-cylinder, fourteen-passenger motor vehicle.

First he designed the vehicle, then he went in search of an engine. The Springfield Gas Engine Company and the Otto Gas Engine Company made only large stationary engines for factories. The Olds Motor Works, Wolverine Motor Works, and Detroit Motor Works offered small three-cylinder models that would not fill the bill. Henry Ford offered to build him two five-passenger cars for $2,700 each, but that still wasn't what Chenoweth had in mind. Finally, with the help of a Mississippi mechanic named C. H. Miles (who later invented the double-seal piston ring) he got his plans together.

In St. Louis they leased the shops of the Borbein Auto Company and began work on the vehicles themselves. In Logansport, Indiana, the Western Motor Company began to hand-build two six-cylinder engines to Chenoweth's design for $735 each. The first motor stage was assembled and tested successfully in St. Louis and shipped on a flat car to Colorado City, way up in Mitchell County, to usher in a new era of public transportation.

On Sunday preachers warned their congregations to stay away from this new device of the Devil. Preachers

W. B. Chenoweth
by Suzy Keller

278

have always been a mite skittish around things they don't understand and can't control.

Others predicted that the wheeled bomb would explode and kill the whole town. The first trip from Colorado City to Snyder was made on Monday, October 29, 1907, with one passenger, W. A. Jones. You might say that Jones was a "captive passenger" because he had helped to finance the venture. This first run of about 30 miles over relatively non-existent roads took 12 hours. The return trip with five free passengers went more smoothly. Things were looking good until a group of citizen vigilantes refused to let he vehicle pass through their community.

Chenoweth wasn't about to give up. The operation was moved to Big Spring, and the second bus arrived. On the Big Spring to Lamesa run it took horse-drawn stages 14 to 15 hours and three changes of horses to cover the necessary 55 miles. The motor stage regularly made it in eight to nine hours.

Success breeds competition. Once Chenoweth proved it could be done, everybody got into the act. There were new vehicle designs and new services. Americans took to automotive transport like a modern gold rush. Those first two six-cylinder busses ended their lives hauling milk for a Fort Worth dairy, but the idea started by W. B. Chenoweth never died.

1912—Katy Had "The Right Stuff"

When author Tom Wolfe wrote his instant classic, The Right Stuff, *about America's Project Mercury Astronauts, he described a special breed of men who had what they called "the right stuff." According to Wolfe, this applied to a "mad monk" collection of test pilots, fighter jocks, and generally nerveless individuals with the ability "... to put his hide on the line and then have the moxie, the reflexes, the experience, and the coolness to pull it back in the last yawning moment and then go up again the next day." They made a movie about Tom's book, and it won a bunch of awards. They should have made one about Katy.*

Katherine Stinson was born in Fort Payne, Alabama, back in 1891. She was a small girl, dark and vivacious, with more than a touch of independence. When Wilbur and Orville Wright made their historic flights in 1903, Katy was twelve years old, and she decided that she, too, would fly. She convinced Max Lillie of Chicago to teach her to fly, and, after only four hours of instruction, she was on her own. In 1912 she became the fourth American woman to get a pilot's license, and, because of her size, she toured the country as "The Flying Schoolgirl."

Back in 1910, the U.S. Army Signal Corps established an aviation center in San Antonio with one officer and eight men. Lt. Benjamin D. Foulois was given the only airplane the Army had—a Wright Brothers biplane with a 25-horsepower, water-cooled, "pusher" engine—and was told to "teach himself how to fly." So, you see, you might say that American military aviation and Katy Stinson lifted off at about the same time. When she was 21, in 1912, more than ten years before Charles Lindbergh ever climbed into a cockpit, Katy Stinson flew the same type plane used by the Army. The next year Katy and her mother formed the Stinson Aviation Company in Hot Springs, Arkansas. Katy's "barnstorming" finally brought her to Texas in 1913, and the company moved to San Antonio that same year.

There really was no "cockpit" at that time. The pilot sat in a bucket seat with nothing between him, or her, and the ground but a web of wires and control cables. A lever in each hand controlled the wings while pedals for both feet controlled the rudder. There were no instruments, and there was nothing to protect the pilot from the wind and weather or the occasional curious bird. Perhaps more than the exploits of Lt. Foulois (the Army aviation facility was withdrawn from Texas to Maryland in 1911 following a less than spectacular showing along the Mexican border), the aerial antics of Katy Stinson over San Antonio proved that the area was a good one for flying. With Army Aviation gone, Katy convinced the authorities at Fort Sam Houston to allow her to use the drill field as a temporary landing strip. Katy taught her sister Marjorie to fly, and then, with their mother, the women opened their own flight school and airport—Stinson Field.

Katherine Stinson, the "Schoolgirl Aviatrix"
by Nathan Smith

Marjorie, Eddie and Katherine Stinson
courtesy Texas Air Museum, Stinson Field

Katy became the first woman to "loop-the-loop" and, also, the first pilot to perform advertising skywriting at night. In 1917, Katy set the world's record for long-distance flying on a trip from San Diego to San Francisco. The 610 miles took nine hours and ten minutes, and the flight was farther and faster than any man or woman had ever flown before.

Katherine Stinson became well known throughout the world. She toured both Europe and Asia, and, in 1916, over 25,000 people turned out in Yokohama, Japan, to watch her skywrite Japanese characters at night with fireworks. In a way, you might say that she was the mother of Japanese aviation because flight schools sprang up all over the islands after her demonstration.

When the United States finally entered World War I, Katy immediately volunteered for military duty. She had already trained more people to fly than were in the Air Corps of the Army. But, you see, she was a woman, and, according to the government, women were not physically or emotionally stable enough to fly airplanes. At least, that was what the men in the Army said. So, Katy raised more than $2 million for the Red Cross by

281

giving flight demonstrations and flew the first scheduled airmail service between Washington and New York. Unable to fly for her country, Katy finally went to France as an ambulance driver while the family at Stinson Field continued to build airplanes and train pilots. The field, now a home for both private and commercial planes, is still there in San Antonio.

The weather in France during WW I took its toll. Katherine Stinson moved to New Mexico for her health after the war and became a noted architect. She lived to see the Mercury Astronauts and see men walk on the moon. She died in 1977, knowing that the Equal Employment Opportunity Act would finally guarantee women a place in aviation, but she never knew that, in 1983, Dr. Sally Ride, a physicist, would be the first American woman in space.

1913—The Legacy of Julius

The decade of the 1870s was a traumatic one for the United States. In the South, "Reconstruction" (that never matched any known definition of the term) ran its course, left ruin in its wake, and, for the most part, the reins of government were in the hands of the "Redeemers." There was an attempt to return to the days before the "War of Northern Aggression." The nation's financial situation was bad, and the vast majority of farmers did not own their land but were trapped in the tenant-farmer and crop-lien system of serfdom. The "Captains of Industry" were making millions in the new wave of the industrial revolution, and the plight of workers in all forms of industry was, perhaps, worse than that of farmers or of the slaves before emancipation. We saw our first serious labor strikes, and there were riots, lynchings, burnings, and other assorted extremes of social unrest. Samuel Clemens, writing as Mark Twain, gave this time period its most enduring label, "The Gilded Age." It was a thin veneer of gold over a form of dried mud.

Chicago can be a frightening place for a 17-year-old cut adrift in a rapidly changing world. That's today. In 1879, it was worse. The completion of the Union Stockyards in 1865 assured Chicago's leadership in American meatpacking. The "Great Chicago Fire" in 1871 destroyed three and a third square miles of business and residential property and assured a long-lasting boom in building. At the hub of transportation, Chicago joined the rest of the United States by lake, rail, river, and canal. The population ranked next to that of New York, and there were representatives of every ethnic group in the United States. That was when young Julius Rosenwald came to town.

Julius was born in Springfield, Illinois, in 1862, and, at age 17, he was well versed in the family clothing business. Jewish immigrants were the backbone of the clothing and retail marketing establishments of frontier America. Wherever they went, they brought good business practices and innovations to a nation where "homemade" was the general rule rather than the exception. Look around you today. You'll see that they still play an important role; Neiman-Marcus, Foley's, and Levi's are good examples.

Julius became a wholesale clothier and, for the next sixteen years, worked his way up through the business. He saw that in order to control quality, distribution, and sales, one had to be personally involved at all levels. One of his customers was Aaron Montgomery Ward, who became the first mail-order merchant to sell general merchandise. In 1895, Julius took what he had learned and joined the partnership of Sears and Roebuck to see if they could beat Ward's business. Mail order wasn't enough. Soon, under the coaching of Julius, Sears-Roebuck sold by mail and through retail centers throughout the country. When Richard Warren Sears retired in 1908, Julius took over as president of what had become the largest mail-order and retail establishment in the world.

So, what does this initiative have to do with Texas? Well, other than exciting almost every home with regular "sit up and rare back" catalogues that offered everything from shoes to windmills, taught generations how to read small print, and adorned most outhouses, you'll have to wait until 1913 to see the real legacy of Julius.

You see, Julius Rosenwald had an abiding interest in education for those less fortunate than himself. Although he, personally, fit the Horatio Alger prototype of "rags to riches," he recognized that there were others who did not have the opportunities to learn that he had. In 1913, he began

Mr. & Mrs. Julius Rosenwald
courtesy Peter M. Ascoli

283

to provide matching-fund grants to schools for black kids throughout the South, especially in Texas. Not since the Freedman's Bureau schools of the late 1860s had such opportunities existed.

In Texas, the Julius Rosenwald Fund created 518 schools. Most of these were in the East Texas Piney Woods, with 22 of them located in Houston County alone. Students who attended these schools (and there are thousands of them throughout the country) remember them as being usually well-built, one-room, one-teacher establishments with fairly standardized playgrounds built around one baseball, one bat, one basketball, and a mulberry tree with a swing. When you think about it, though, that is about all that most rural schools had. The schools Julius built had a tendency to endure.

One of the Rosenwald schools built near Ratcliff in 1920 served well until county consolidation in 1955. It then became a community center and hosted a variety of weekly civic functions. In 1968 it was moved to the town of Kennard and became the focal point for the new Project Head Start Program—something Julius would have liked. Then, in 1985, it was moved back to its original site in the Albin Chapel community, about one mile south of Ratcliff. With a new paint job, it became "The Little Red Schoolhouse" and acquired a historical marker all its own to commemorate not only the durability of the building but also the concern and planning of Julius Rosenwald, who brought both Sears and education to early Texas.

1916—Cyclone's Fleas

Politics seems to bring out both the best and the worst in all of us. The old saying about there being two things you don't want to watch being made—sausage and politics—is quite true. There are things that go into both of them that we'd rather not know about. Politics is also high comedy and high drama, and, somewhere along the way, there should be awards for creative acting. If we gave such awards, one surely would have gone to a fellow called "Cyclone."

Now folks, I just don't know why I've not told you before about James Harvey Davis. Maybe it is because he was a politician, and I generally don't trust folks who regularly lie to me. But, that won't wash because I've told you about others. Or, it may be because he didn't die until 1940, and I thought that he was not really "historic." Well, that is wrong, too, because I've told you about some other "modern" topics. I guess that he just slipped through the cracks, and that is something that should not have happened.

First, the bare details that you can find in various compendiums of biographical lore: James Harvey Davis was born near Walhalla in South Carolina in 1853 and came to Texas with his folks to settle over in Wood County. He taught school for a while, married Belle Barton, fathered four children, and practiced law. Back when the Farmers' Alliance was a strong voice in government and local affairs, supporting the rights of the small landowner and tenant farmer against oppressive government and big business, he traveled throughout the South as

James Harvey Davis
photo from "A History of Texas and Texans" by Francis W. H. Johnson, courtesy UTSA's Institute of Texan Cultures at San Antonio

a lecturer and Alliance organizer. That's when he got the name that he relished for the rest of his life. You probably never heard of James Harvey Davis, but "Cyclone Davis" may ring a bell, especially if you are over fifty years old.

Cyclone was devastating. His words were to the point, and he used words that his listeners could understand. Most of the folks he talked to were farmers and poor folks with limited opportunities for education. They may have liked the sound of the rolling voices of trained orators, but they didn't really understand what was being said. But, when Cyclone spoke, they knew what he said, and they liked it. Even after the death of the Populist Party in 1896, people still listened. Cyclone was never a man to be silent when he believed in something. This willingness to represent the common folks led him to the Congress, where he served in the House of Representatives from 1915 to 1917.

Cyclone Davis was in favor of prohibition. That topic was, and still is, a hot topic in Texas, where we are about equally divided on whether or not we can, or should, legislate the private morals of the people. Here's what Cyclone said in a debate on the topic:

> *"In our discussions, I have invariably admitted that saloons increased the business of a town, and I have described the character of business they increased: the business of sin and shame, vice and venality, rows and riots, fusses and fights, moans and groans, ..."*

At this point, George C. Pendleton, the adversary in the debate, interrupted Cyclone with a comment of his own:

> *"Cyclone, there is no use to make a ridicule of this matter, you will admit having seen saloons in some of the most prosperous towns you ever saw?"*

As I said, Cyclone seldom minced words:

> *"Yes, Sir, I have seen saloons in many prosperous towns; but, Sir, I have likewise seen fleas on some of the biggest, fattest dogs I ever saw, but I never have been wise enough to believe them fleas made that dog fat. I was silly enough to believe them fleas just lived off the fat that the dog already had, and the more business them fleas done, the worse off that dog was."*
>
> *"So, being a prohibitionist my theory is to abolish the flea, but you anti-prohibitionists insist that it would never do to interfere with the personal liberty of the flea: allow him to do business with the dog six days in the week, but make him rest on Sunday. Allow him to do business with a full-grown dog, but forbid him doing business with little puppy-dogs."*
>
> *"Now, Sir, let me say seriously, the only way a flea's business affects a dog is to disturb his peace, make him howl and scratch and make him mangy."*

Old Cyclone had a few more choice thoughts on the subject and on dishonest politics in general, but we'll let them slide because they've put a few folks in jail lately for offending someone's "inner child" by speaking their mind. That debate, however, found its way into newspapers all over the country and raised chuckles even in the saloons he fought against. Maybe if modern politicians added some of Cyclone's spirit to their debates, they'd be more interesting.

1917—"Birdie"

The odds are pretty good that you've never heard of Birdie Harwood. That's too bad, because she blazed the way for a lot of capable and public-minded women. Before women "got the vote" in 1919, very few women served their communities, counties, states, or the federal government in any elected capacity. There were a few appointments, but, with an all-male electorate, even these were very rare.

Ophelia Crosby was born up in Blanco County back in 1872. That was a few years before Crosby County was named for her grandfather, who came to Texas from Alabama in 1845 and ran the General Land Office until 1867. Ophelia's father was a prominent rancher who had been a captain in the Confederate Army. She grew up on the range, in the shadow of cowboys and cattlemen. They called her "Birdie" because of her chipper attitude and curiosity about everything. She learned to ride on the shoulders of "Ab" Blocker, one of the greatest of the trail drivers, and was confidant

Ophelia Crosby Harwood
courtesy Marble Falls Public Library, Marble Falls, Texas

in the company of folks from Ben Thompson, the famous gunman, to Ira Aten, the respected Texas Ranger. When she graduated from Ab's shoulders to horses, she rode a sidesaddle designed for Mollie Goodnight and impressed both the rough and tumble cowboys and Austin society. "Birdie" Crosby married Dr. George Harwood on May 12, 1892, and moved with him to Marble Falls, where he practiced medicine for the next 43 years.

Birdie was not content to be just a wife and a mother. From the beginning she took an active interest in the functioning of city and state government. She once wrote, *"No good woman is out of place doing those things which are so vital to the welfare of her children and her home."* As her children grew, so did her interest in things outside the home. She wrote, *"A woman's first duty is to her home and children. When she has raised them up to take their place in the world, it is then her duty to turn to her state and there help make and enforce the laws that will make it a fit abiding place for them."* It wasn't that Birdie was "pushy"—she just had bright ideas about how society should function for the good of all and didn't mind telling others about them.

The early 20th century was still difficult for independent women in America. Although there were advances in medicine and in the things of the home, a woman's place in society was basically unchanged. Most folks thought women were too dainty and fragile in mind and body to participate in what was basically a man's world of business and government. Somehow, that didn't bother Birdie. While other women marched in suffragette picket lines, she knocked on the doors of offices.

In April of 1917, two years before suffragettes got the vote, an electorate made up solely of men elected Ophelia "Birdie" Harwood mayor of Marble Falls. She was the first woman to become the mayor of a city in Texas.

Birdie served her city well. After the death of her husband in 1934, she stepped down from the mayor's office to become municipal judge. She never failed to demonstrate that a woman was capable of expanding beyond the role set for her in society. She continued to lead parades riding her sidesaddle, and, when she died in 1954, she had seen women take their place in both government and industry.

On July 24, 1993, the City of Marble Falls honored Birdie with a combined celebration. There were lots of people and good times and some solemn moments when folks remembered the way things used to be. There was also the presentation of a new award. Harriet E. Myers, the first woman president of the 53,000-member State Bar of Texas, received the first annual Birdie Harwood Award created to honor a special woman who achieved a position of status in a domain that was once exclusively masculine. I guess you could say that Birdie, on her sidesaddle, helped lead the way.

1921—The Silver Wings of "Queen Bess"

Some folks like to work in the cotton fields; some like to fly with the birds. Sometimes you can't tell which is which, or I guess in this case it is "who is who," unless you give them the opportunity and watch for a while. The key, I think, is faith and determination. How many people have chosen to stay in life's fields rather than, with faith, follow the dream of the Psalmist to "take the wings of the morning ..." and see what else life has to offer.

Bessie Coleman was one of those folks who did not enjoy working in the cotton fields. Back in 1892 when she was born, there wasn't much choice for a tenant farmer's family. Over 80% of all cotton farmers worked on farms that they did not own and grew the crops that the owners wanted. There wasn't much land left over to grow something to eat, and, at the end of the year, the odds were that the tenant owed more money to the store than came from his share of the crop. Tenant farming was just as much a

Bessie Coleman's flight certificate from the
Federation Aeronautique Internationale, June 15, 1921
courtesy UTSA's Institute of Texan Cultures at San Antonio

kind of slavery as any in the *ante-bellum* South. Tenant farmers were tied to the land with debts that kept getting bigger each year. Tenant farmers were not happy people.

Bessie was born over in East Texas in those piney woods, where the life of a tenant was even worse than it was in many other places. As a child, she worked in the fields all day to help with the crop and, at night, did laundry for folks who could pay her a few cents to help out. But, even with the extra money, it wasn't easy. You see, Bessie Coleman was an African-American, and her future looked very bleak. Then, in 1915, when she was 23, Bessie Coleman ran away from the cotton fields. She left East Texas and headed for Chicago. She had a dream of somehow being special and amounting to something. At first, it didn't look like she'd made it. She ended up as a manicurist in a beauty shop that catered to other, more affluent, African-American clients. But, even that was better than picking cotton and doing other folks' laundry. Then there was a fair, and Bessie, for the first time, watched an airplane swoop and dive like the birds she had watched over the fields of Texas. Bessie Coleman wanted to fly.

No one in Chicago would teach her. Not only was she a woman, she was also black. Then came the "war to end all wars," followed by the post-war boom that we call the "Roaring Twenties." In Chicago many folks prospered and put their money in the stock market. Bessie saved her money and went to France.

France has never been as color-conscious as the United States. At the little town of Le Crotoy in the Somme Valley, Bessie Coleman, one-time cotton hand and manicurist, attended L'Ecole d'Aviation des Freres Caudron, the leading private aviation school in the nation. Then, in 1921, she became the world's first licensed black female pilot. This was two years before Amelia Earhart received her wings.

When Bessie returned to the United States, life was still not easy. Very few people wanted to watch an African-American woman fly, and there were no airline or airmail delivery jobs open. For five years, with a few months out to return to France for advanced training, "Queen Bess," as her fans called her, toured the country giving exhibition flights for other African-Americans at rural fairs and celebrations and lecturing on dreams and how to reach them in segregated schools and churches. She reminded folks that *"background and beginnings don't matter"* any more than the color of a person's skin. What mattered were a person's will and determination and self-confidence. In order to fly, she said, you've got to leave the ground. No matter who you are, you have to make your own horizons.

Queen Bess wore the traditional leather coat, leggings, and helmet of the French Flying Corps, along with her white silk scarf and silver wings. In most ways, she was a fashion plate for a romantic view of a romantic profession, while Amelia Earhart was capturing attention in baggy overalls. It made no difference. Queen Bess was making a statement for herself, for her fans, and for her race. To them, she was what dreaming and flying were all about.

Bessie Coleman died at age 34 in a crash at Jacksonville, Florida. Few, if any, major newspapers carried the story, but the black press grieved. She was the first, and she had charted a course and gone boldly toward a new frontier. In 1977, a group of African-American female pilots who hadn't been born when Queen Bess died formed a flying club in her honor. In 1992, Chicago declared May 2 as Bessie Coleman Day, and her sister female pilots flew the "missing man formation" over her grave.

1923—Red's Raid on the King Tut

Some of you may remember the oil boom days around Navarro County during the "Roaring Twenties." On January 7, 1923, the J. H. Burke Number One well blew in just southeast of Corsicana, and, in April, the Johnson well began producing 12,000 barrels a day. Before you could say

Marvin "Red" Burton, Texas Ranger
courtesy the Texas Ranger Hall of Fame and Museum, Texas Ranger Research Center, Waco, Texas

"boomtown," the Corsicana Daily Sun *announced that its home represented "the wealthiest [per capita] business city in the United States." If you were there, you remember the streets clogged with traffic and every wide spot in the road filled with tents, lean-tos, and shanties for the oil field workers, lease speculators, and other assorted types of humanity that flocked to the area.*

If you were in Navarro County, you also probably remember that, even during prohibition, the streets ran with illegal liquor, and that, for a small fee, somewhere, you could buy any depraved diversion your heart desired.

Things got pretty bad. Local law enforcement officers found themselves not just outnumbered but outgunned and not in favor with those staunch local citizens who were busy making money through assorted illicit businesses. Even deacons with doughnut shops were bootleggers. That is when the local minions of the law called for help from the State and "Red" Burton entered the picture.

Marvin "Red" Burton was a Texas Ranger with a reputation for fearlessness in "bootlegger busting" up around Dallas. In January of 1924, he was cleaning up a few problems over around Glen Rose, south of Fort Worth, but he sent in a team of undercover agents to check out operations. The team leader was one Richard Watson whom the *Corsicana Daily Sun* later described as *"a quiet, innocent appearing and friendly youth."* Little did folks know that he had as much experience as Red and that his team of operatives could sweet-talk their way into almost any speakeasy in the country. They set up shop in mid-January and went to work buying and drinking their way to a string of future indictments.

Red arrived on February 7th, and they compared notes. The team reported illicit liquor manufacturing and sales in every community in the county, accompanied by gambling and prostitution. The list of names involved folks wanted on fugitive warrants from other states, many well-known pillars of the community, and a lot of regular folks in between.

The raids started at Navarro, a little town south of Corsicana, and continued for three days and nights. *"This is a Ranger raid! Now back up to the wall and stick up your hands!"* There was none of the bumbling grandstanding that came to characterize alcohol agent raids in the future, and no one was butchered in the process. The raids were well timed and efficient. Soon, wagons were busy hauling prisoners to the county jail, while others, filled with gambling devices, liquor, and illegal weapons, were headed for evidence rooms. When the smoke cleared, the jails were filled, and the grand jury handed down fifty felony indictments.

But, some big fish got away. That bothered Red. His unbeaten team reported that, somewhere, there was still a well-protected bar frequented only by elite members of the Corsicana economic society. There were rumors, but no one knew for sure where it was. A secret search warrant was issued.

On Saturday afternoon, when business was booming, Red and that *"friendly youth"* Dick Watson ambled into the Corsicana National Bank. After a serious and lively discussion with the Rangers, the vice president was encouraged to open the main bank vault.

There it was amongst the lock-boxes! "King Tut's Room" was regally carpeted and contained *"a regular bar ... with all the fixtures for a saloon,"* including two carloads of whisky and a full compliment of eager depositors who felt secure behind the ten-ton door. There was no back door through which folks could slip away. More wagons came and went loaded with the assorted withdrawals from the vault.

Reform movements rarely last forever and national prohibition was repealed. No doubt, the banks of today are strictly legitimate in all that they do. But, there are still those who remember Red's raid that put a stop to "banking with pleasure" in King Tut's Room.

1924—Stout Jackson

There are many legendary strong men in the world. Hercules from mythology and Samson from the Bible come to mind. When I was growing up, every comic book had a coupon you could send with a dollar to get a book by Charles Atlas that would tell you how he changed "from a 97-pound weakling into the most perfectly formed man in the world." Angelo Siciliano arrived in New York in 1903 and was, indeed, a puny teenager. He didn't adopt the Atlas name until 1922, when he won a body-building competition using methods he learned by watching lions stretch in the zoo. You can still buy his program, although I notice that it now costs $49.95. It is a good program, but, before the world heard of Charles Atlas, there was Stout Jackson.

Strongman Thomas Jefferson "Stout" Jackson
by Gary Manthei

Folks, let me tell you about Stout Jackson. If you look in the newspaper or telephone book, the odds are that you will find a variety of "stout shops." These are places where those of us who are just a bit wider than we would like to be can find clothes that fit a bit more loosely than a surgical glove. That just shows you what happens to words. I looked up *stout* in the dictionary, and it said, *"courageous, brave, strong in body or construction; as in stout-hearted, a stout person or a stout ship."* That's the definition we're talking about. You might say that Stout Jackson was, well, he was stout.

He wasn't always that way. Thomas Jefferson Jackson was born in 1890 on a little ranch up northwest of Fort Worth and sort of looked like the runt of the litter. Although he was an active youngster, he was small and began life taking the general abuse handed out to most folks who are either little or weak. Do you remember those body-building ads where some muscle-headed hunk kicked sand on the little fellow at the beach? Well, that's about what it was like.

Early on, however, Tom Jackson decided he didn't like it. He started doing special exercises. I don't know what they were because he didn't advertise, but he drank at least a quart of milk every time he sat down to the table. Wasn't long until folks began to notice a change. Not everybody noticed, however. One day at school the local bully picked on "little Tommy" one time too many. Tom Jackson clear-cut his timber down to the ground, burned his brush, and plowed up the ashes. Someone must have said, *"Wow, he sure is stout!"* because the name stuck. By the time he graduated from high school, he still weighed only 155 pounds, but he liked to turn horseshoes into corkscrews with his bare hands, and he had already lifted 1,500 pounds with a back lift.

They could always use a "stout" hand around the ranch but Tom "Stout" Jackson decided to go on the road. He had a team of mules and a wagon and began to hit the county fairs, billing himself as *"Jackson, Stoutest Man on Earth."* His first stop was the fair at Joplin, up in Jack County. He drew 101 customers at fifteen cents apiece. It was a beginning. For several years he toured North Texas and Oklahoma and just kept getting stronger. Then he branched out to cover other western states about the time that Angelo Siciliano was watching the lions at the zoo.

Stout Jackson had little use for the standard bar bells that folks use to "pump iron" today. He said that the rural folks in his audiences just couldn't relate to them. He used things that they were familiar with. He'd usually start his show by borrowing a rope from some cowboy in the audience. Cowboys depended on those ropes, and still do. Those ropes pulled cows from bog holes and flipped steers for branding. Stout would double the rope, loop it around his hips and shoulders, and break it. Where cars were popular he would stand on two inner tubes and stretch them up over his head. With a special harness and a brace, he'd resist the pull of a team of mules. Then, just for fun he'd twist horseshoes and toss anvils. But his favorite was the back lift. Bent at the hips and with his hands resting on a block of wood, Stout Jackson would straighten his legs and back and lift platforms crowded with men. In March of 1924, at Bob Holmes' Gin in

Lubbock, he back-lifted a platform holding 12 standard bales of cotton for a total of 6,472 pounds. Now folks, that was stout!

The Great Depression and money worries took most of his paying audience, so, with his wife, Stout moved to South Texas, where he designed and built movie theaters and organized entertainment for predominantly Mexican-American audiences. He weathered well. When he was in his 70s, he could still bend 60-penny spikes with his hands.

Stout Jackson died in Austin in 1976 at the age of 86. I would like to have seen a meeting between him and another of our legendary strong men, Strap Buckner. Together they could probably have straightened out the kinks in the Colorado River.

1926—The Pennies of "Old Pushbroom"

San Antonio is an exciting place to visit. It always has been. From its beginnings as a roadside rest stop along the Spanish road that ran from the mission and presidio complex of San Juan Bautista, just below today's Eagle Pass, to the mission of San Miguel de Linares de los Adaes at today's Robeline, Louisiana, it has seen the ebb and flow of empire. It was a provincial capital, a major battlefield in two wars, and a mustering point for armies in at least six more. It was headquarters for the western expansion of the cattle industry and the railroad. It was, and is, the meeting place for more than a dozen cultures. It has always been exciting. It has not always been clean.

Now folks, I really don't know too much about Otto Phillip Schnabel. No doubt, if I lived in San Antonio and had access to the local libraries, I could learn more in short order. So far, he has managed to stay out of the publications that list those who made a major impact on Texas. Next time around, he should be at the head of one of the lists dealing with beauty, cleanliness, virtue, etc.

O. P. first appeared on the business scene of San Antonio back in 1919 as a manager for the Jefferson Standard Life Insurance Company. In ten years he built up a considerable business, but, during the Depression, it was hard to sell insurance of any kind. Then came World War II, and business boomed again. After the war and almost thirty years of hard work, O. P. rewarded himself with a trip to Europe in 1947.

Now, way back in 1926, O. P. had started his first campaign against litter in the streets of San Antonio. He had a business card, as all insurance salesmen do, but his was different. Along with the usual particulars,

295

Otto Phillip Schnabel & Paul Villaret, air raid wardens, 1942
courtesy UTSA's Institute of Texan Cultures at San Antonio (San Antonio Light Collection)

he included a wish for a good day, a request for a clean city based on the absence of litter, and a bright new shiny penny. He made sure that the area around his office was clean and began picking up litter wherever he saw it. People began to joke that the initials "O. P." stood for "Old Pushbroom," and that was probably in his mind when he went to Europe.

In 1947, most of Europe was a shambles. From Rome to Paris and on to London and Berlin, cities large and small and even tiny market villages were piles of ashes. Clearing the rubble would take a decade and rebuilding much longer, but what impressed O. P. most was the spirit of those who still operated small businesses. Those towns untouched by war gleamed like the new pennies he handed out with his cards. Every morning, streets were cleaned and sidewalks scrubbed. In areas of devastation, while the demolition of unsound buildings took place next door, small businessmen cleaned their windows, swept their premises, and planted flower boxes. The idea, "as bright as a new penny," and the spirit of the people stuck in his mind, and, when O. P. returned to San Antonio, he looked at it with new eyes.

O. P. Schnabel started where everyone has to start, with himself. He made sure that every place he went was cleaner when he left it. Then he started his campaign to really enlist others with more than a bright penny and a request. Soon after his return, he founded the Beautify San Antonio Association. It became one of the first major anti-litter campaigns in America. Through the efforts of the Association, the city acquired trash cans for street corners and, even more importantly, arranged for them to be emptied. From the streets, Old Pushbroom's Association moved to private property and offered rewards to those businessmen who showed the spirit he had seen in Europe and who beautified their own grounds. From San Antonio, he moved to the state and founded the Beautify Texas Council. Although he died in 1987, the spirit of Old Pushbroom lives on. Whether the folks involved recognize it or not, the "Don't Mess With Texas" campaign is a modern spin-off of what started with Old Pushbroom's pennies.

Keeping San Antonio and Texas clean is expensive. O. P. once estimated that he had, personally, passed out over $70,000 in pennies. Today it costs millions of dollars a year. You can do your part. Old Pushbroom's quest reminds me of the words to an old gospel song, *"Brighten the corner where you are."*

1928—Miss Lillie

The last time I pulled in to that big truck stop just east of San Antonio on I-10, I got to thinking that there probably wasn't a rig on the lot that cost less than twice the value of my house. Then I got to thinking about the folks that drive those rigs and keep us supplied with almost everything we use. Without those big rigs on the highways, every store in every city would soon close. It's something to think about. Without daily deliveries, most grocery stores would be down to paper plates in three days.

About that time one of the drivers climbed down from the cab and, after straightening her skirt, walked with grace into the dining room. It sort of reminded me of that long-gone commercial that started out with, "You've come a long way ..." And that, of course, made me think of Miss Lillie.

Back in 1897 they still called Hempstead, over in Waller County, north of Houston, "Six-Shooter Junction." It seems that folks in those parts had ways of feud, foul play, and frolic that kept the courts and undertakers busy and encouraged passengers on the trains to sit on the floor with their heads below window level when the porter announced, *"Hempstead.*

297

Hempstead. Change cars for the Austin branch and be prepared to meet your God."

That's the way things were on January 9th when Miss Lillie came to town, a three-week old "taken baby" from John Sealy Hospital in Galveston, adopted by Fannie and George McGee. As time passed and Lillie grew, excitement seemed to follow her wherever she went. She was a big child, looking older than her years, and she found her way, with a child's inventiveness, in and out of enough of Hempstead's daily turmoil to satisfy anyone. When George McGee died and Fannie took a job as a nurse for a living, Miss Lillie was in the 5th grade. She quit school to become, at age 13, the youngest, full-time night telephone operator in Texas.

Lillie was happy. She supported her adopted mother by working all night. Between calls she read to stay awake and take the place of her lost schooling. In the mornings she slept, and in the afternoons and evenings she joined the other young people of town in the round of picnics, rodeos, and dances at the armory. Then came scarlet fever, a throat operation that left her with a husky baritone voice, and the permanent partial loss of hearing that often accompanied that illness.

Her early marriage at age 15 to a traveling auditor didn't work out. Then came her second marriage to Willard Drennan on July 17, 1917. For ten years both Willard and Lillie worked hard just to keep food on the

Lillie Drennan
by Suzy Keller

table—then came the boom from the Raccoon Bend Oil Field on the Brazos. Hempstead was transformed overnight. With an abandoned and then repaired open-cab Model T Ford truck, the Drennan Truck Line began operation, hauling supplies to the oil field. Business boomed, and the truck line grew. Miss Lillie kept the books, sometimes drove a second truck, rounded up business, and ran the office, while Willard and other hired drivers hauled most of the loads. During the 1920s, a soft drink bottling plant added its weight, and income, to the family business.

Things were too good. Willard decided that with so much money coming in he didn't need to work, and he began to play around in Houston and down in Mexico. Lillie's second divorce was granted in 1929. That year Miss Lillie Drennan became the first woman licensed by the State of Texas (and in the United States) to operate a common carrier motor truck and the first woman to receive a permit from the Railroad Commission of Texas to operate her own national truck line. Talk about a legend; Miss Lillie was even bigger than that. She always wore knee-high oil field boots, heavy cavalry riding britches, and a leather jacket, topped off with a ten-gallon hat in the style of Tom Mix and William S. Hart. She carried a .45 "New Service" Colt revolver and had a reputation for delivering her loads no matter what the road or weather or who got in the way. In the cutthroat hauling business she held her own and prospered. If it took colorful language, she explained that, *"Me and God have an understanding."* If it took forty hours of driving in two days, she did it with black coffee and never had an accident. Through the dark days of the Great Depression, Miss Lillie and the Drennan Truck Line kept on trucking. Throughout the United States, at freight terminals and roadside diners, oil workers and truckers knew of "Miss Lillie of Six-Shooter Junction." When World War II broke out, Brigadier General John Porter used her help to plan for and train the first Women's Army Corps Transport Drivers for the Quartermaster Corps. She was still going strong in 1950 when she demonstrated her abilities for the Texas Motor Transportation Association "Roadeo" in Dallas.

From Model Ts to the gender of the drivers, trucking has indeed come a long way. For a great part of that distance, Miss Lillie led the pack.

Miss Lillie retired from the Drennan Truck Lines in 1952 at age 55, with 27 years of trucking under her belt, and began writing newspaper and magazine articles. She rarely wrote about trucking. Instead, she wrote about plants and flowers and gardening—something she'd never had time for before retiring—and operated a little novelty and package store until her death in 1974.

I was right. *"You've come a long way ..."*

1928—Ma Thornton and the "Soup" Wagon

Every time you invent something new, you automatically invent a bunch of jobs that will support it. Invent an automobile and you create a need for metal workers, upholsterers, painters, mechanics, battery makers, folks that mount tires, and a whole lot more. The more complex the invention, the more jobs it produces. This also leads to specialization. In most fields we've moved away from the individual craftsman who did the entire job from start to finish. Some of the necessary specializations are quite interesting.

You might say that Mrs. W. A. Thornton was just a normal wife and homemaker, helping her husband do a job that needed to be done. Then again, you might think that she was a little bit different, a specialist. I guess it all depends on your perspective. You see, Ma Thornton drove a "soup" wagon.

Actually, the story begins back in 1847 when a chemistry student in Paris, with the unlikely name of Sombrero, mixed a few common ingredients in a laboratory and invented nitroglycerin. The 1874 issue of *The American Cyclopaedia* said that it was the greatest advance in explosive technology since the invention of gunpowder. The ingredients may have been common, but the result wasn't. Until the splitting of the atom, nitroglycerin, also known as "fulminating oil," "nitroleum," "trinitrine," "glonoine," "nitro," or simply "soup," was the most powerful—and hazardous—explosive known. It was powerful, all right. One drop would flip a 300-pound anvil. As far as hazard goes, 28 pounds of pressure or a temperature of 118 degrees would set it off. Folks, soup was not something with which to play games.

Ma Thornton's Soup Wagon
by Suzy Keller

In 1864, Alfred Nobel, up in Sweden, mixed soup with an absorbent clay, wrapped it in red paper, and called it "dynamite." That revolutionized the mining and construction industries and made things a lot safer, but it also cut down on the power of the explosive. For really big bangs, soup was still the answer.

Then along came the oil industry. Without going into a lot of details, drillers learned that, sometimes, if you set off a big explosion in the very bottom of a reluctant well, it fractured the rock formation and allowed the oil and gas to flow more freely. This realization led to the creation of another oil patch specialist, the "well-shooter."

Well-shooters were a breed apart and excited the same morbid curiosity as an automobile wreck. Realizing that to step on a single drop of soup usually meant the loss of a leg or instant death, these folks regularly poured, by hand, from two-quart cans, up to 700 quarts of soup into long metal cylinders called torpedoes and lowered them to the bottom of drilled wells, where they were detonated by timing devices or simply a long-fused stick of dynamite. The resulting explosion, perhaps a mile underground, blew large quantities of debris from the well and opened massive fractures in the rock. If they were lucky, they also got oil. Well shooters were a legendary bunch, and we'll talk more about them some day. But, for now, first things first.

You see, well-shooters couldn't shoot if they didn't have the soup. Railroads wouldn't carry the stuff. In remote areas it came by backpack or pack mule. For a while, it traveled in specially built wagons. By the 1920s it usually arrived at the well in a car or truck with sensitive springs and insulation. In 1919 a car carrying soup exploded on the Weatherford Road just west of Fort Worth and completely atomized the car, the driver, an unlucky hitchhiker, and the bridge, and it also flattened a garage and injured people a quarter of a mile away. Unfortunately, things like that happened frequently, especially on rough roads and in the summer, when it was hot.

Ward A. "Tex" Thornton was among the best of the well-shooters during the oil boom days of the 1920s. Folks talk a lot about him wherever old-time roughnecks gather, but you don't hear much about his wife. Tex would have had a hard time without her, because she delivered the soup. When Tex checked out a well and made his calculations, he'd give her a call, and, pretty soon, she'd come bouncing into the oil patch in her modified Studebaker loaded with enough soup to level a city block. When folks saw her coming, they found urgent business elsewhere.

Tex also fought oil-well fires. He'd position a torpedo of soup on a trolley cable, move it over a burning well, and wait for the inevitable explosion to snuff out the flame. In 1928 he snuffed a fire in Corpus Christi only to have it re-ignite about 15 minutes later. The blast and re-ignition made a crater about 200 feet wide and just as deep. Meanwhile, the fire roared on. The situation called for another and bigger blast, but Tex was out of soup, and there was no more in the area. No problem. A telephone call did the trick.

Back home in Amarillo, the helpful Ma Thornton loaded her soup wagon with enough nitro to wipe out a town and started her 700-mile trip over the unpaved and rutted roads of the long diagonal. Some nosey news hound got the word, and soon armed committees of "concerned citizens" blocked roads at county lines to keep her out of their areas. Although they stayed at a respectable distance, newspapermen hounded her all the way, reporting each turn. It took back roads and a week of travel, but she made it. The fire was snuffed again with an even larger explosion, and the newsies played the publicity for as much as they could get.

Then the Thorntons went back to work. After all, they were both doing their part to get the job done.

2003—Lest We Forget

People still come to Texas. Projections are that our population will continue to grow due to a variety of factors. A lot of the folks who come will be looking for the same things as those who came one, two, or three hundred years ago. They want security, a new start where there is opportunity and freedom from an oppressive government. Predictably, many will have to fight in some way to get and protect what they want. Freedom is never "free."

It was ever thus, and ever will be. Peace is often not peaceful in its attainment. In September of 1835 Stephen F. Austin, released only a month before from prison in Mexico, addressed the folks meeting for the "Consultation" at San Felipe. "We must seek peace, if it can be had on constitutional grounds. But, to seek peace, we must prepare for war." *The opportunities we have today were bought for us at a high price. We should also be willing to pay a price for the future.*

If you visited Arlington National Cemetery on a Memorial Day you faced emotional and literal overkill. As one poet put it, *"Those endless rows of snowy stones"* represent *"A buried world of light and love; and who can count the cost thereof?"* On any day it is an experience. On Memorial Day, we just don't have the ability to comprehend what we are seeing. It is too much.

The best place to get an emotional handle on Memorial Day is in the small country cemeteries. Whether they are in upstate New York, a Kansas wheat field, or in the woods and prairies of Texas, you have a better chance to view those graves with flags not as faceless among thousands but as fathers, sons, husbands, lovers, and yes, some of these fly the flag, too—as mothers, daughters, and sweethearts. All of them are claiming their last bit of their "promised land" for which they were willing to fight.

I spend a lot of time telling you about people who, in their own way, contributed something to our Texas heritage. Well, I can't name them all, but all of those whose graves have the little flags did their part too. No matter what creed, color, or gender they may be, they are a part of all of us.

I won't name names or tell you exactly where it is because they're entitled to their peace, but about 15 years ago I first visited one of those little cemeteries up in the Piney Woods while looking for a particular church. The church is gone now from that little hill, but there is an old arbor with vines where folks can stand and sing and listen and remember. It wasn't rich country, just sand, red clay, pine trees, and a few cows. A dirt road with ruts at the creek crossings led back to the highway two and a half miles away. Someone had started a house nearby but was unable to finish it, and some of the tarpaper flapped in the wind. The cemetery was in good shape, though, well kept, so I walked around.

The first thing that struck me was the number of markers that listed a military affiliation. I mean, after a while, you can recognize them at a distance. There were a lot of them in this peaceful little place. All around them were other markers. Some were wooden, with the little plastic nametags you squeeze out by hand. Some were hand-chiseled sandstone, and some were hand-cast concrete with the marks of the forms still on them. There were a few markers made from the pre-cast concrete splash-pans you put under the down-spout at your house, and there were a couple of the tall concrete posts that the highway department once used to mark the right-of-way. There was a certain uniformity in disharmony. The oldest marker I found was dated 1828, before Texas became a Republic. She was sixteen and married when she died. Her husband apparently never remarried and was buried beside her when he died, sixty years later.

But, to get back to those that will, or should, show a flag on Memorial Day. In this tiny cemetery there are two state markers for San Jacinto veterans. Within ten feet of each other were one from Company "F" of the 25th Texas Cavalry, CSA, and one from Company "E" of the First Pennsylvania Light Artillery, USA. Did they at last become friends here in the woods before they became neighbors in death? There is one from the First United States Volunteer Cavalry. They were the dismounted "Rough Riders" that stormed up Kettle Hill with Teddy Roosevelt. Two more served with the 85th United States Infantry in France, during the "war to end all wars" that didn't. Seven served in the Army during World War II and three in the Navy. One listed the Korean Conflict, and there was a kid, fresh from boot camp, representing that mess in Viet Nam. So far, there are none representing Panama, or Grenada, or Somalia, or Lebanon, or Afghanistan, or Iraq, or anywhere else our sons and daughters, mothers and fathers, and other kin have gone to protect our liberties and those of others. As you can tell, I go back there every year or so to check on new arrivals. I've never seen any people, just markers.

Almost every rank is represented in that little cemetery. There are apprentice seamen, privates, corporals, sergeants, and a flock of officers up to the rank of colonel. No admirals or generals seemed to pass this way. These were just folks like you and your neighbors. Some of them rode horses or walked; some drove trucks; one flew an airplane. Some sailed *"in harm's way"* in big ships or feisty little boats with big bites. Most of them fought, and at least one cared for the wounded.

On Memorial Day, all of these should have flags; they went when they were called. But, you know, there should also be flags for those who waited for them to come home. There should be flowers, lots of flowers. But, most of all, before next Memorial Day we ought to take the time to visit and read the markers in our local cemeteries, even of those folks we don't know, "lest we forget."

illustration by Gary Manthei

Afterword

Being Texan is not complete. It never will be, as long as there is a Texas and there are Texans, or those who exhibit "Texan-like" attitudes. In this book I have only introduced you to a few of those people who have made us what we are. There are thousands more. In fact, you too should have your own story here. For many years I required students to research their own family histories and recount, in writing, some portion that they found significant. These "family narratives" from several thousand students are on file in the Anthropology Department of Texas A&M University—perhaps the only collection of its type in the United States.

This is the second edition of *Being Texan* and includes a few more stories to fill some general time slots. I will never run out of stories, only the time to tell them. Meanwhile, collect your own. *You* are a part of the story.

Jeff Carroll
Bryan, Texas
May 2009

Appendix I

Facilitator's Guide

Being Texan is designed not only for the casual reader, but also to serve as a supplement for use in classroom settings and for homeschoolers. The stories are arranged chronologically so that, in sequence, they illustrate many of the topics found in a standard textbook. Each story also represents a variety of the "Texas Essential Knowledge & Skills" (TEKS) for the teaching of Social Studies in Grade 4 and for the teaching of Texas History and Geography at the 7th grade level and advanced Texas studies at the 9th through 12th grade levels, as required by the Texas Education Agency. (See Appendix IV) No one story can cover all of these elements of knowledge and skill, but together all of them are covered many times over.

The creative student, teacher, or facilitator can readily apply the stories to TEKS in other fields as well. For instance, a story about why people in Texas were willing to drive cattle two thousand miles to market and why the trail-drive routes moved further west each year fits not only into the study of history, but also involves math, economics, government, science, and even biology.

Supplemental Aids

Each story stands alone, although some relate to others. In fact, most of them originated either as newspaper columns or as scripts for the *Legendary Texas* program on National Public Radio. Some of them also appeared in the *Legendary Texas* series of books (*Unsung Heritage, The Promised Land, These People We Call Texans, Following the Star,* and *From South Pass To The Rio Grande*). However, to get the most educational benefit from them, the student or facilitator should have several references available and access to a computer and the internet.

You should have access to textbooks on Texas history and Texas geography. This allows you to fit the individual stories into the overall "big picture" and introduces you to the "scholarly text" that the stories illustrate.

You should have at least one standard Texas road map and an assortment of felt markers. As time goes by, you may want more than one or several specialized maps marked to show different things. The *Texas Official Travel Map* is available free from offices of the Texas Department of

Transportation. While there, you might as well also ask for the free *Texas Travel Guide*.

You should have a fairly recent copy of the *Texas Almanac*. These are filled with interesting facts and contain thumbnail sketches of Texas counties. New ones are published every year to bring them up-to-date, but older ones are almost as valuable in helping you find particular towns, counties, and other details.

You should be familiar with and know how to access *The Handbook Of Texas*, published by the Texas State Historical Association. Texas is the only state to have its own encyclopedia of history and geography. The six-volume set is not for everyone because it is relatively expensive, but many schools and libraries have sets, *and* it is available and up-dated regularly on-line. If you have computer and web access, go to any one of the big search engines and ask it to find "*The Handbook of Texas*." Once you have located it, the *Handbook* has its own search engine to allow you access to more than you probably ever wanted to know about Texas.

Coordinating The Program

In order to win approval by committee, most textbooks today are *very* politically correct. The stories in *Being Texan* are not necessarily so and present themselves through the eyes of the times in which they happened. Differences of opinion should be expected and looked for. Critical thinking can take place only when there is a presentation of more than one perspective. A particularly valuable exercise is to compare and contrast the perspectives of the stories and the text and then search for clues to other viewpoints in supplemental sources such as *The Handbook Of Texas* and the *Texas Almanac*. Students *and* teachers must remember that history *is not* an exact science.

Remember also that the author of these stories is also a teacher who has used them successfully to generate discussion for many years.

Many of the stories contain specific locations such as counties, cities, and towns, and many speak of traveling from one to another. Valuable activities include locating these sites on a map, calculating distances, and comparing and contrasting what is there today with what was there at the time of the story. This type of exercise alone fulfills several of the TEKS requirements and involves a certain amount of research. Creative writing exercises might describe what participants in the stories saw or heard along a particular route of travel or a diary or journal of the trip. Several students might create a one-act play based on a particular story. One private school using these stories has students choose a particular character without revealing the identity to anyone else, then prepare both a costume and a list of "Who am I?" questions to test their classmates. The use of these resources to make the past come alive is limited only by the imagination, and the culmination of a particular study might include a visit to the actual site of the action.

Appendix II

Survival Values in Learning

In one way, the *Being Texan* stories stand on their own. They are short enough for use in many situations, can be read simply for pleasure, and used to illustrate a variety of topics. In addition, however, they can serve as a springboard to other disciplines. Central to any use other than pleasure reading is the fact that, with a planned discussion strategy, they can encourage within the individual the ability to obtain, organize, translate, interpret, and apply bodies of knowledge or information. In short, the stories can be a rather painless path to critical reasoning.

Take a few minutes and study the chart on "Survival Values in Learning" at the end of this article.

This information is relatively old, but is in the public domain and refers to mental processes that, we are told, don't change. According to this chart, in any learning environment, the retention rate of nonsense syllables and filler material used in lectures, etc. drops to about 18% after one month and levels off at about 10% in three months. That is where it stays. Factual material, such as dates and even names of people, shows a retention rate of only about 42% after one month and then drops to 35%. This is bad news for those who teach only factual bits of information without any conceptual glue to hold them together.

Conceptual schemes, such as cause-and-effect relationships, time-line progressions and space-time relationships, fare a bit better. From a peak retention rate of about 55% after one month they drop to about 50%.

Keep in mind that educational psychologists agree that you cannot teach much material without the use of concepts and facts. However, if that is all we teach, our overall success rate will be relatively low.

Take a look at the top of the chart. Motor skills, which drop to about 75% after one month, hang on at 70% for the rest of your life. In truth, you don't forget how to ride a bicycle and a little wobbly practice after even 50 years will bring you back into original form. Unfortunately, motor skills are not usually part of a social science education, *unless we put them there* with hands-on involvement.

The real winners in retention are the thinking-skills processes and attitudes. This is not always good. Every student is an example of Newton's Law of inertia.

Every student comes to the teacher with attitudes about individual subjects, the process of studying, and themselves—created in some other learning environment at some other time. The same applies to thinking skills. Once these attitudes and thinking skills (or lack thereof) are fixed, they assume the inertia of rest and it may take a really big pry-bar to move them. That is why, to get full value from the stories, you and I both need a strategy to lift facts and concepts to the level of thinking skills and new attitudes. Unfortunately, critical-thinking skills are something that we often do not enjoy applying. We have been conditioned by media, politicians, preachers, and family to accept what we are told without thinking about it too much. That way, all of those stand a better chance of controlling what we think and believe, which often influences votes, donations, and actions. If we teach nothing else, we should teach students to think for themselves.

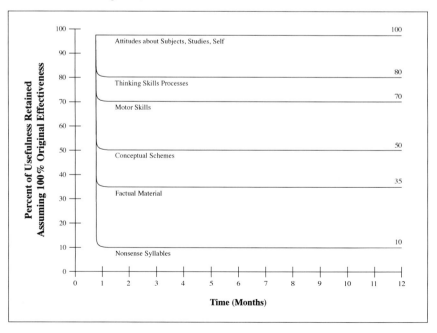

VI

Appendix III

Discussion Strategies

Discussion implies a two-way transfer of ideas. This can best be facilitated by the use of a planned questioning strategy involving only four general types of question. These questions, however, must be used in sequence to get the most benefit. Here are some general rules–of–thumb that should apply to ALL questioning strategies.

1. Be patient. *Never* rush a question. If you don't have time to do it correctly, don't do it. This is especially true with new students who have never had the opportunity to participate at this level. Someone has always told them what and how to think. They are afraid to voice their opinions until they think they know what you want them to say. If you have prepared your strategy correctly, they won't know what your opinion is. They are on their own and must think for themselves. This is often quite painful. In effect, when you ask a question, wait as long as necessary to get an answer. The student must start from scratch and think about it before venturing an answer. *Wait!* (I know, this is hard on you, too.) In most cases, all you can think of while waiting is how much valuable time is passing.

2. Having posed a question, repeat it occasionally while you are waiting, but *do not change the wording in any way.* The change of even one word can (and will) short-circuit the answering process. The student will notice it and wonder if the question has changed and if the thought process needs to change as well. This is one good reason for writing down the questions you ask—so you don't forget.

3. Be accepting of all answers in the beginning. This will also be difficult for you. The first responses you receive may be so far from what you wanted that you feel compelled to correct the student immediately. *Don't!* It will put a stop to any further interaction. The student will think, "I'm dumb. My answer wasn't good enough." Or, the student may think, "I thought that was a good answer, but the teacher wanted to argue. I won't fall into that trap again." There is a time and place for eliciting more correct answers, but you need to wait for it.

4. If you are in a classroom setting and writing the student responses on the board, *do not paraphrase* what the student said. If necessary, say, "I didn't quite get all of that. Please say it again." Or ask, "How can I say that so I can get it all on the board?" Then, write exactly what the student says. It verifies and justifies and rewards the student for a response.

OK! Are you ready for the questions?

The first type of question is the *Open Question.*

The Open Question is designed to allow everyone to participate at any level and to elicit a large body of information on which to focus later. An example of an Open Question dealing with some of the *Being Texan* stories could be: *"What do you think were some causes for the Texas War for Independence?"*

Another could be: *"What do you think were some reasons Anglo-Americans moved to Texas?"*

Do not be satisfied with only one or two answers. The rest of the discussion depends on getting a large body of information with which to work. Remember to accept *all* answers, no matter how off-target they may seem at the time. You can correct that later.

One open question often leads to another open question that focuses attention on one of the responses. So, we can call it:

The *Focusing Question*

The Focusing Question is also open, but directs attention to a particular topic and is usually a response to one of the answers elicited in the first type of question. For instance, you might ask: *"You said that the instability of the Mexican government was one of the reasons for the Texas War for Independence. In what ways do you think this was a reason for the war?"*

Or, you might say: *"You said that the availability of land was one reason why Anglo-Americans came to Texas. In what ways do you think this was different from what was found in the United States?"*

Again, you can elicit a large body of information and follow many open questions with focus questions, bringing in even more information for the mind to work with. Notice, however, that as the questioning progresses, it asks for more specific response.

Then comes the third type of question:

The *Interpretive Question*

This is where you break into really higher cognitive processes. The student is asked to compare and/or contrast two or more concepts, feelings, relationships, or ideas.

For instance, using the two general topics we've talked about above, you might ask: *"In what ways might the causes of the Texas War for Independence and the Anglo-American arrival in Texas be related?"*

Or: *"How might you account for the fact that many Tejanos fought beside Anglo-Americans for Texas independence?"*

This will probably be the place where you get rid of extraneous material you gathered in the open questions. Ask for the relationships. The students may see some that you never thought of. At the same time, they may see how something they suggested earlier really doesn't fit with how the topic has progressed.

The first few times you try to create this kind of questioning strategy, it will not be easy. This will be a learning process for you as well. However, after a few tries, both you and the students will get to where you enjoy it. Trust me, and trust the process. It works. Some real plusses for this process is that it not only takes the teacher out of the role of always telling the student what to think, but it also gives the student the satisfaction of participating as a supplier of information on which the lesson is built, rather than just as a recorder of facts.

Now comes the last type of question:

The *Capstone Question*

Believe me, after you've perfected your questioning, you're going to start getting more response from the students than you can easily handle. You and they may get so carried away with the exhilaration of the process that you run out of time. *Don't.* Always save time for the Capstone Question. This is where you allow the student to summarize for his or her understanding and bring closure to the discussion. The question itself is usually very simple, but it might take a lot of time for the student to process it.

"Based on our discussion, what can we say about the Texas War for Independence?"

"How might we summarize the relations between Mexicans and Anglo-Americans in 1835?"

Now it's your turn. If you want to try your questioning strategy on me first, I invite you to send me an e-mail at carrollj@suddenlink.net. It may take a while, but I *will* respond. Choose any story you want. Tell me what it is so we're on the same page, and send me two examples of Open Questions, Focus Questions, Interpretive Questions, and Capstone Questions based on that story. Then, for each of your questions, give me some possible answers to your questions. Remember that you need to have in mind some of the more obvious answers on which to build your continuing questions. Establish a dialogue with me about what you've done, and, if there are enough responses, with your permission, we may be able to print a Teachers' Guide in the future. Trust the process. *It Works!*

Appendix IV

TEXAS ESSENTIAL KNOWLEDGE & SKILLS (TEKS)

In 1998, the Texas Education Agency replaced the lists of "Essential Elements" of Texas education with the far more complex and comprehensive listing of "Texas Essential Knowledge & Skills" (TEKS). Each story in *Being Texan* refers to one or more of these elements of knowledge and skills. For instance, in the third story, "Homefolks," you will find that it meets the requirements for TEKS 1: A&B at the 4th grade level and the stories "Martyr" and "Rio Grande Thanksgiving" apply to TEKS 2: A, B & C. For those in systems that require lesson plans and supplemental materials keyed to TEKS, it is a relatively simple matter to match the stories to the requirements.

For those who may not have a copy, here are the TEKS for Social Studies in the Grade 4 and Grade 7 levels.

§113.6. Social Studies, Grade 4.

(a) Introduction.

(1) In Grade 4, students examine the history of Texas from the early beginnings to the present within the context of influences of the Western Hemisphere. Historical content focuses on Texas history including the Texas revolution, establishment of the Republic of Texas, and subsequent

annexation to the United States. Students discuss important issues, events, and individuals of the 19th and 20th centuries. Students conduct a thorough study of regions in Texas and the Western Hemisphere that result from human activity and from physical features. A focus on the location, distribution, and patterns of economic activities and of settlement in Texas further enhances the concept of regions. Students describe how early Native Americans in Texas and the Western Hemisphere met their basic economic needs and identify economic motivations for European exploration and colonization and reasons for the establishment of Spanish missions. Students explain how Native Americans governed themselves and identify characteristics of Spanish and Mexican colonial governments in Texas. Students recite and explain the meaning of the Pledge to the Texas Flag. Students identify the contributions of people of various racial, ethnic, and religious groups to Texas and describe the impact of science and technology on life in the state. Students use critical-thinking skills to identify cause-and-effect relationships, compare and contrast, and make generalizations and predictions.

(2) To support the teaching of the essential knowledge and skills, the use of a variety of rich primary and secondary source material such as biographies; novels; speeches and letters; and poetry, songs, and artworks is encouraged. Selections may include a children's biography of Stephen F. Austin. Motivating resources are also available from museums, historical sites, presidential libraries, and local and state preservation societies.

(3) The eight strands of the essential knowledge and skills for social studies are intended to be integrated for instructional purposes with the history and geography strands establishing a sense of time and a sense of place. Skills listed in the geography and social studies skills strands in subsection

(b) of this section should be incorporated into the teaching of all essential knowledge and skills for social studies. A greater depth of understanding of complex content material can be attained when integrated social studies content from the various disciplines and critical-thinking skills are taught together.

(4) Throughout social studies in Kindergarten-Grade 12, students build a foundation in history; geography; economics; government; citizenship; culture; science, technology, and society; and social studies skills. The content, as appropriate for the grade level or course, enables students to understand the importance of patriotism, function in a free enterprise society, and appreciate the basic democratic values of our state and nation as referenced in the Texas Education Code, §28.002(h).

(b) Knowledge and skills.

(1) History. The student understands the similarities and differences of Native-American groups in Texas and the Western Hemisphere before European exploration. The student is expected to:

(A) identify Native-American groups in Texas and the Western Hemisphere before European exploration and describe the regions in which they lived; and

(B) compare the ways of life of Native-American groups in Texas and the Western Hemisphere before European exploration.

(2) History. The student understands the causes and effects of European exploration and colonization of Texas and the Western Hemisphere. The student is expected to:

(A) summarize reasons for European exploration and settlement of Texas and the Western Hemisphere;

(B) identify the accomplishments of significant explorers such as Cabeza de Vaca; Christopher Columbus; Francisco Coronado; and René Robert Cavelier, Sieur de la Salle and explain their impact on the settlement of Texas;

(C) explain when, where, and why the Spanish established Catholic missions in Texas;

(D) identify the accomplishments of significant empresarios including Moses Austin, Stephen F. Austin, and Martín de León and explain their impact on the settlement of Texas; and

(E) identify the impact of Mexico's independence from Spain on the events in Texas.

(3) History. The student understands the causes and effects of the Texas Revolution, the Republic of Texas, and the annexation of Texas to the United States. The student is expected to:

(A) analyze the causes, major events, and effects of the Texas Revolution, including the battles of the Alamo and San Jacinto;

(B) describe the successes and problems of the Republic of Texas;

(C) explain the events that led to the annexation of Texas to the United States;

(D) explain the impact of the Mexican War on Texas; and

(E) identify leaders important to the founding of Texas as a republic and state, including Sam Houston, Mirabeau Lamar, and Anson Jones.

(4) History. The student understands the political, economic, and social changes in Texas during the last half of the 19th century. The student is expected to:

(A) describe the impact of the Civil War and Reconstruction on Texas;

(B) explain the growth and development of the cattle and oil industries;

(C) identify the impact of railroads on life in Texas, including changes to cities and major industries; and

(D) describe the effects of political, economic, and social changes on Native Americans in Texas.

(5) History. The student understands important issues, events, and individuals of the 20th century in Texas. The student is expected to:

(A) identify the impact of various issues and events on life in Texas such as urbanization, increased use of oil and gas, and the growth of aerospace and other technology industries; and

(B) identify the accomplishments of notable individuals such as Henry Cisneros, Miriam A. Ferguson, Audie Murphy, Cleto Rodríguez, and John Tower.

(6) Geography. The student uses geographic tools to collect, analyze, and interpret data. The student is expected to:

(A) apply geographic tools, including grid systems, legends, symbols, scales, and compass roses, to construct and interpret maps; and

(B) translate geographic data into a variety of formats such as raw data to graphs and maps.

(7) Geography. The student understands the concept of regions. The student is expected to:

(A) describe a variety of regions in Texas and the Western Hemisphere such as political, population, and economic regions that result from patterns of human activity;

(B) describe a variety of regions in Texas and the Western Hemisphere such as landform, climate, and vegetation regions that result from physical characteristics; and

(C) compare the regions of Texas with regions of the United States and other parts of the world.

(8) Geography. The student understands the location and patterns of settlement and the geographic factors that influence where people live. The student is expected to:

(A) identify clusters of settlement in Texas and explain their distribution;

(B) explain patterns of settlement at different time periods in Texas;

(C) describe the location of cities in Texas and explain their distribution, past and present; and

(D) explain the geographic factors that influence patterns of settlement and the distribution of population in Texas, past and present.

(9) Geography. The student understands how people adapt to and modify their environment. The student is expected to:

(A) describe ways people have adapted to and modified their environment in Texas, past and present;

(B) identify reasons why people have adapted to and modified their environment in Texas, past and present, such as the use of natural resources to meet basic needs; and

(C) analyze the consequences of human modification of the environment in Texas, past and present.

(10) Economics. The student understands the basic economic patterns of early societies in Texas and the Western Hemisphere. The student is expected to:

(A) explain the economic patterns of various early Native-American groups in Texas and the Western Hemisphere; and

(B) explain the economic patterns of early European immigrants to Texas and the Western Hemisphere.

(11) Economics. The student understands the reasons for exploration and colonization. The student is expected to:

(A) identify the economic motivations for European exploration and settlement in Texas and the Western Hemisphere; and

(B) identify the economic motivations for Anglo-American colonization in Texas.

(12) Economics. The student understands the characteristics and benefits of the free enterprise system in Texas. The student is expected to:

(A) describe the development of the free enterprise system in Texas;

(B) describe how the free enterprise system works in Texas; and

(C) give examples of the benefits of the free enterprise system in Texas.

(13) Economics. The student understands patterns of work and economic activities in Texas. The student is expected to:

(A) explain how people in different regions of Texas earn their living, past and present;

(B) explain how geographic factors have influenced the location of economic activities in Texas;

(C) analyze the effects of immigration, migration, and limited resources on the economic development and growth of Texas;

(D) describe the impact of mass production, specialization, and division of labor on the economic growth of Texas;

(E) explain how developments in transportation and communication have influenced economic activities in Texas; and

(F) explain the impact of American ideas about progress and equality of opportunity on the economic development and growth of Texas.

(14) Economics. The student understands how Texas, the United States, and other parts of the world are economically interdependent. The student is expected to:

(A) identify ways in which technological changes have resulted in increased interdependence among Texas, the United States, and the world;

(B) identify oil and gas, agricultural, and technological products of Texas that are purchased to meet needs in the United States and around the world; and

(C) explain how Texans meet some of their needs through the purchase of products from the United States and the rest of the world.

(15) Government. The student understands how people organized governments in different ways during the early development of Texas. The student is expected to:

(A) compare how selected Native-American groups governed themselves; and

(B) identify characteristics of Spanish and Mexican colonial governments and their influence on inhabitants of Texas.

(16) Government. The student understands important ideas in historic documents of Texas. The student is expected to:

(A) identify the purposes and explain the importance of the Texas Declaration of Independence, the Texas Constitution, and the Treaty of Velasco; and

(B) identify and explain the basic functions of the three branches of state government.

(17) Citizenship. The student understands important customs, symbols, and celebrations of Texas. The student is expected to:

(A) explain the meaning of selected patriotic symbols and landmarks of Texas, including the six flags over Texas, San José Mission, and the San Jacinto Monument;

(B) sing or recite Texas, Our Texas;

(C) recite and explain the meaning of the Pledge to the Texas Flag; and

(D) describe the origins and significance of state celebrations such as Texas Independence Day and Juneteenth.

(18) Citizenship. The student understands the importance of voluntary individual participation in the democratic process. The student is expected to:

(A) explain how individuals can participate voluntarily in civic affairs at state and local levels;

(B) explain the role of the individual in state and local elections;

(C) identify the importance of historical figures such as Sam Houston, Barbara Jordan, and Lorenzo de Zavala who modeled active participation in the democratic process; and

(D) explain how to contact elected and appointed leaders in state and local governments.

(19) Citizenship. The student understands the importance of effective leadership in a democratic society. The student is expected to:

(A) identify leaders in state and local governments, including the governor, selected members of the Texas Legislature, and Texans who have been President of the United States, and their political parties; and

(B) identify leadership qualities of state and local leaders, past and present.

(20) Culture. The student understands the contributions of people of various racial, ethnic, and religious groups to Texas. The student is expected to:

(A) identify the similarities and differences within and among selected racial, ethnic, and religious groups in Texas;

(B) identify customs, celebrations, and traditions of various culture groups in Texas; and

(C) summarize the contributions of people of various racial, ethnic, and religious groups in the development of Texas.

(21) Science, technology, and society. The student understands the impact of science and technology on life in Texas. The student is expected to:

(A) identify famous inventors and scientists such as Gail Borden, Joseph Glidden, and Patillo Higgins and their contributions;

(B) describe how scientific discoveries and technological innovations have benefited individuals, businesses, and society in Texas; and

(C) predict how future scientific discoveries and technological innovations might affect life in Texas.

(22) Social studies skills. The student applies critical-thinking skills to organize and use information acquired from a variety of sources including electronic technology. The student is expected to:

(A) differentiate between, locate, and use primary and secondary sources such as computer software; interviews; biographies; oral, print, and visual material; and artifacts to acquire information about the United States and Texas;

(B) analyze information by sequencing, categorizing, identifying cause-and-effect relationships, comparing, contrasting, finding the main idea, summarizing, making generalizations and predictions, and drawing inferences and conclusions;

(C) organize and interpret information in outlines, reports, databases, and visuals including graphs, charts, timelines, and maps;

(D) identify different points of view about an issue or topic;

(E) identify the elements of frame of reference that influenced the participants in an event; and

(F) use appropriate mathematical skills to interpret social studies information such as maps and graphs.

(23) Social studies skills. The student communicates in written, oral, and visual forms. The student is expected to:

(A) use social studies terminology correctly;

(B) incorporate main and supporting ideas in verbal and written communication;

(C) express ideas orally based on research and experiences;

(D) create written and visual material such as journal entries, reports, graphic organizers, outlines, and bibliographies; and

(E) use standard grammar, spelling, sentence structure, and punctuation.

(24) Social studies skills. The student uses problem-solving and decision-making skills, working independently and with others, in a variety of settings. The student is expected to:

(A) use a problem-solving process to identify a problem, gather information, list and consider options, consider advantages and disadvantages, choose and implement a solution, and evaluate the effectiveness of the solution; and

(B) use a decision-making process to identify a situation that requires a decision, gather information, identify options, predict consequences, and take action to implement a decision.

§113.23. Social Studies, Grade 7.

(a) Introduction.

(1) In Grade 7, students study the history of Texas from early times to the present. Content is presented with more depth and breadth than in Grade 4. Students examine the full scope of Texas history, including the cultures of Native Americans living in Texas prior to European exploration and the eras of mission-building, colonization, revolution, republic, and statehood. The focus in each era is on key individuals, events, and issues and their impact. Students identify regions of Texas and the distribution of population within and among the regions and explain the factors that caused Texas to change from an agrarian to an urban society. Students describe the structure and functions of municipal, county, and state governments, explain the influence of the U.S. Constitution on the Texas Constitution, and examine the rights and responsibilities of Texas citizens. Students use primary and secondary sources to examine the rich and diverse cultural background of Texas as they identify the different racial and ethnic groups that settled in Texas to build a republic and then a state. Students analyze the impact of scientific discoveries and technological innovations such as barbed wire and the oil and gas industries on the development of Texas. Students use primary and secondary sources to acquire information about Texas.

(2) To support the teaching of the essential knowledge and skills, the use of a variety of rich primary and secondary source material such as biographies and autobiographies; novels; speeches, letters, and diaries; and poetry, songs, and artworks is encouraged. Selections may include a biography of Barbara Jordan or Lorenzo de Zavala and William B. Travis' letter "To the People of Texas and All Americans in the World." Motivating resources are also available from museums, historical sites, presidential libraries, and local and state preservation societies.

(3) The eight strands of the essential knowledge and skills for social studies are intended to be integrated for instructional purposes with the history and geography strands establishing a sense of time and a sense of place. Skills listed in the geography and social studies skills strands in subsection (b) of this section should be incorporated into the teaching of all essential knowledge and skills for social studies. A greater depth of understanding of complex content material can be attained when integrated social studies

XIX

content from the various disciplines and critical-thinking skills are taught together.

(4) Throughout social studies in Kindergarten-Grade 12, students build a foundation in history; geography; economics; government; citizenship; culture; science, technology, and society; and social studies skills. The content, as appropriate for the grade level or course, enables students to understand the importance of patriotism, function in a free enterprise society, and appreciate the basic democratic values of our state and nation as referenced in the Texas Education Code, §28.002(h).

(b) Knowledge and skills.

(1) History. The student understands traditional historical points of reference in Texas history. The student is expected to:

(A) identify the major eras in Texas history and describe their defining characteristics;

(B) apply absolute and relative chronology through the sequencing of significant individuals, events, and time periods; and

(C) explain the significance of the following dates: 1519, 1718, 1821, 1836, 1845, and 1861.

(2) History. The student understands how individuals, events, and issues prior to the Texas Revolution shaped the history of Texas. The student is expected to:

(A) compare the cultures of Native Americans in Texas prior to European colonization;

(B) identify important individuals, events, and issues related to European exploration and colonization of Texas, including the establishment of Catholic missions;

(C) identify the contributions of significant individuals including Moses Austin, Stephen F. Austin, and Juan Seguín during the colonization of Texas;

(D) identify the impact of the Mexican federal Constitution of 1824 on events in Texas;

(E) trace the development of events that led to the Texas Revolution, including the Law of April 6, 1830, the Turtle Bayou Resolutions, and the arrest of Stephen F. Austin; and

(F) contrast Spanish and Anglo purposes for and methods of settlement in Texas.

(3) History. The student understands how individuals, events, and issues related to the Texas Revolution shaped the history of Texas. The student is expected to:

(A) explain the roles played by significant individuals during the Texas Revolution, including George Childress, Lorenzo de Zavala, James Fannin, Sam Houston, Antonio López de Santa Anna, and William B. Travis; and

(B) explain the issues surrounding significant events of the Texas Revolution, including the battle of Gonzales, the siege of the Alamo, the convention of 1836, Fannin's surrender at Goliad, and the battle of San Jacinto.

(4) History. The student understands how individuals, events, and issues shaped the history of the Republic of Texas and early Texas statehood. The student is expected to:

(A) identify individuals, events, and issues during the Republic of Texas and early Texas statehood, including annexation, Sam Houston, Anson Jones, Mirabeau B. Lamar, problems of the Republic of Texas, the Texas Rangers, the Mexican War, and the Treaty of Guadalupe-Hidalgo; and

(B) analyze the causes of and events leading to Texas statehood.

(5) History. The student understands how events and issues shaped the history of Texas during the Civil War and Reconstruction. The student is expected to:

(A) explain reasons for the involvement of Texas in the Civil War; and

(B) analyze the political, economic, and social effects of the Civil War and Reconstruction in Texas.

(6) History. The student understands how individuals, events, and issues shaped the history of Texas from Reconstruction through the beginning of the 20th century. The student is expected to:

(A) identify significant individuals, events, and issues from Reconstruction through the beginning of the 20th century, including the factors leading to the expansion of the Texas frontier, the effects of westward expansion on Native Americans, the development of the cattle industry from its Spanish beginnings, the myth and realities of the cowboy way of life, the effects of the growth of railroads, the buffalo soldiers, James Hogg, Cynthia Parker, and Spindletop; and

(B) explain the political, economic, and social impact of the cattle and oil industries and the development of West Texas resulting from the close of the frontier.

(7) History. The student understands how individuals, events, and issues shaped the history of Texas during the 20th century. The student is expected to:

(A) define the impact of "boom and bust" and trace the boom-and-bust cycle of leading Texas industries throughout the 20th century, including farming, oil and gas, cotton, cattle ranching, real estate, and banking;

(B) evaluate the Progressive and other reform movements in Texas in the 19th and 20th centuries;

(C) trace the civil rights and equal rights movements of various groups in Texas in the 20th century and identify key leaders in these movements, including James Farmer, Hector P. García, Oveta Culp Hobby, and Lyndon B. Johnson;

(D) analyze the political, economic, and social impact of major wars, including World War I and World War II, on the history of Texas;

(E) trace the emergence of the two-party system in Texas during the second half of the 20th century.

(8) Geography. The student uses geographic tools to collect, analyze, and interpret data. The student is expected to:

(A) create thematic maps, graphs, charts, models, and databases representing various aspects of Texas during the 19th and 20th centuries; and

(B) pose and answer questions about geographic distributions and patterns in Texas during the 19th and 20th centuries.

(9) Geography. The student understands the location and characteristics of places and regions of Texas. The student is expected to:

(A) locate places and regions of importance in Texas during the 19th and 20th centuries;

(B) compare places and regions of Texas in terms of physical and human characteristics; and

(C) analyze the effects of physical and human factors such as climate, weather, landforms, irrigation, transportation, and communication on major events in Texas.

(10) Geography. The student understands the effects of the interaction between humans and the environment in Texas during the 19th and 20th centuries. The student is expected to:

(A) identify ways in which Texans have adapted to and modified the environment and analyze the consequences of the modifications; and

(B) explain ways in which geographic factors have affected the political, economic, and social development of Texas.

(11) Geography. The student understands the characteristics, distribution, and migration of population in Texas in the 19th and 20th centuries. The student is expected to:

(A) analyze why immigrant groups came to Texas and where they settled;

(B) analyze how immigration and migration to Texas in the 19th and 20th centuries have influenced Texas;

(C) analyze the effects of the changing population distribution in Texas during the 20th century; and

(D) describe the structure of the population of Texas using demographic concepts such as growth rate and age distribution.

(12) Economics. The student understands the factors that caused Texas to change from an agrarian to an urban society. The student is expected to:

(A) explain economic factors that led to the urbanization of Texas;

(B) trace the development of major industries that contributed to the urbanization of Texas; and

(C) explain the changes in the types of jobs and occupations that have resulted from the urbanization of Texas.

(13) Economics. The student understands the interdependence of the Texas economy with the United States and the world. The student is expected to:

(A) analyze the impact of national and international markets and events on the production of goods and services in Texas;

(B) analyze the impact of economic phenomena within the free enterprise system such as supply and demand, profit, government regulation, and world competition on the economy of Texas; and

(C) analyze the impact of significant industries in Texas such as oil and gas, aerospace, and medical technology on local, national, and international markets.

(14) Government. The student understands the basic principles reflected in the Texas Constitution. The student is expected to:

(A) identify how the Texas Constitution reflects the principles of limited government, checks and balances, federalism, separation of powers, popular sovereignty, and individual rights; and

(B) identify the influence of ideas from the U.S. Constitution on the Texas Constitution.

(15) Government. The student understands the structure and functions of government created by the Texas Constitution. The student is expected to:

(A) describe the structure and functions of government at municipal, county, and state levels;

(B) identify major sources of revenue for state and local governments; and

(C) describe the structure and governance of Texas public education.

(16) Citizenship. The student understands the rights and responsibilities of Texas citizens. The student is expected to:

(A) summarize the rights guaranteed in the Texas Bill of Rights; and

(B) identify civic responsibilities of Texas citizens.

(17) Citizenship. The student understands the importance of the expression of different points of view in a democratic society. The student is expected to:

(A) identify different points of view of political parties and interest groups on important Texas issues;

(B) describe the importance of free speech and press in a democratic society; and

(C) express and defend a point of view on an issue of historical or contemporary interest in Texas.

(18) Citizenship. The student understands the importance of effective leadership in a democratic society. The student is expected to:

(A) identify the leadership qualities of elected and appointed leaders of Texas, past and present, including Texans who have been President of the United States; and

(B) analyze the contributions of Texas leaders such as Henry B. González, Phil Gramm, Barbara Jordan, and Sam Rayburn.

(19) Culture. The student understands the concept of diversity within unity in Texas. The student is expected to:

(A) explain how the diversity of Texas is reflected in a variety of cultural activities, celebrations, and performances;

(B) describe how people from selected racial, ethnic, and religious groups attempt to maintain their cultural heritage while adapting to the larger Texas culture; and

(C) identify examples of Spanish influence on place names such as Amarillo and Río Grande and on vocabulary in Texas, including words that originated from the Spanish cattle industry.

(20) Science, technology, and society. The student understands the impact of scientific discoveries and technological innovations on the political, economic, and social development of Texas. The student is expected to:

(A) compare types and uses of technology, past and present;

(B) identify Texas leaders in science and technology such as Roy Bedichek, Walter Cunningham, Michael DeBakey, and C.M. "Dad" Joiner;

(C) analyze the effects of scientific discoveries and technological innovations, such as barbed wire, the windmill, and oil, gas, and aerospace industries, on the developments of Texas;

(D) evaluate the effects of scientific discoveries and technological innovations on the use of resources such as fossil fuels, water, and land;

(E) analyze how scientific discoveries and technological innovations have resulted in an interdependence among Texas, the United States, and the world; and

(F) make predictions about economic, social, and environmental consequences that may result from future scientific discoveries and technological innovations.

(21) Social studies skills. The student applies critical-thinking skills to organize and use information acquired from a variety of sources including electronic technology. The student is expected to:

(A) differentiate between, locate, and use primary and secondary sources such as computer software, databases, media and news services, biographies, interviews, and artifacts to acquire information about Texas;

(B) analyze information by sequencing, categorizing, identifying cause-and-effect relationships, comparing, contrasting, finding the main idea, summarizing, making generalizations and predictions, and drawing inferences and conclusions;

(C) organize and interpret information from outlines, reports, databases, and visuals including graphs, charts, timelines, and maps;

(D) identify points of view from the historical context surrounding an event and the frame of reference that influenced the participants;

(E) support a point of view on a social studies issue or event;

(F) identify bias in written, oral, and visual material;

(G) evaluate the validity of a source based on language, corroboration with other sources, and information about the author; and

(H) use appropriate mathematical skills to interpret social studies information such as maps and graphs.

(22) Social studies skills. The student communicates in written, oral, and visual forms. The student is expected to:

(A) use social studies terminology correctly;

(B) use standard grammar, spelling, sentence structure, and punctuation;

(C) transfer information from one medium to another, including written to visual and statistical to written or visual, using computer software as appropriate; and

(D) create written, oral, and visual presentations of social studies information.

(23) Social studies skills. The student uses problem-solving and decision-making skills, working independently and with others, in a variety of settings. The student is expected to:

(A) use a problem-solving process to identify a problem, gather information, list and consider options, consider advantages and disadvantages, choose and implement a solution, and evaluate the effectiveness of the solution; and

(B) use a decision-making process to identify a situation that requires a decision, gather information, identify options, predict consequences, and take action to implement a decision.

Bibliography

This bibliography is far from all-inclusive. It would be difficult to list all sources that went into the creation of these stories. Some of them are simply unavailable to the public. Others are so esoteric and long out-of-print that they are additionally hard to access. And, most folks don't have the time or inclination to struggle through rolls of microfilm looking for a four-inch item in an 1840 newspaper. What I have elected to do is to list a number of available sources and make a few comments about each one to give you an idea about the content. However, before I do that, here are some comments about sources in general.

Newspapers: The files of old newspapers are a treasure trove of what was important to people at the time they were printed. Most "hometown" papers and many metropolitan ones printed letters from folks who had written home to touch base with their families. In addition, news items of the day came from many sources and even the commercial advertisements tell a lot about the lives of ordinary people. Rarely have I ever read a paper more than 50 years old and not found the basis for a story. This would be a good writing exercise for students.

Records of the County Clerk: Not only do court records tell you who did what to whom, but they also tell about wills, property transfers, marriages, divorces, property inventories, and even cattle brands.

City and County Histories: Almost every county has a history book, and the same applies to many cities. Look for the older ones. They are far more interesting, because they usually have a lot more about people and less about politics.

Here are some books I think would be of interest to both the teacher and the casual reader:

Bedichek, Roy. Adventures With A Texas Naturalist. Austin: University of Texas Press, 1947.
This is an excellent collection of fact and philosophy.

Boatright, Mody C. Folklore of the Oil Industry. Dallas: Southern Methodist University Press, 1963.
Oil is important to Texas, and the "oil patch" has its own set of heroes and tall tales.

Crawford, Ann Fears, and Ragsdale, Crystal Sasse. Women In Texas: Their Lives, Their Experiences, Their Accomplishments. Burnet, Texas: Eakin Press, 1982.
This covers the lives and accomplishments of thirty important Texas women.

Crisp, James E. Sleuthing The Alamo. New York: Oxford University Press, 2005.
This is historiography at its best, a "must read" for those who "Remember The Alamo."

Dobie, J. Frank. Coronado's Children. New York: Grosset & Dunlap, 1930.
I think this is the book that first interested me in history. A lot of folks don't like it today because it is far from "politically correct." It is, however, reflective of the time when it was written. All of Dobie's books are good, and have been reprinted several times. I won't list them here, but look for them.

Duval, J. C. Early Times In Texas. Austin: H. P. N. Gammel & Co., 1892.
You probably won't find an original of this, except in a library, but it has been re-printed several times. It is not politically correct, and hardly a "scholarly" work, but a fascinating read.

Fehrenbach, T. R. Lone Star: A History of Texas and the Texans. New York: American Legacy Press, 1983.
This one is large, but easily read. They made a TV mini-series based on it back in the 1980s. I recommend it to folks who want a good general overview of the "Texas Mystique."

Fowler, Gene. Crazy Water. Fort Worth: Texas Christian University Press, 1991.
This is a collection of stories about many of the Texas health resorts based on mineral water. Texas has hundreds of mineral springs where many generations of folks "took the water" and sought health. They began dropping from favor around the middle of the 20th century when the government began to put fluoride in our water supplies.

Friend, Llerena B. Sam Houston, The Great Designer. Austin: University of Texas Press, 1954.
This is another one that you probably won't find in the original, but which has been reprinted. It was the long-time standard biography of Houston.

Haislet, John A., ed. Famous Trees of Texas. College Station: Texas Forest Service, 1983.

As the name implies, these trees in Texas are famous either for their size or for the parts they played in history.

Hardin, Stephen L. Texian Iliad: A Military History of the Texas Revolution. Austin: University of Texas Press, 1994.
This is just what the title implies, but it is an easy read and there are excellent illustrations.

Horgan, Paul. Great River: The Rio Grande in North American History. New York: Rinehart, 1954.
This book won both the Pulitzer and the Bancroft awards in history. The very size of the book is intimidating, but it is an easy read. It has been reprinted several times.

Luchetti, Cathy. Home On The Range: A Culinary History of the American West. New York: Villard Books (Random House), 1993.
This is not confined to Texas, but applies to women all over the West. It is a good companion to the Carol Padgett book listed later.

Mabry, Robert, Jr. Texas Flags. College Station: Texas A&M Press, 2001.
Designed to accompany a museum display, this gives excellent coverage of many of our most noted flags.

Maxwell, Robert S. and Baker, Robert D. Sawdust Empire. College Station: Texas A&M University Press, 1983.
Like oil, timber is one of our most important resources, but we don't usually hear much about it. This covers the history of the lumber industry in Texas, a history often left out of textbooks.

Metz, Leon C. Roadside History of Texas. Missoula, Montana: Mountain Press Publishing Co., 1994.
This is a good traveling companion as one wanders through the highways and byways of Texas. It is a part of a large series of similar books on other states. If you're going on a long road trip, pick up those states involved to keep passengers occupied.

Newcomb, W. W. Jr. The Indians of Texas. Austin: University of Texas Press, 1961.
This is probably the best overall book on Texas Indians.

O'Neal, Bill. Encyclopedia of Western Gun-Fighters. Norman: University of Oklahoma Press, 1979.
As the title implies, this is a collection and comparison of many of the gunfighters of the Old West.

Padgett Carol, ed. Keeping Hearth & Home in Old Texas. Birmingham, Alabama: Menasha Ridge Press, 2001.
This is a delightful "practical primer for daily living" which includes everything from recipes to etiquette.

Reid, Stuart. The Secret War for Texas. College Station: Texas A&M University Press, 2007.
For years I wondered about the shadowy involvement of the British Empire in the politics of Texas and Mexico. This tangled web of intrigue stretches from the Napoleonic wars to the Alamo and beyond that to the annexation of Texas as the 28th state in the Union and the foreshadowing of secession.

Robertson, Pauline Durrett and Robertson, R. L. Panhandle Pilgrimage. Amarillo: Paramount Publishing Company, 1978.
This is an excellent source of information about the Panhandle and is profusely illustrated.

Shafer, Harry F. Ancient Texans. Austin: Texas Monthly Press, 1986.
This is the best available book on the life and time of ancient Texans in the Trans-Pecos region. Beautifully illustrated.

Smithers, W. D. Chronicles of The Big Bend. Austin: Madrona Press, 1976.
This one covers mostly the presence of the U.S. Military along the border in West Texas during the early 20th century. Profusely illustrated.

Sonnichsen, C. L. I'll Die Before I'll Run: The Story of the Great Feuds of Texas. Lincoln: University of Nebraska Press, 1951.
This is the best of the books on Texas feuds. Be careful. You will be prone to take sides.

Stephens, A. Ray and Holmes, William M. Historical Atlas of Texas. Norman: University of Oklahoma Press, 1989.
This is an excellent, large-format atlas of maps dealing with Texas history. I especially appreciate the base maps that show county boundaries.

Syers, William Edward. Off The Beaten Trail. Waco: Texian Press, 1971.
This is an excellent collection of Texana in short easy pieces.

Tarpley, Fred. 1001 Texas Place Names. Austin: University of Texas Press, 1980.
Have you ever wondered where Dry Duck Creek got its name?

Turner, Ellen Sue and Hester, Thomas R. A Field Guide To Stone Artifacts of Texas Indians. Austin: Texas Monthly Press, 1985.
If anyone has ever shown you an "Indian arrowhead," this book will help you identify it. It probably should be on the reference shelf of every elementary and secondary schoolteacher.

Walraven, Bill, and Walraven, Marjorie K. The Magnificent Barbarians: Little Told Tales of the Texas Revolution. Austin: Eakin Press, 1993.
As the title suggests, this one is filled with short episodes of the war.
However, its greatest value is in "Appendix A" which contains the lists of "U.S. Army Deserters or Discharges With Names Similar to Those of Men Who Served in the Texas Revolution" and "Appendix B" with a list of Tejanos who served on the Texian side.

Weniger, Del. The Explorers' Texas, The Lands and Waters. Austin: Eakin Press, 1984.
Many "historians" don't like this because Weniger is not a historian.
He is a biologist who has won several awards normally reserved for historians.

Winegarten, Ruthie. Texas Women, a Pictorial History. Austin: Eakin Press, 1986.
This covers hundreds of women of all ethnicities in Texas and the photographs allow the reader to put faces on the people.

Ximenes, Ben Cuellar. Gallant Outcasts, Texas Turmoil, 1519—1734. San Antonio: The Naylor Company, 1963.
The Spanish claimed Texas for over 300 years. And yet, this crucial time period gets little coverage in textbooks. It will be difficult to find this book outside of a library, but it sheds much-needed light on shadowed enterprise.

Resources

The following organizations and individuals graciously contributed period images, photographs, and research information to this edition of *Being Texan:*

Mr. Peter M. Ascoli
private collection

Brazoria County Historical Museum
Angleton, Texas

Jeff Carroll
private collection

Center for American History Prints and Photography Collection
University of Texas
Austin, Texas

Daughters of the Republic of Texas Library at the Alamo
San Antonio, Texas

Fannin County Museum of History
Bonham, Texas

Library of Congress Brady-Handy Collection
Washington, D.C.

The Lockhart Post Register
Lockhart, Texas

Marble Falls Public Library
Marble Falls, Texas

Texas Air Museum, Stinson Field
San Antonio, Texas

Texas Ranger Hall of Fame and Museum, Texas Ranger Research Center Library
Waco, Texas

Texas State Library Archives Commission
Austin, Texas

University of Texas at San Antonio Institute of Texan Cultures Library
San Antonio, Texas

Wharton County Historical Museum
Wharton, Texas

Index

-C-

-H-

-L-

-N-

-U-